Combat History of Sturmgeschütz-Brigade 276

Assault Gun Fighting on the Eastern Front

Edited by
Heinz Fleischer

Translated by Allen Brandt and Robert J. Edwards

Combat History of Sturmgeschütz-Brigade 276

Assault Gun Fighting on the Eastern Front

Edited by
Heinz Fleischer
Translated by
Allen Brandt & Robert J. Edwards

Copyright © 2000

The material in this book is copyright by J.J. Fedorowicz Publishing, Inc., and no part of it may be reproduced, stored in a retrieval system, or transmitted in any form or by any means whether electronic, mechanical, photocopy, recording or otherwise without the written consent of the publisher.

Published by
J.J. Fedorowicz Publishing, Inc.
104 Browning Boulevard
Winnipeg, Manitoba
Canada R3K 0L7
Web: www.jjfpub.mb.ca
E-Mail: jjfpub@escape.ca
Telephone: (204) 837-6080
Fax: (204) 889-1960

Printed in Canada
ISBN 0 - 921991 - 54 - 1

Printed by
Friesens Printers
Altona, Manitoba, Canada

Publishers' Acknowledgements

We wish to thank Allen Brandt for bringing the manuscript to our attention and for his translation of the German text. Also our thanks and appreciation to *Herr* and *Frau* Fleischer for their hospitality in inviting John and Mike into their house for a most interesting afternoon of discussions and reminiscences. Matt Hall has provided another superb signing box; George Bradford was gracious enough to provide his excellent scale drawings of the *Sturmgeschütze* which the brigade used and can be seen in the period photographs accompanying this book.

Finally, we wish to thank you, the reader, for purchasing this book and all of you who have written us with kind words of praise and encouragement. It gives us the impetus to continue translating the best available German-language books and produce original titles. Our catalog of books is listed on the following pages and can be viewed on our web site at www.jjfpub.mb.ca. We have also listed titles which are near production and can be expected in the near future. Many of these are due to your helpful proposals.

John Fedorowicz, Mike Olive and Bob Edwards

Editor's Notes

Modern American Army terminology is generally used wherever an equivalent term is applicable. In cases where there may be nuances where we think the reader might enjoy learning the German term, we have included it parenthetically.

In cases where the German term is commonly understood or there is no good, direct English equivalent, we have tended to retain the German term, e.g., *Schwerpunkt* (point of main effort), *Auftragstaktik* (mission-type orders) etc.

In an attempt to highlight the specific German terminology, we have italicized German-language terms and expressions. Since most of the terms are repeated several times, we have not included a glossary. Since we assume the reader will already have a basic understanding of German rank terms and the terminology used for vehicles, we have likewise not included any separate annexes to the book to explain them.

Unit designations follow standard German practise, i.e., an Arabic numeral before the slash (e.g., *3./Sturmgeschütz-Brigade 276*) indicates a company or battery formation. A Roman numeral indicates the battalion within the regiment.

Other Titles by J.J. Fedorowicz Publishing

The Leibstandarte (1. SS-Panzer-Division): Volumes I, II, III, IV/1 and IV/2
European Volunteers (5. SS-Panzer-Division)
Das Reich (2. SS-Panzer-Division): Volumes I and II
The History of Panzerkorps "Großdeutschland": Volumes 1, 2 and 3
Panzer Soldiers for "God, Honor, Fatherland": The History of Panzerregiment "Großdeutschland"
Otto Weidinger
Otto Kumm
Manhay, The Ardennes: Christmas 1944
Armor Battles of the Waffen-SS, 1943-1945
Tiger: The History of a Legendary Weapon, 1942-1945
Hitler Moves East
Tigers in the Mud
Panzer Aces
Footsteps of the Hunter
History of the 12. SS-Panzer-Division "Hitlerjugend"
Grenadiers, the Autobiography of Kurt Meyer
Field Uniforms of German Army Panzer Forces in World War 2
Tigers in Combat, Volumes I and II
Infanterie Aces
Freineaux and Lamormenil—The Ardennes
The Caucasus and the Oil
East Front Drama — 1944
The History of the Fallschirm-Panzer-Korps "Hermann Göring"
Michael Wittmann and the Tiger Commanders of the Leibstandarte

The Western Front 1944: Memoirs of a Panzer Lehr Officer
Luftwaffe Aces
Quiet Flows the Rhine
Decision in the Ukraine: Summer 1943
Combat History of the schwere Panzer-Jäger-Abteilung 653
The Brandenburgers—Global Mission
Field Uniforms of Germany's Panzer Elite
Soldiers of the Waffen-SS: Many Nations, One Motto
In the Firestorm of the Last Years of the War
The Meuse First and Then Antwerp
Jochen Peiper: Commander, Panzerregiment "Leibstandarte"
Sturmgeschütze vor! Assault Guns to the Front!
Karl Baur: A Pilot's Pilot
Kharkov
Panzer Aces 2
Panzertaktik! Armor Tactics of the German Armed Forces
The Combat History of schwere Panzer-Abteilung 503
Normandy 1944, German Military Organization, Combat Power and Organizational Effectiveness

In Preparation (Working Titles)

The Combat History of schwere Panzerjäger Abteilung 654
Tragedy of the Faithful, The History of the III. SS-Panzer-Korps
Drama Between Budapest and Vienna
Kursk 1943, A Photo Album
Of Good Conscience, The History of the 4. SS-Polizei-Division
Funklenkpanzer, A History of German Remote- and Radio-Controlled Armor Units

J.J. Fedorowicz Publishing

Signing Box by Matt Lukes

Table of Contents

1. Report by *Leutnant* Gerd Albert
   (His assignment to *Sturmgeschütz-Brigade 276* from its formation in July 1943 to 11 November 1943). 1

2. November 1943: Boneterevka Sector — Fighting Partisans…….
   (After-action report by *Obergefreiter* Willi Wenk, *3./Sturmgeschütz-Brigade 276*, motorcycle messenger and *Sturmgeschütz* loader). 20

3. "Memories….." of war during operations conducted by *Sturmgeschütz-Brigade 276*
   (After-action report by *Hauptmann* Friedrich Stück). 22

4. Operations in the Pripjet Marshes…….
   *(*After-action report by *Hauptmann* Friedrich Stück*)* *32*

5. The End of January 1944 on the Rowno—Korosten Road…..
   *(*After-action report by *Hauptmann* Friedrich Stück*)* *35*

6. Heavy Defensive Fighting from 23 December 1943 to 21 March 1944…
   Sturmgeschütz-Brigade 276 with *Heeresgruppe "Süd"* under *Generalfeldmarschall* von Manstein…
   The Pocket at Kamemez-Podolsk from 23 March 1944 until the breakout on 6 April 1944 under *Generaloberst* Hube
   (After-action report by *Obergefreiter* Heinz Fleischer, *Sturmgeschütz* driver, *3./Sturmgeschütz-Brigade 276*). 42

7. The Beginning of August 1944 in the Willkowischken Sector…..
   (After-action report by *Obergefreiter* Willi Wenk, *3./Sturmgeschütz-Brigade 276*, motorcycle messenger and *Sturmgeschütz* loader). 50

8. Operations on the Schloßberg, Willuhnen, Neustadt—
Schirwindt Road on 16 August 1944
(After-action report by *Obergefreiter* Heinz Fleischer,
Sturmgeschütz Driver, *3./Sturmgeschütz-Brigade 276*). 53

9. *Major* Norbert Braun's Last Operation as Commander of
Sturmgeschütz-Brigade 276 on 21 August 1944 in the
Bramerhusen Section
(After-action report by *Obergefreiter* Heinz Fleischer,
Sturmgeschütz driver, *3./Sturmgeschütz-Brigade 276*). 57

10. An Engagement with four *Sturmgeschütze* in the Village of
Zoliesia, 28 August 1944
(After-action report by *Obergefreiter* Heinz Fleischer,
Sturmgeschütz driver, *3./Sturmgeschütz-Brigade 276*). 60

11. The Fighting on 16 October 1944 during the Russian
Offensive in East Prussia...
(After-action report by *Obergefreiter* Heinz Fleischer,
Sturmgeschütz driver, *3./Sturmgeschütz-Brigade 276*). 64

12. "Front Leave 1945"....
(Report by *Hauptmann* Friedrich Stück). 70

13. Fighting on 19 January 1945 with five *Sturmgeschütze* about
thirty kilometers northwest of Ciechanow and nine kilometers
south of the Soldau—Lautenburg road
(After-action report by *Obergefreiter* Heinz Fleischer,
Sturmgeschütz driver, *3./Sturmgeschütz-Brigade 276*). 73

14. After-action report from 2-12 February 1945 in the Area of
Operations of Schwetz, Julienhof, Belino, Bislau and Tuchel
(After-action report by from *Obergefreiter* Heinz Fleischer,
Sturmgeschütz driver, *3./Sturmgeschütz-Brigade 276*). 78

15. Tuchler Heide: Mid-February 1945....
(After-action report by *Hauptmann* Friedrich Stück). 80

16. Operations on 18/19 February 1945 in the Tuchler Heath and the Village of Altfliess…
(After-action report by *Obergefreiter* Heinz Fleischer, *Sturmgeschütz* driver, *3./Sturmgeschütz-Brigade 276*). 90

Photo Section 97

17. Operations at Mewe from 27 February until 5 March 1945...
(After-action report by *Obergefreiter* Heinz Fleischer, *Sturmgeschütz* driver, *3./Sturmgeschütz-Brigade 276*). 185

18. The *3. Batterie* of *Sturmgeschütz-Brigade 276* Employed as Infantry and in the Heavy Defensive Fighting around the City of Danzig…
(After-action report by *Obergefreiter* Heinz Fleischer, *Sturmgeschütz* driver, *3./Sturmgeschütz-Brigade 276*). 195

19. *Sturmartilleristen* of *Sturmgeschütz-Brigade 276* Employed as Infantrymen from 2-15 April 1945 in the Landau, Scharfenberg, Wotzloff and Gottsfalde Sectors…
(After-action report by *Obergefreiter* Heinz Fleischer, *Sturmgeschütz* driver, *3./Sturmgeschütz-Brigade 276*). 199

20. From the End of February until the End of the War in May 1945….
(Report by *Hauptmann* Friedrich Stück). 205

21. Surrender on 9 May 1945 and the Path into Soviet Captivity from Schiewenhorst to Deutsch Eylau…
(Report by *Obergefreiter* Heinz Fleischer, *Sturmgeschütz* driver, *3./Sturmgeschütz-Brigade 276*). .229

Appendices

1. A Capsule History of *Sturmgeschütz-Brigade 276* 237
2. Report of Internment by the Swedes and Transfer to Russian Captivity (Anonymous) 241

Foreword

This book is a chronicle about the formation and history of *Sturmgeschütz-Brigade 276*. It is not a novel containing fabricated stories, rather a collection of unembellished experiences which were endured and later written about by comrades of *Sturmgeschütz-Brigade 276*. Every name, every place and every detail is real; all experiences reported herein are the truth, as seen through the eyes of the authors during the years 1943-1945. This book should serve as a memorial to our comrades who were killed in action as well as an admonition for the living. *Sturmgeschütz-Brigade 276* was formed in Altengrabow near Jüterbog in the summer of 1943. The brigade was formed from members of the *2. Batterie* of *Sturmgeschütz-Brigade 190*. The symbol for *Sturmgeschütz-Brigade 276* was a shield containing a jumping black panther.

Under the leadership of *Hauptmann* Rünger, the brigade quickly grew into a tightly knit unit. Experienced *Sturmartillerie* officers led the individual batteries. In the late fall of 1943, *Sturmgeschütz-Brigade 276* departed from the train station in Jüterbog to the East in the area of *Heeresgruppe "Mitte"*. The first operations took place south of Briansk. Immediately after the first operation, *Hauptmann* Rünger and his adjutant were killed during a Stalin Organ attack. *Hauptmann* Schulte, commander of the *1. Batterie*, temporarily led the brigade until *Major* Norbert Braun took over as the new commander.

On 21 August 1944, *Major* Braun was killed by a round fired from a Russian antitank gun near Turcinai—Bramerhusen. The first operations south of Briansk were followed by the defensive fighting in the Korosten, Schitomir, Schepetowka, Jampol, Proskurow, Schmerinka, Winniza and Rowno—Goszcza—Korec sectors. They ended in the Kamenez—Podolsk pocket. About 90% of the personnel and a few trucks, amphibious cars and communications vehicles from the headquarters battery were saved.

In the middle of April 1944, the brigade, which at that time was employed as an infantry unit, escaped the pocket while fighting in the vicinity of Butschatsch. Afterwards, the brigade was transported by train to Deutsch Eylau (West Prussia) where it was to be reformed. After the reformation, *Sturmgeschütz-Brigade 276* was loaded onto trains at Deutsch Eylau on 1 and 2 August 1944 and was employed at Willkowischken. With the *349.* and *549. Volksgrenadier-Divisionen*, we liberated Willkowischken. Due to the superior strength of the Russians, we were pushed back in the direction of Wirballen, Schirwindt, Eydkau, Schloßberg and Ebenrode. During the defensive fighting, the brigade recorded heavy casualties.

We were then sent in a southerly direction until reaching the Pultusk—Ciechanow sector, where we spent the Christmas in 1944. On 14 January 1945, the Russians attacked with strong forces and the brigade had to retreat in a northwesterly direction.

Sturmgeschütz-Brigade 276 was then employed in the Kulm, Kulmsee, Schwerz, Graudenz, Tuchler Heide, Mewe and (Preußisch) Stargard sectors where it experienced heavy defensive fighting and sustained many casualties. Between 20 and 24 March 1945, the brigade lost its last four Sturmgeschütze north of (Preußisch) Stargard. Thereafter Sturmgeschütz-Brigade 276 ceased to exist. Starting 25 March 1945, the brigade was employed as an infantry unit, during which it sustained very high casualties. Starting 1 February 1945, Hauptmann Werner Stück became the commander of the unit.

It must be said that all of the comrades of *Sturmgeschütz-Brigade 276* — just like every other German Soldier in East and West Prussia —had only one thought: To fight to the last man, so that the helpless, the women and the children, as well as wounded German soldiers, could be saved by escaping to sea. We continued to fight for this reason alone, although we all knew that the war had been lost some time ago.

Heinz Fleischer

1. Report by Leutnant Gerd Albert

(His assignment to *Sturmgeschütz-Brigade 276* from its formation in July 1943 to 11 November 1943)

On a beautiful summer day at the end of June 1943, I was sitting in a train that was on its way to Altengrabow near Jüterbog. I had with me my orders for my transfer to the newly-formed *Sturmgeschütz-Brigade 276*. My thoughts circled around my certain past and a completely uncertain future. The advance in 1942 with *Artillerie-Regiment 9* from our winter position near Kaganowitscha (southern Ukraine), passing through Taganrog Rostow — Krasnodar until reaching Novorossisk (on the Black Sea), was behind me. There were unbelievable marches on foot. We had marched on foot because the horses from the horse-drawn vehicles had all died as the result of a severe lack of feed and water. No one had been allowed to sit on the horses and the comrades who could not control their thirst in the glowing heat collapsed. The few wells we found contained either brackish water or water that had been poisoned. Between Rostow and Krasnodar we found some tractors on a collective farm with which we were able to tow our *LFH* (light field howitzers: 10.5 cm). We were also able to sit on them. From then on we felt like princes. The reader will have noticed by now my reasons for telling this tale: I was a real lover of horses and also a pretty good rider and therefore I swore at that time never to go to war again as a member of horse-drawn troops.

After I was graduated from the *Artillerie-Waffenschule* (Artillery Military Academy) Jüterbog with a promotion to *Leutnant* (at the age of 18!) and had completed an officer's training course, I found out that the *Sturmartillerie* was looking for volunteer officers. My dream came true very quickly. My hopes were confirmed with enrollment in a retraining course for the *Sturmartillerie*. The course took place at Burg near Magdeburg: I was now with an elite troop that consisted only of volunteers … which had no use for horses! At Burg we had also learned about the meaning and purpose of the *Sturmartillerie* and about the technical and tactical aspects, as well as the special supply considerations. Everything had been very interesting, even if during this train ride I quietly doubted whether everything we learned could be applied to the real world.

Something else occupied my thoughts: During the farewell gathering the commander of the *Sturmgeschütz* school, *Oberst* Hoffmann-Schönborn, had mentioned (among other things), that up until now most of the officers of the *Sturmartillerie* had been killed in action. He also mentioned that this branch of service was still relatively young and in the process of being formed. But with my youthful optimism I was able to suppress these thoughts, even though it was also clear to me that the war had become much harder in comparison to the war that I had experienced in 1942. After all of the more or less boring courses in Altengrabow were over, I reported to our commander, *Hauptmann* Rünger, and to the commander of the *3. Batterie*, *Oberleutnant* Tobler, to whom I was assigned as a platoon leader.

The first goal was to form a unit from the thrown-together "stockpile" of men, a third of whom were battle-proven *Sturmartilleristen* from the *2. Batterie* of *Sturmgeschütz-Brigade 190* and two thirds of whom were volunteers from every possible branch of service (the majority being artillery men). And within three weeks the brigade was already in possession of all its equipment. Everything was brand new, from the field kitchen and vehicles to the most modern *Sturmgeschütze*. These were naturally the imposing nucleus of the brigade, thirty-one in all, and included a commander's Sturmgeschütz, three battery commander's *Sturmgeschütze* and three *Sturmgeschütze* for each platoon. Each battery consisted of three platoons; one of which was equipped with 10.5 cm howitzer guns while the remaining two were equipped with long-barreled 7.5 cm guns. The asphalt covered barrack square at Altengrabow was the last time we would ever see this combined mass of firepower.

At the end of July 1943 we loaded up on the transport trains (one train per battery) that were to take the brigade to the Eastern Front. Just as the transport through Poland had begun, the Sturmgeschütz ammunition holders, which were built with every bit of German perfection and lined the inside of the *Sturmgeschütze*, were removed. Apparently the *"alte Hasen"* (combat-proven veterans), who knew of every possible life saving fact for any emergency, stated that one could load twice as many rounds (about 80), when the rounds were simply stacked on the floor. The result was that the loader could barely find enough space in the fighting compartment and had to remain bent under the closed hatch.

As the *2. Batterie* arrived in its area of operations south of Brjansk, it could no longer detrain at the train station where the *1. Batterie* had arrived. Upon its arrival, the *3. Batterie* had to detrain at a train station still further west and was immediately put into defensive action against Russian troops that had broken through on a wide front along the boundary between our *Heeresgruppen "Mitte"* and *"Süd"*(!). This was a small foretaste of the hell that the brigade was to experience in the upcoming days and weeks. Almost everything that we had learned during the re-training at Burg had faded into gray theory. For example, I did not experience a single operation with my entire battery, much less the brigade.

The platoons were without any form of communication with each other and had to depend on themselves. This included rations, munitions and fuel. They received their orders from the command posts of the infantry divisions to which they were attached (often for only days or even hours) and more or less acted as a fire brigade. They also sometimes received their orders directly from the corps headquarters. In this general chaos they often did not know where the Germans or Russians were. As a result, those of us at the front were constantly out of ammunition and rations after a few days. In order to get them, I moved to the rear in my *VW "Schwimmwagen"* (amphibious vehicle) — a great vehicle, by the way — and found our battery supply trains. After we loaded up a few food canisters, and after I believed I had arranged for munitions through the corps headquarters (!) by telephone, we moved — *Gefreiter* Hagemann as driver and I — once again to the front. Prior to departing, I had reported to the operations officer of the corps that my platoon was still unmolested in the village where I had left it.

In the two villages on the way to our destination it occurred to me that the residents had hurriedly fled into their houses as we approached. During our trip to the supply trains we had seen neither German nor Russian soldiers. But now we felt decidedly uneasy. Due to the heavy vegetation on either side of the road, we could not see the crossing until we were 25 meters from it. It was secured by Russian troops lying on the ground with a machine gun and three machine pistols. There was now no possibility of escaping from the village by backing up. I ordered my driver to stop the *"Schwimmwagen"* and to wait for my possible return.

I climbed out and approached the four Russians very slowly. I wondered why none of them fired at me, since they saw me and had to have recognized me in the broad daylight. When I was less than 10 meters in front of them, the first one drew his Kalaschnikow. My scream "Hands up!" (in Russian, of course) could only have had some kind of symbolic meaning. After I took out all four Russians with my 7.65 mm pistol — in the order they attempted to engage me — I grabbed the machine gun. I wanted to have proof of this unbelievable story. As fast as I could I ran back to my *VW Schwimmwagen* with this souvenir, especially since the Russians in the village had obviously been awakened and were making themselves noticeable with their gunfire.

I wondered next how the *Schwimmwagen* had rolled forward into the wall of a house, but then saw that my driver had been shot dead. He was still sitting upright at the steering wheel. I was able to pull him into the passenger's seat and then started the stalled engine. Despite a few hits to the *Schwimmwagen* and a flat tire, I was able to escape from the village.

I moved to our supply trains as fast as I could in the deep sand and arrived without incident. Once again I did not see any German or Russian soldiers. I found my platoon the next day. It was engaged in combat much further west. Our supply trains were also able to save themselves, even though they were far east of the line that one had called the "front" at that point.

There wasn't a front anymore. The Russian armies pushed westward and were only slowed down by supply problems and the *Kampfgruppen*. These *Kampfgruppen* varied in strength and had no

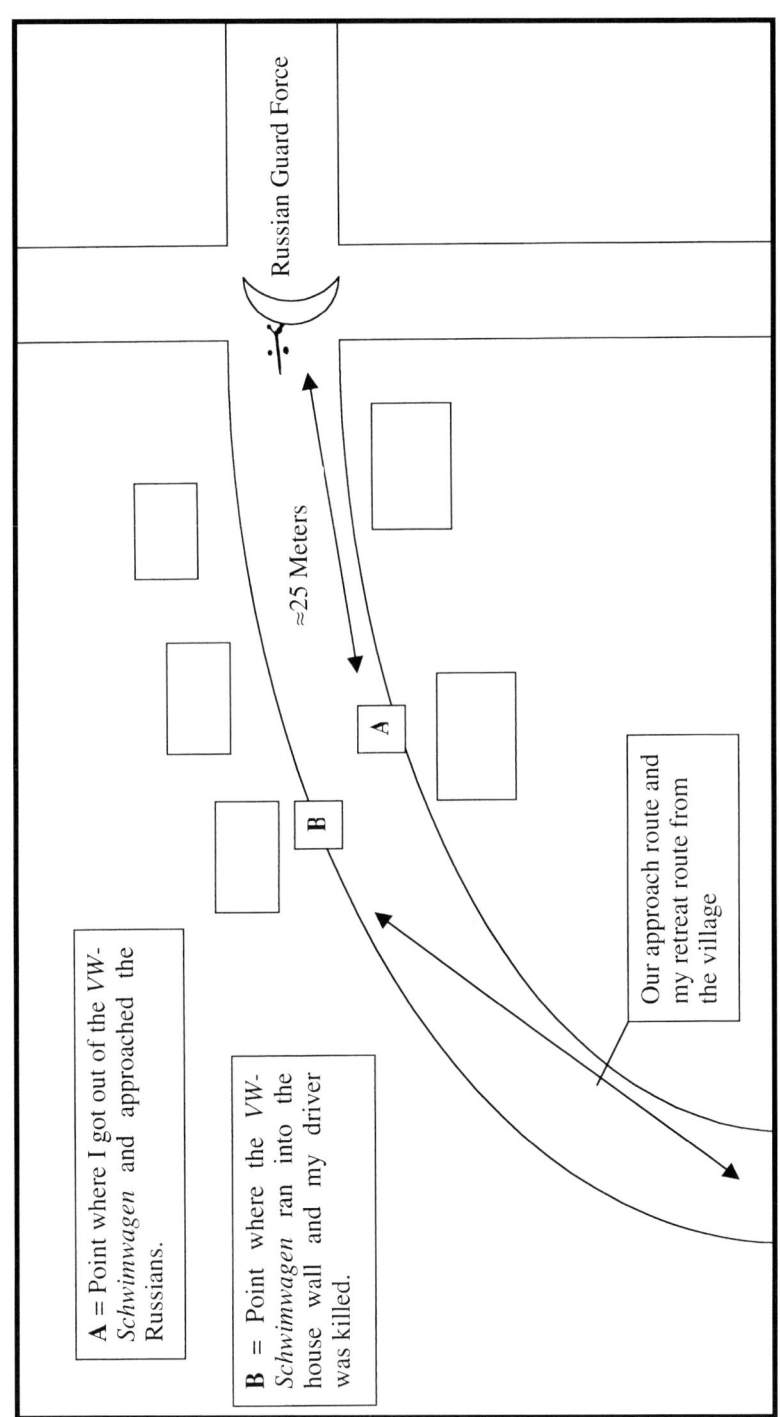

communications with one another to the left or right. They were frequently formed out of necessity and seldom by any higher commands. They had to hold off the clearly superior opponent, wherever and however this was possible, often by fighting to the last man.

We, as the "fire brigade", were ordered from one *Kampfgruppe* to another, between which there were untold kilometers where neither Russians nor Germans could be found. It was an unimaginable "no-man's land", especially to the north, where *Heeresgruppe "Mitte"* had its sector. Our platoons were largely dependent on themselves and often had absolutely no radio communication with the battery commanders, much less the brigade. Our commander, together with his adjutant, had been killed during the very first days of fighting, just like a platoon leader from our battery. The platoon leader, *Leutnant* Ulpta, had had his head blown off by a Russian antitank rifle as he stuck it through the commander's hatch so that he could see where he was.

It should be mentioned that the *Sturmartillerie* had lost many platoon leaders and assault gun commanders in this way! But such tragic facts were first learned about only after days or weeks had passed. Given the context, that may not have been such a bad thing after all!

In the chaos of war we also received orders that were scarcely compatible with the employment doctrine of the *Sturmartillerie*. For example, one day I was sent to a tributary of the Desna River with the order to start a relief attack on the opposite side together with an infantry battalion that was waiting there. For far and wide there was no bridge to be found, but the river was supposedly so shallow that we could have easily crossed over with the infantrymen riding on our *Sturmgeschütze*. When we arrived at the river, we couldn't find any German infantrymen, despite all of our efforts. But we were covered with intense mortar fire from the other side. The far side was — at most — 50 meters and, due to the fact that it was covered with bushes and trees, nothing could be seen behind the vegetation. As I sat there in my *Sturmgeschütz* — it was perpendicular to the water on the bare embankment — I still couldn't see any Russians. Then a mortar round blew off our left track — which our driver (Morawitz) brought to our attention —the assault gun was no longer mobile. Immediately thereafter the fire coming from the Russians was reinforced with small arms fire, and I got out of the assault gun. I didn't have any other choice.

My two assault gun commanders, *Wachtmeister* Seelbach and Taschka, came to help me, crawling flat on the ground. I had purposely left their assault guns behind as I moved to the river's edge, so that they wouldn't be forced to expose themselves. The thought of having another gun tow my assault gun back up the embankment was quickly dismissed, especially since there was no cover for some distance.

Instead, we decided to fix the track with the spare links we always carried with us. It was very hard work, and it was a wonder we were successful and none of us were even lightly wounded in the enemy mortar and infantry fire. It is almost unnecessary to mention that we pulled back without ever crossing the river (the depth of the river remained unknown), but we were happy to have saved our skins. The Russians did not have any desire to pursue us.

A little later I received an order to move my platoon at night about 40 kilometers to the south, so we could help an infantry division that was in a precarious situation. I carefully worded my thoughts and stated that: a. a *Sturmgeschütz* would not be able to perform to its full potential at night, b. we only had five or six rounds remaining and more munitions could not be acquired and c. we were completely uncertain what could surprise us on the way to the infantry division (which was a given due to the lack of information concerning the situation). To this I received the answer (with a hint at the consequences of disobeying orders) that we could certainly move back should we encounter serious danger. Further, the infantry would be happy if they could receive some "moral support" which our mere presence would certainly provide. It should be mentioned that *Sturmartilleristen* of all brigades received such orders and others similar to them. We survived the night without casualties, but we never did "find" the infantry division.

A few days later I was ordered to an infantry regiment in a broad depression that had been attacked by superior Russian forces. We were to move our three *Sturmgeschütze* without infantry support (as so often!) up a hill located on the left flank of the regiment. We were to attack the enemy from there. It was afternoon as we moved out, without (as we thought) being seen. After going about two kilometers up the hill, we suddenly reached a crest which could only be recognized from a few meters distance. I had advanced too far past the crest and my assault gun tipped forward into a well-sited antitank ditch. The antitank ditch was guarded and defended by Russians in battalion strength (as we had determined by then), obviously to protect their flank. My driver, Morawitz, had barely started to get our *Sturmgeschütz* moving again when he screamed, "The Russians are on our gun!" (I myself couldn't see through the periscope because we were at too much of an angle.)

What should I do? I pulled out five or six egg-type hand grenades that were inside our assault gun and held them in my hand as long as I could before throwing them through the barely opened hatch and onto the *Sturmgeschütz*. But the effect of this was only short-lived (according to Morawitz) and we were still stuck in the ditch. Therefore, I called my two other assault guns forward. Suspecting the worst, I had left them to the left and right of me behind the edge of the ditch. While my gun was still in front of them, I ordered them to fire their machineguns until Morawitz had managed to get over the opposite edge of the antitank ditch. While climbing up and over the other side, he had ground a path for the other two assault guns (*Wachtmeister* Seelbach and *Wachtmeister* Taschka). We were fortunate that our opponent didn't have any weapons that were capable of putting us out of action. They fought to the last man. Assuming that they were all dead, we climbed out of our assault guns, but their wounded lying in the field continued to shoot at us. Without being able to help much (partly due to the onset of dusk) we could see our infantry in close combat with charging waves of Russians.

I only wanted to use this as an example of how it often went for *Sturmartilleristen* when they, without infantry support, had to operate more or less as tanks. Our *Sturmgeschütze* were never meant, nor were they built, for these or similar tasks.

On the Dnjepr our front was supposed to have been stabilized. We saw a respectable system of antitank ditches that had been dug by the *Organization Todt*. When we crossed the river from the east on a large

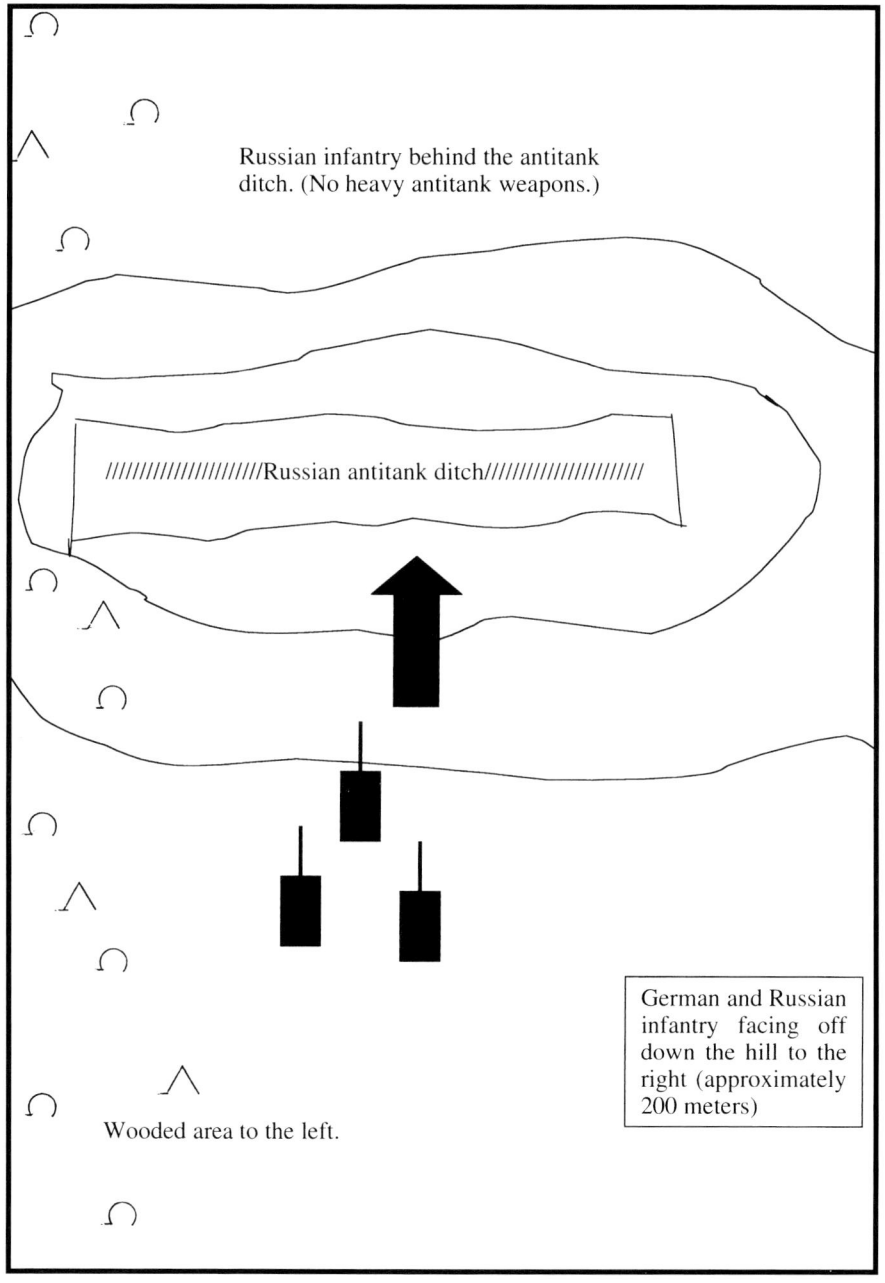

bridge that had been built by our combat engineers and was located north of the Kiev reservoir, we met up with *Leutnant* Beckmann's platoon from our *2. Batterie*. We were a considerable force that had never been assembled before — together we had six intact *Sturmgeschütze*. Both of our platoons were sent twenty kilometers upstream, where the Russians had already built a small bridgehead. Together with an infantry battalion that was already there, our mission was — at the very least — to prevent the bridgehead from getting any larger. If we had to, we were to fight to the last man, so that retreating German divisions would be able to cross the bridge.

When I wanted to contact the battalion commander in the late afternoon, he had already been killed, together with two thirds of his men. A large village was stormed two times by our brave infantry and then lost again. It was, for all practical purposes, the Russian bridgehead. Despite the onset of dusk, we decided to attack. At that point we suddenly saw Russian tanks of various types and a game of cat and mouse began among the houses.

Since our maneuverability as well as our optics and the accuracy of our assault guns — and, perhaps, also our mental agility — were superior to those of the Russians on this firm ground, we were able to knock out every opponent we saw without suffering any casualties. This continued until the sun finally went down. The last Russian tank we knocked out was a KV I which our driver, Morawitz, was only able to recognize as a silhouette when it was just a few meters away. He could see it because he sat lowest in the vehicle. In the darkness, however, we were unable to hold our half of the village, especially since, in the meantime, the number of our infantrymen had sunk to well under one hundred, about half of whom were badly wounded. Therefore we pulled back undetected to a line located about two hundred meters outside the village, from where we could easily recognize any attacking Russian infantry. After we knocked out another T 34 from this position, an absolute silence suddenly set in. Not a single flare climbed skyward. On the enemy side perhaps because the Russians had too much respect for us, and on our side because we recognized our inferiority and didn't want to give away our position.

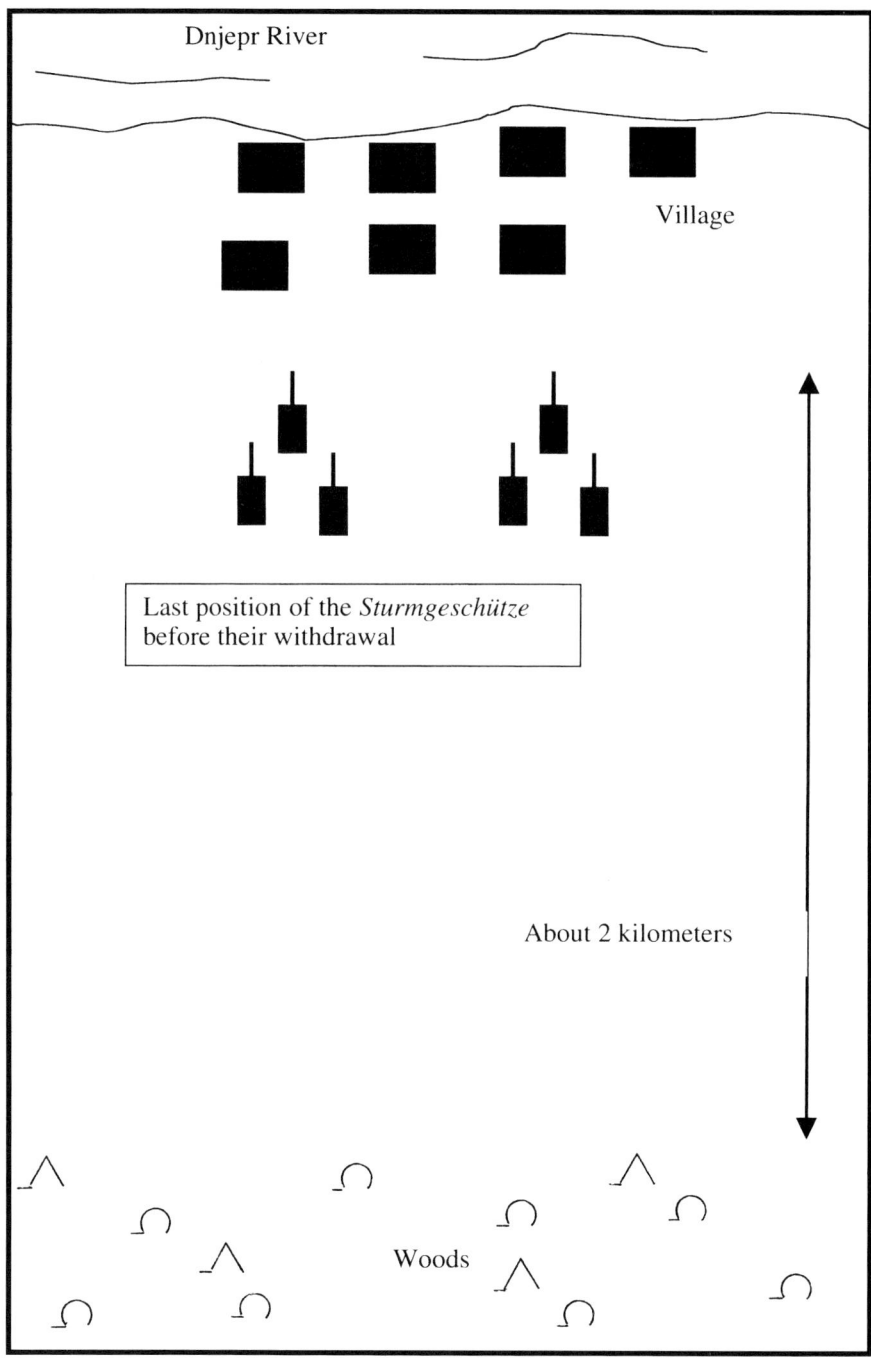

After about two hours — our nerves were almost completely shot — we heard at a considerable distance — first from the north and then from the south — columns of Russian tanks rolling past us to the west. This lasted for hours. Our radio operators (= loaders, machine gunners!) hadn't had any contact to the rear for a long time. Under these conditions we decided —*Leutnant* Beckmann from the infantry and I — despite it being against orders, to move with mounted infantry to the west at dawn and thus abandon our really hopeless position. The Russians in the village allowed this to happen without firing a round, which only served to nourish our fears even more: Were we already encircled? How could the innumerable Russian tanks have crossed the powerful Dnjepr River?

(Not until much later did I find out that the Russians had built bridges over the Dnjepr during the night which were twenty centimeters under the surface of the water. That kept our long-distance reconnaissance planes, which we had seen many times from the village, from observing the bridges. With the equipment they had at the time, it would have been impossible. As mentioned previously, there was a large no-man's land between the *Kampfgruppen* so that the Russians could build the bridges unimpaired. The enemy bridgehead proved to have been a successful deception by the Russians!)

We soon came to a trackless forest. The situation did not allow us to move around it. After a few kilometers, the trees became increasingly dense and the ground increasingly marshy. We took off the side skirts from our *Sturmgeschütze* — side skirts were used to weaken the effects of enemy fire on the sides — and built a route meter for meter that went deeper and deeper into the bog. The loud noise of the *Sturmgeschütz* engines not only served to disturb the peacefulness of this primeval forest, but also gave away our position to the enemy. After we had become considerably tired, our infantrymen (who were given the task of securing our retreat) reported that Russians were approaching us through the trees. They were then seen at distance of only 50 to 100 meters…and we had once again bottomed out with our *Sturmgeschütze. Leutnant* Beckmann and I conferred: The wounded who were unable to walk were placed at the required distance from the assault guns. They were prepared to be blown after the machine guns had been removed. Every one of us took our personal weapons and ammunition, as much as we could carry. (Food and water had already run out while in the village — except for a single bottle of schnapps, which we all finished off in defiance of reason). The few healthy infantrymen were to hold up the Russians until the assault guns could be blown.

It was certainly one of my most traumatic experiences during the war to leave behind the wounded who, for the most part, knew what their fate was going to be. It would have indeed been impossible for us to carry them in this situation and over an unknown distance. And we were completely sure, based on our experiences, that the Russians would take no prisoners in this situation — everyone knew that. Therefore a few of them urgently asked for the coup de grace, which none of us could give them. I can still clearly see their horrified faces today. The Russians attacked from the rear just as we blew up our six assault guns. To our amazement they didn't follow us very far, perhaps because their shock after the explosion was too large or they were curious about what had been left behind. It is more probable, though, that they had orders not to risk any more casualties after their tank units had broken through to the west. They could assume that they had us in the bag. At any rate, we were able to hurriedly escape with the few infantrymen and after a long march we were able to report to my completely surprised battery commander, *Oberleutnant* Tobler. He had already reported us as missing after he tried to recover us with a large prime mover and a few men he had rounded-up from the trains. They had given up the situation as hopeless after coming into contact with the enemy.

Leutnant Tobler ordered a large meal for us at the field kitchen (baked potatoes with tinned meat). We were extremely hungry and half-dying of thirst and as soon us we ate this meal, it went right through our systems and out the back door. By the way, none of our superiors made a stink about blowing up the six *Sturmgeschütze* which, surprisingly, were quickly replaced. They were only happy we had not held out "to the last man" and had returned to the brigade without being wounded.

Leutnant Beckmann and his platoon were only able to enjoy this respite for a few days. They ran into a Russian ambush during a counterattack. A relief attack came too late. They found all of the members of the platoon staked (!) to a garden fence in a remote village and no sign of their three *Sturmgeschütze*. To whomever this seems unbelievable, he should know that *Sturmartilleristen* were especially feared and hated due to their successes. Russian tank units had orders to avoid encounters with our *Sturmgeschütze* if at all possible. Due to that we could not count on any mercy if taken prisoner.

The northern-most divisions of *Heeresgruppe "Süd"* had been pushed further and further to the southwest in the fall of 1943, the result being that they were encircled in the area of Kamenez — Podolsk in the winter. This included *Sturmgeschütz-Brigade 276*. At the beginning of November 1943, we reached the area east of Shitomir and Korosten. On the rail line between these two large cities stood the last artillery train of the *Wehrmacht*. This train could only be saved by passing through Korosten since Shitomir had once again fallen into Russian hands. But the Russians had already crossed over the rail line with limited forces between the artillery train and Korosten, which is why the *291. Infanterie-Division* counterattacked there. During the day it was able to free the rail line even though suffering heavy casualties. At night, however, it was pushed back. This back-and-forth struggle went on for days.

The commander, to whom I was ordered to report, was happy that I had appeared with at least three *Sturmgeschütze*, but complained about the poor training and lack of experience of the young soldiers of his newly-formed regiment. The nightly cries of "hurrah" by the numerous and superior enemy forces were, according to him, enough to send his infantrymen fleeing over the rail line back to the west. We planned the counterattack for early next morning. That evening I had concerns that our *Sturmgeschütz* tracks could be thrown off while crossing the rail line's steep embankment covered with heavy vegetation.

Luckily I found a path with a crossing on the regiment's left flank. We used this to make our crossing the next morning, as the infantry moved out for the attack. The Russians, who had not sufficiently pro-

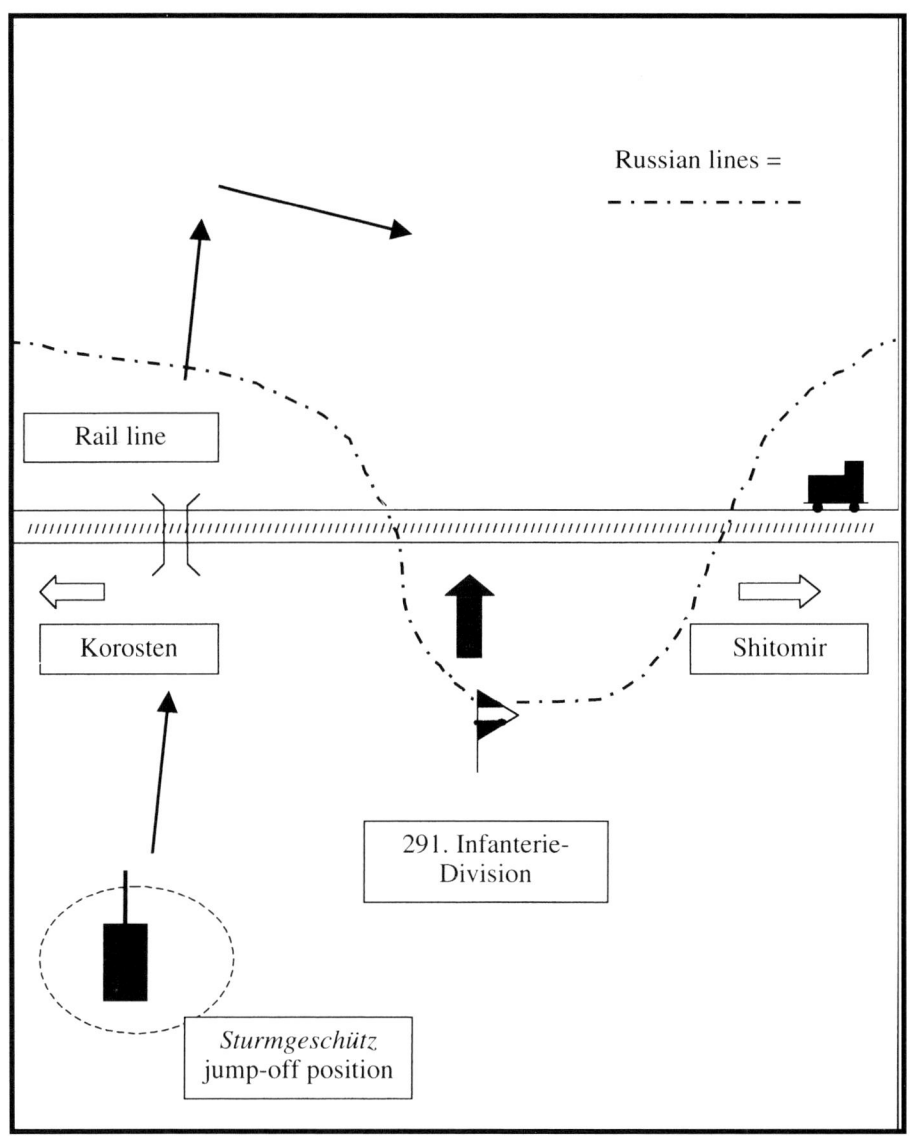

tected their right flank, were obviously surprised that we moved by them at great speed. Since we did not encounter any armor-piercing weapons, we turned around and went into position. The rest can be imagined: We fired all of our rounds and the infantry did the rest to annihilate the entire Russian unit. The enemy did have it in for our artillery train, however. The Russians renewed their attack the following night and captured the rail line once again with considerably strengthened forces and before our artillery train could be saved. The terrible game had to start all over again. I was once again ordered to the commander of the infantry regiment. There was nothing more to discuss about our combined attack: There was no other way for our *Sturmgeschütze* to successfully negotiate the train tracks.

On the other hand, I was not able to conceal my concerns:

If the Russians were even close to being as clever as we were, they must have mined the rail crossing with mines and set up antitank guns to prevent a crossing. The Russians, to our great regret, had long since started employing antitank gun regiments. To make a long story short: As I rolled first over the rail crossing with a barely repressed fear — which one sometimes refers to as "courage" — nothing happened. We rolled on further east than we had done the day before and repeated our attack with the infantry. The Russians did not attack the rail line, however, before our valuable artillery train was saved. It should be mentioned that it had the capability of inflicting tremendous damage, at least for those days. The infantry commanders were very happy and promised me a high award, which I was to receive from my brigade, but I never did, because I had to leave the brigade shortly thereafter. But my intent wasn't to write about awards! I almost forgot to report how I was wounded for the first time on 10 October 1943.

I had to report to a commander of a *Pionier-Bataillon* (combat engineer battalion) that had held the Russians up for days during which it had suffered very heavy casualties. A combined attack was executed which was to bring relief to the engineers, who did not have contact with German troops to their left or their right. Another intent of the attack was to teach the Russians some respect.

In the foggy half-darkness — the terrain was partially marshy — it took a while before we made out a *Landser* waving to us. For us this was a considerable relief, since up to this time we were not sure if we had moved around in front or behind of the Russians during our search for the engineers. In the entire area not one shot was heard, it was unusually calm. As a precaution I had our three *Sturmgeschütze* go back to the hilly terrain and where there was partial cover. I then proceeded by foot for about a 100 meters to the waving engineer. While approaching him he increasingly motioned to me to lay down and crawl. I did what he said, but I didn't see the point of it…at least not yet. I briefly discussed the attack with the commander whose battalion no longer even had the strength of a company. Finally he demanded that I crawl back to my assault guns, since there were numerous Russian sharpshooters not less than 80 meters away from us in the thick weeds who would be able to see us.

After I crawled back the same stretch and still no shot had been fired far and wide, it seemed that this tiresome method of getting back to my assault gun was taking too long. I also thought about the distance I still had to crawl and decided to stand up. As soon as I got up I felt a blow to my left knee that was so strong I fell back down. A later diagnosis showed that this was a direct shot through the knee that didn't hit any bones or tendons. I was very lucky, since the Russians had been using primarily illegal "dum-dum" bullets (which exploded after meeting their target). If I had been hit by one of them, I certainly would have at least lost my lower leg. I then continued my crawl back to my *Sturmgeschütze* and led the attack, as promised, with complete success, even though I had an increasing amount of blood in my boot. When we ran out of ammunition, we knew that the enemy would no longer undertake anything in this position. The commander of the *Pionier-Bataillon* was, by the way, awarded the Knight's Cross a few days later and was killed a few days thereafter….he was one of the best officers I had ever known.

I arrived at the field hospital at Schepetowka. During his morning rounds, the chief doctor confirmed what I had known: "Lucky, typical ticket home — get ready to be transported with the hospital train waiting at the train station." I turned this offer down, not because I wanted to play the "hero," but rather because I knew that being sent back to the front from a replacement unit would mean that I would never meet up again with my comrades in the *3./Sturmgeschütz-Brigade 276*. My comrades and I, for better or worse, had gone through thick and thin. And I didn't want to lose that because of a simple wound that was a "ticket home." The chief doctor did not understand and shook his wise head. After exactly one week, my comrades from my battery picked me up with my still stiff knee. Later, my knee began to discharge puss and was operated on without anaesthetic by our brigade doctor, Dr. Kaverau, before it finally and completely healed.

On 24 November 1943, I was finally pulled out of the events on the Eastern Front by a Russian heavy antitank gun. During the afternoon of the preceding day, a meeting took place southwest of the major city of Korosten. I had never seen so many high officers present in one place at the front. The city was to be retaken on the next day by all forces available. I received the mission to move out for the attack with strong infantry forces at dawn from the vicinity of where the meeting took place. For this attack I had available the last four *Sturmgeschütze* of the battery.

I began to have doubts during the meeting. Although no round was fired, I knew what we could expect when we moved down the 1500 meter slope without cover to the periphery of the city. Especially since the enemy had already occupied the city for a week. I was unable to discern a larger meaning for the operation after all I had experienced in all the previous weeks and months. Were prestige victories which were meant to impress the people back home the only goal? Was it worth the enormous amount of casualties we had to trade for conducting such operations?

We were ready to move out before dawn. For the first time ever I put on my helmet, which was actually supposed to be a requirement before any operation. But for what? After the usual flares were fired, it all started. As we approached the crest of the terrain, from where we had observed the city the day before, my assault gun, which the Russians had seen as the first to appear, trembled. It was the result of a terrible detonation… I heard a scream from our loader …. felt my head jerk back … and fell down in pleasant unconsciousness. Only years later did I find out what happened: The first round from an antitank gun struck our *Sturmgeschütz* in the ideal location between the cannon and the superstructure. My driver, Morawitz, is to this day of the opinion that this round badly wounded the gunner, Blauwitz, the loader and myself. Morawitz climbed over the gunner and then me in order for us to climb out. Then, with the help of *Wachtmeister* Taschka, whose loader was also lightly wounded, he pulled the three of us out of the assault gun while exposing himself to enemy fire!!!

Later I saw our *Sturmgeschütz* in a picture (which is no longer available); it had been hit by about a half-dozen antitank rounds and had burned out. A layman cannot comprehend the physical task that comrades Taschka and Morawitz accomplished when they pulled us out of that assault gun. No less worthy was the unselfish comradely behavior of these two. They did not receive a single word of recognition nor were they awarded with medals. They were simply heroes! While our loader died next to the cannon, Taschka and Morawitz dragged the gunner and me back to the rear and arranged for our evacuation.

In order to complete the picture, I would like to close my report with the fact that after this day — 24 November 1943 — until almost the end of the war, I received treatment in a half-dozen field hospitals. My hearing, despite many operations, could not be saved. Also, despite all of the surgeries I have had, to this day I still have more than 50 pieces of shrapnel in my body (various x-ray technicians have given up trying to get an exact count.)

2. November 1943: Boneterevka Sector – Fighting Partisans.......

(After-action report by *Obergefreiter* Willi Wenk, *3./Sturmgeschütz-Brigade 276*, motorcycle messenger and *Sturmgeschütz* loader).

*H*auptmann Tobler had just been killed a few days ago and was buried. The terrain was heavily forested. In this area many partisans had dug themselves in. Barely a day went by during which the partisans did not mine the so-called roads or during which small groups of them were shot by German soldiers. In the process, we also had dead and wounded.

Our *Spieß*, *Hauptwachtmeister* Ernst Hufnagel, had a four-wheel drive vehicle upon which a twin machinegun was mounted. He drove it every day to drop off rations to the combat elements. Besides that, he and two comrades used this vehicle to engage partisans.

I was a motorcycle messenger and spent most of my time with the combat elements. My job was to pass on orders or reports that could not be sent over radio. One time, when I was released from duty up front for a few days leave and arrived at the trains, the *Spieß* asked me if I wanted to come along on a partisan hunt.

My reply was, "If you give me a bottle of schnapps, I'm your man." The driver was *Obergefreiter* Niederlechner. For these operations we were additionally equipped with machine pistols, Pistol 08's, egg-style hand grenades and a lot of ammo.

There were difficult roads and terrain. But it didn't matter to this four-wheeler. Besides, I got a bottle of schnapps for every operation.

The partisans figured that the Germans would only go so far in this difficult terrain. Because of this they felt very sure of themselves and barely ever posted guards. As a result, we could often surprise them and take prisoners according to rank whom we turned over to the regiment. The others were shot. For partisans there was only one choice: Death.

We also knew that for us three there was a great danger in being taken prisoner, which also meant that we would be killed. We also knew that if we were wounded, the result would be the same. There were risky situations where I thought to myself, "It's over." But as a result of our operations we insured that the partisan activity in this sector was greatly reduced. We were also able to destroy many of the partisans' weapons and mines. Lastly, we were also able to gain information which was useful for other operations.

3. "Memories….." of war during operations conducted by Sturmgeschütz-Brigade 276

(After-action report by *Hauptmann* Friedrich Stück).

During the first days of January the order was issued for my transfer to the Eastern Front and to *Sturmgeschütz-Brigade 276*. After the usual search for a unit in the field with help from the "control points," I arrived at the brigade's headquarters at Schepetowka on 12 or 13 January 1944. I was greeted and reported to the commander, *Major* Braun. There were temporary accommodations, dinner with the other officers, etc. The staff considered what they would do with the "newcomer." Its intentions to assign me to command the staff battery didn't please me at all. (My training concentrated more on operations with a gun battery). But, since only two batteries were in action — four assault guns of the *3. Batterie* had been split between them — there really wasn't much other use for me. But later…. things became quite different!

What happened during these days? (Obviously I had just as little understanding of the so-called "big situation" on the front, just like the rest of the soldiers, except for, perhaps, the higher staff officers. I understood the meaning and context of the course of events only later, after publications describing them appeared). After the fall of Kiev, four Soviet armies under the leadership of General Vatutin were able to advance the 1st Ukrainian Front in a wide arch from its location in the Pripjet marshes in December 1943 through Korosten, Fastow and Tscherkassy on the Dnjepr. Only weak forces were able to oppose these Russian forces along the greatly endangered boundary between *Heeresgruppen "Süd"* and *"Mitte"*. Opposing these forces were only small mobile battle units (these units were in a weary state and also had to act as the fire brigades) and weak infantry forces. To the latter belonged the so-called *Korps-Abteilung C* (Corps Detachment C). It should also be mentioned that the Russian forces they were opposing were further supported by strong partisan units that were located in the marshes.

A short time after my transfer from *Sturmgeschütz-Ersatz-Abteilung 300* (Assault Gun Replacement Battalion 300) at Neiße to *Sturmgeschütz-Brigade 276* and my arrival on 12 or 13 January at the brigade headquarters at Schepetowka, *Major* Braun told me the following: "The brigade has been directed to immediately send the *1. Batterie* on the Rowno—Nowgorod—Wolynsk road to the area around Korec in response to an urgent call for help by *Korps-Abteilung C*." The *1.* and *2. Batterien* had been committed elsewhere and could not be called back. The *3. Batterie* was located with the supply trains and their vehicles (which were in the vicinity). It had handed over all of its battle-ready *Sturmgeschütze* to the other batteries.

Brigade order: I was to take over command of the *3. Batterie* and immediately prepare all of the elements for movement (except for the assault gun sections) and head for the north the next morning. Destination: Korec, about 50 kilometers away as the crow flies. On the way, four *Sturmgeschütze*, which were to be pulled out of the line from where they were fighting with the other batteries, were to meet up with our column. Not an easy task! It was only thanks to the energetic action of all of the members of the battery (only a few of whom I had thus far gotten to know), the effective support of *Leutnant* Kany and especially of the *Spieß*, *Hauptwachtmeister* Hufnagel, that the given order could be carried out.

Departure: Early morning, 14 January 1944. Weather conditions: cloudy skies, lightly hazy, light frost, some old snow drifts, terrain slightly hilly to flat, partly forested, sparsely populated, roads in some areas firm (with frost) and good for movement. I was concerned that no current information about the enemy or friendly situation in the area of operations was known. It was soon obvious that for far and wide no German troops could be seen.

After a few hours the quickly moving column, whose vehicles were travelling close together, was forced to take a break. In front of us was a depression, deep and wide; the path on the slope was steep and covered with ice. There were also piles of snow at the bottom. This obstacle was barely passable for the *Sturmgeschütze*. It would be even more difficult to overcome for the other vehicles. They would need to be towed and this would rob us of a lot of time.

Therefore, the head of the column turned around, traveled back a short stretch — following the increasingly flatter course of the depression — and turned off to the northwest. This was done in order to overcome the natural barrier at a more favorable place or, if necessary, to go around it. This decision soon took on a special meaning: On the north side of the depression, a few tanks suddenly appeared, some of which were moving in the forested landscape. It was hard to tell if they were German or Russian tanks. Who would have suspected that enemy tanks would be here, about 20 kilometers southwest of Korec and west of our planned route? This question was answered quickly: Tank rounds fired from a village northwest of us, obviously aimed at the Panje wagons. Decision: *Sturmgeschütz* element take position, assault guns free to fire at the pack of tanks (four T-34s were clearly visible) at an approximate distance of two thousand meters (with more probably hidden); all following elements move quickly around the village from the south (cover provided by houses, trees and bushes), then continue the march to the northwest to the road near Goszcza!

The advance was successful. The *Sturmgeschütze* drew fire from the Russian guns and, despite being at a long distance, they were able to achieve several clearly recognizable and effective hits, without being hit themselves. While taking position (choosing positions that provided good cover) and firing their weapons, the assault gun crews conducted themselves as only seasoned veterans would be expected to. Bravo! But the other elements performed excellently as well; there was no panic and they did not perform in a sloppy or senseless manner. As an absolute "beginner" as a *Sturmgeschütz* battery leader, I came to a very comforting and happy conclusion: This "bunch" was really OK!

But onwards. The Russian tanks stopped and after a while it was obvious that they had pulled back. Two remained where they were, but didn't fire any more. Were they knocked out? Let's hope so! Then came a negative report: "A vehicle and crew are missing." It must have probably broken down or lost its way before reaching the depression. *Hauptwachtmeister* Hufnagel moved immediately with his vehicle (a *Kfz. 2* mounted with anti-aircraft machine guns) to about the place before the depression where the road curved off. Upon arriving, he was suddenly fired at with rifles and machine pistols from a group of houses that were surrounded by vegetation. As a result, he had to turn back. Parts of a destroyed car, which he was able to see, led to the conclusion that our comrades had run into an ambush and were captured or killed. The uncertainty concerning the fate of the men who were missing placed a heavy burden on the comrades and a noticeable depression set in.

I myself was still burdened with the question of how I would be able to complete the mission after the recent encounter and the unknown situation concerning the enemy: Travel on the quickest route to *Korps-Abteilung C* at Korec. The detour through Annopol and Goszcza would certainly cost a few hours which could no longer be made up by traveling at a faster pace. On the other hand, it would have been a horrible idea if I had decided to "guide" the entire battery through the impassable depression with the *Sturmgeschütze* towing the other vehicles. The result would have been that we would have been surprised — that means attacked — by enemy tanks accompanied by infantry. The other alternative was to turn to the east before reaching the depression, without knowing that Korec had already been taken and the Russians had advanced on both sides of the rail line. Under those conditions, that route would have certainly led to a disaster.

In retrospect, it is still interesting to consider several things: First, one must consider whether the clash with the Russian tanks had hindered a planned Russian advance to Goszcza and Rowno. Second, it must be remembered that the unfortunate and unsuccessful search for the missing *Sturmgeschütz* had clarified how far enemy infantry had already advanced. The outcome of both of these events contributed considerably to our understanding of the local situation and greatly influenced the fact that the battery reached the road without further casualties!

During the afternoon of 1 January 1944 the four *Sturmgeschütze* as well as the headquarters and munitions elements moved east in the direction of Korec. The supply trains and the maintenance section set up at Goszcza. After about a half an hour I was stopped in front of a group of houses to the right of the road and led to a group of staff officers of the *59. Armee-Korps*. I was urgently awaited and correspondingly greeted. But then it got serious: Situation briefing and operations order! As mentioned previously, Korec had fallen into the hands of the Russians and since then they were advancing further, paralleling the road.

A *Kampfgruppe* of *Korps-Abteilung C* (a formation consisting of several run-down divisions) and parts of the headquarters staff of the *59. Armee Korps* were surrounded in a village north of the road about 10 kilometers west of Korec. The road itself was supposedly free of enemy forces. My opinion: The surrounded units would break out with all forces at once and withdraw to a new main line before the enemy could strengthen his encirclement with new forces. Retreating to the new main line would also prevent the Russians from gaining freedom of movement on the road.

Battery mission: After coordinating the tactical details, as well as the timing of the operation, the assault guns were to rush ahead in the direction of Korec under the cover of darkness. They would advance as far as the branch in the road that led to the defended village. The battery would engage enemy forces by pressing forward during the breakout phase in the sector south of the road so our forces would not be endangered! *(Note: What were the cute little rules that were taught at the Sturmgeschütz school? "Sturmgeschütze are only to fight escorted by infantry; they are not intended for night operations" and so on and so on…)*

It began as planned: We moved east quickly and encountered no resistance. But then a wild firefight began which was caused by those breaking out; the firefight was intensified by returning enemy fire. We weren't able to see any targets clearly and so we fired at "muzzle flashes" in the assigned sector. We didn't have to move far before we came upon the lead elements of the *Kampfgruppe* which proceeded to pass us by. The entire operation went quickly and according to plan. I can't say whether we had hit much with our continuous fire while securing the flank during the breakout (but how did the Austrians put it: "…. the psychological effect was immense….!")

Korps-Abteilung C was able to construct something similar to a main line on both sides of the road near the village of Babin (?). Staffs and supply troops set up to the rear in the direction of Goszaza. We were able to rest for a few hours later.

Sixteen January 1944 in the morning: Situation briefing with the *Korps-Abteilung C* staff. Enemy situation: The Russians did not pursue the retreating *Kampfgruppe* during the night, but in the meantime had occupied a village about six kilometers east of the new main lines and brought up reinforcements, presumably tanks as well. Friendly situation: Our forces were weak. We barely had any more infantry and because of that had signals and supply troops fighting as infantry. We had no heavy weapons except a few light and medium antitank guns and a single 2 cm four-barreled anti-aircraft gun mounted vehicle. I couldn't make out anything else. These weak forces could only occupy a narrow strip of land on both sides of the roadway for their mission of preventing an enemy breakthrough to the west on the improved road.

As far as I knew, there was no contact with our troops to the north or south of this narrow strip (just as we had experienced the day before!).

Note: Later publications provide documentary evidence that between Schepetowka and the Pripjet Marshes there was a gap in the main lines of more than 80 kilometers. This gap was only inadequately covered and secured by weak Kampfgruppen.

The battery was to be deployed directly to the left and right of the roadway and forward along a blocking position near the village of Babin. It was to be positioned there specifically to defend against armored enemy forces. After the discussion of the situation concluded, I moved forward during daylight to coordinate things with the commander of the troops engaged there and also to orient myself. In the meantime, *Leutnant* Kany arranged for the "care" of the assault guns at the forward logistics support point. He then moved them towards Babin to the point where the road branched off. Based on coordination with an unknown *Major*, the commander of a *Kampfgruppe*, the three *Sturmgeschütze* were to be integrated into the defense and to act as "corset stays" along the thinly occupied blocking position on the road. *Leutnant* Kany briefed the assault gun crews, who, above all, had to have an open field of fire on the road. My own assault gun took position on the road approaching the village that was near the command post.

The tactical measures were based on thoughts and observations submitted by the leadership of the *Kampfgruppen*. I agreed with their opinions: The success of enemy attacks was completely dependent on the weather, which influenced the condition of the terrain (the condition of the built-up areas, the ability of the ground in marshy depressions to support vehicular traffic, etc.). Attacks with tanks accompanied by infantry could only be carried out on firm ground, which meant on the road or from the depressions in the terrain. These marshy depressions in the land ran south of the raised road and were located between this road and the village of Babin and continued on far to the east. The village of Babin was in the shape of a T and built on hilly terrain. Correspondingly, riflemen armed with light weapons and the light four-barreled anti-aircraft gun on the *SFL* (*Selbstfahrlafette* — self-propelled chassis) were, for the most part, at the end of the "T" in the village in the eastern part. Light antitank guns, on the other hand, were on the northern edge of the village with fields of fire overlooking the depressions and the road.

After all tasks were calmly carried out and no enemy activity was noticed, the *Major* (the leader of the *Kampfgruppe*) invited me for a drink with his staff. Meeting place: Command post in a small cottage on a snow-covered, rising defile.

Those present greeted me in a very cheerful and cordial manner. (A bottle of German champagne — *Sekt* — still had to be brought from the commander's captured "Ziss" truck for the promised "passing of the bottle" but, as it later turned out, we would be forced to do without it.)

During the pleasant atmosphere of the reception, I became a bit concerned. Would we be able to fulfill the high expectations of these comrades? They had been fighting for many weeks in hard defensive fighting that had cost many casualties. Sooner than expected we had to provide an answer to this question. The "Ziss" had just arrived, driving into the defile. Behind it was my wheeled vehicle. Suddenly, sounds of battle — and a red flare! That meant enemy tanks! The tanks could only approach on the road. I immediately left the command post to go to my car for the drive to my assault gun. No, perhaps it would be go directly to my assault gun which was located out of sight behind a long, black, wooden shed (directly above the crossing of the "T" in the village). But it all happened differently than I thought! There were barely any sounds of fighting from the direction of the road, but tanks were firing wildly in the upper half of the village and one could also hear the loud noises made by their tracks. Damn! They had indeed moved over the marshy depressions; the village road's steep incline posed no barrier for them.

Then, suddenly, a T 34/85 that was about eight meters away from me moved right before my nose. He stopped shortly before the slope and then, instead of turning to the right and towards my assault gun, he turned to the left and continued on into the rising narrow defile. It's first victim was my car, he then flattened the "Ziss" truck (which had the bottle of *Sekt* inside it). But then this first tank bogged down. We fired round after round at it using armor piercing and high-explosive rounds — whatever was at hand. Then the second tank: It halted above the embankment and fired into the houses on the incline. It then followed its "leader" on the same path and at the same distance from us. It also turned off to the right, offering us the whole of its rear end. Fire, fire, fire…. There was smoke and dust all over the place in the interior of our assault gun and I could no longer see through the optics. I stuck my head through the hatch. The gunner and the driver must have gotten black & blue from the kicks they received from me in my efforts to "help" them steer and aim. Elevation for the gun was no longer needed. Only traversing adjustments were necessary — fire, fire!

The second tank remained stationary and was smoking, but the first one rolled back and rammed his own comrade. That was it for the both of them! What then happened can barely be described. A third tank passed right in front of my hull, turned again to the left and into the depression to the side of the defile where it turned 180° and then approached us directly. It fired at us, but the rounds were over or to the side. A quick shift to the new target and then: Fire! And then the indescribable happened: Suddenly his cannon looked like a huge broom. Was this a direct hit into his barrel or had one of his own rounds exploded? But he still kept moving towards us. Was he going to try and ram us? Fire at the driver's vision slot! Fifteen meters in front of us the third tank suddenly turned off, began an attempt to climb the slope of the incline and slid back again. Then there was a huge explosion; his whole turret flew in the air!

But in the meantime bullets were whizzing past my ears. Two people had gotten out of the first tank, a Russian Major and a senior non-commissioned officer, and had crawled into a storage shed from where they shot at me with machine pistols. I quickly ducked my head back into the assault gun. The two of them — large and good-looking soldiers — were later fetched from the shed. After caring for their wounds, they were sent to the rear.

But it still wasn't over yet: A fourth T 34/85 remained stationary on top of the incline, firing — to where, I don't know, at least no shots were fired at us, but we were firing at him. With high-explosive rounds! (Our armor-piercing rounds were "history"). We were firing at a distance of 40 to 50 meters. The distance obviously didn't prevent our rounds from having an effect, at least as far as the crew was concerned. They stopped firing and moved backward down onto a narrow alley way and some of them got out of the tank. But then an antitank gun nailed the tank with one of its rounds. It had previously changed position because a fifth T 34 was racing down the main street of the village. It proceeded to put a five-centimeter hole in the turret and that was its coup de grâce. The fifth tank then moved back quickly along the village road and into the depression. The surface, which had thawed in the meantime, slowed down the tank considerably. After the fourth Russian tank had been knocked out, the sound of rounds being fired could be heard from the direction of the blocking position on the road.

I moved up to the road with my assault gun, but already at about the halfway point I could observe what was happening here: *Leutnant* Kany's assault gun had brought the fifth Russian tank to a standstill and then he proceeded to knock it out with precise aim, despite being at a great distance.

What else happened? The infantry of the *Kampfgruppe* that was in the village had gone into cover during the Russian tank breakthrough,

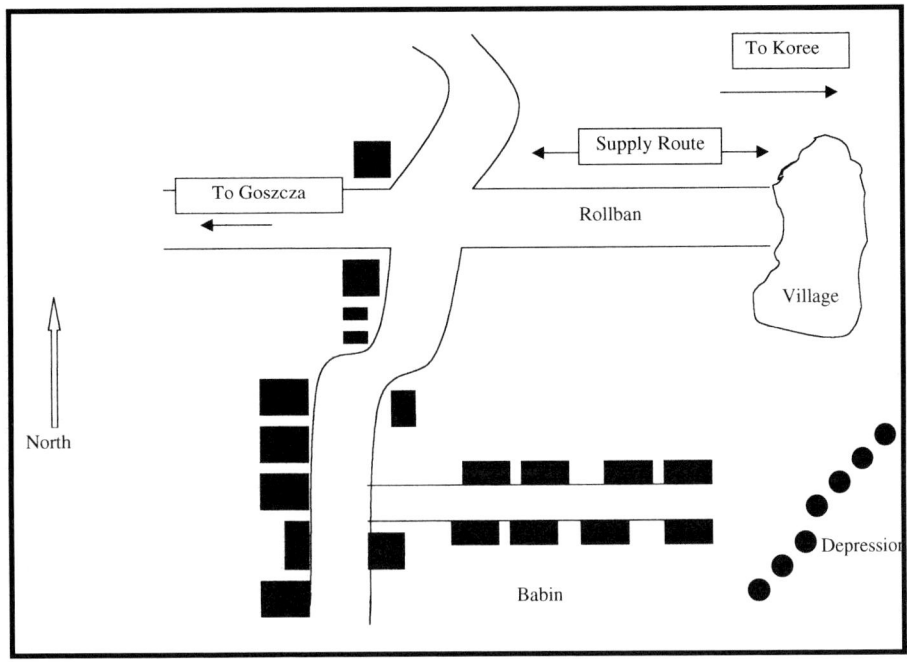

but they stayed in their positions. Perhaps the quick destruction of the feared Russian tanks helped their fighting morale. In any case, together with the antitank gun and the anti-aircraft gun, they defended against the Russians who attacked from the east and southeast. They separated them from their tanks and forced them to withdraw to their jump-off positions. That's all there is to relate. I could not say later how long the entire matter had lasted. We had used practically all of our approximately 80 rounds; maybe that's a sign of how long it lasted? We probably earned the recognition of *Korps-Abteilung C* and also perhaps of the *Armee-Korps*. There was no *Sekt* to pass around, but that didn't do anything to damage our bond of camaraderie. My own observation: I came to the realization that during a critical situation, my *Sturmgeschütz* soldiers, of whom I was very proud, had done everything right and as was expected. My thanks to all comrades of the *3. Batterie*!!

4. Operations in the Pripjet Marshes.......
(After-action report by Hauptmann Friedrich Stück)

End of January 1944. The *3. Batterie* had been employed with *Korps-Abteilung C* on the road running between Rowno, Nowgorod and Wolynsk since the middle of January. It had contributed to substantially halting the Russian advance and breakthrough towards Rowno. This was especially due to the destruction of the lead tank elements on 16 January, about 20 kilometers west of Korec. A few days later I received the order to advance without delay to the north into the outer edges of the Pripjet marshes with my combat-ready *Sturmgeschütze*. Once there, I was to try and establish contact with German elements. Enemy situation: Unknown. Friendly situation north of the road: Unknown. Infantry or combat engineers available to accompany our armor: None! Weather: misty, no precipitation, light frost. Three *Sturmgeschütze* without cover as a "reconnaissance battalion?" An operation in contravention of every rule! My objections and protests fell on deaf ears: Orders are orders! The *Sturmgeschütze* moved out into an oppressive unknown. Soon there were no German soldiers to be found anywhere, but there was nothing to be seen of the enemy either.

The rolling, partly forested landscape, with sandy, marshy or snowed-covered trails and the poor visibility required us to really pay attention to our surroundings. After a few hours we saw small groups of people and Panje wagons to the right of us a few hundred meters away. Friend or foe? Civilians? Hard to tell. I tried an old artilleryman's trick: a round right in front of them. The answer came soon thereafter: rifle and machinegun fire; a few incoming mortar rounds that were not sited very well. After a few rounds from our guns, they fled and the horse-drawn teams galloped away. Were they partisans or regular troops? In any case, they were Russians! With a turn to the northwest and with the assault gun crews' increased attentiveness, we continued further until we stood before a creek that cut deeply into the land. West of it was a village.

A still intact wooden bridge was in front of us and in the village there was no movement to be seen. Also, as we approached, there was no fire, just an uncanny stillness! Two assault guns covered the bridge while another one, with only the driver inside, crossed it. The bridge held and continued to hold for the other assault guns as well. Covering each other, we climbed up the slope to reach the main road of the village. At last we saw some old people and some small children. We asked, "Russki soldatski?" They responded with noticeable restraint, perhaps fear. Oh well, my "Russian" had always been lacking (…and my writing of it was also pathetic, it only mimics my spoken Russian). But then came the answer: A shrug of the shoulders, a shake of the head and "Njet!" Further questions: "Nemjenski Soldatski?"…."Njet; Nish nai; Bajelschi!" So the comrades had left one or two days ago. Carefulness was required, therefore the assault gun crews combed through the entire village and the nearby area. Result: "Village is free of the enemy!"

We were able to make contact with the radio station at the battery trains which, in the meantime, had moved to Rowno. From the garbled radio messages it was concluded that the Russians were now on both sides of the road and were advancing west. How far west remained unclear. Russian forces were already located between us and the road, which was between 25 and 30 kilometers away. Due to that we were blocked from going back the way we came. Would the amount of fuel we had be enough for the continuation of our trek through the marshy landscape and also for a very long trip back? Without receiving supplies this was completely out of the question! To bring up supply elements through trackless terrain, which could possibly be occupied by the enemy, would have been absolutely irresponsible. Decision: No "overnight" in the village.

Departure before the onset of darkness; sneak back to the main road! Next: Over the wooden bridge. Two assault guns had already gotten over when the third one cracked the beams. The assault gun was tilting dangerously and threatened to come off the bridge. With luck, skill and hard work it was saved. Then a night march began that no one will ever forget. The drivers had to drive in the blind during the night, led by the "much-loved" prodding and poking of the gunner or the commander, while one or two other crewmen showed the column the way with flashlights. They also secured our unit with small arms to the sides and rear. They were on foot, kilometer after kilometer, hour after hour. For a while I was able to relieve my driver, who was given a little breather by marching with the others. (After all, we had enjoyed good training on the *Panzer III* at Neiße!) From time to time we stopped, the engines were turned off and we posted men to listen for noise in the extremely dark and misty night. We wanted to pinpoint any noise from fighting or other sources. There was nothing! Just uncanny silence.

In the morning hours, not too far from Goszcza, the main road was reached without incident. The assault gun crews, especially the drivers, were totally exhausted, hungry, and barely approachable. But obviously they were happy to be back in safety again after our "enemy reconnaissance mission" which was the product of a senseless order. But who knew for how long it would last. My men were right; our *Sturmgeschütz* unit wouldn't have to wait long for its next assignment.

Why is it that I can remember this operation and the following ones that took place along the main road even though they contained hardly any successful engagements or similar activities? Perhaps the lack of activity is why I remember it so well. The physical strain during those last few days was very high; our unit was constantly in danger of getting stuck in the marshes or getting caught in an ambush without any hope of help or prospects for survival. Nothing happened: We sent a short report to *Korps-Abteilung C* and an even-shorter report to our far-away brigade. There was not a single reason for recommending someone from the battery for an award for bravery or any other sort of achievement. Far from the view of the headquarters it was once again "All Quiet on the Eastern Front" for the men of the *3. Batterie*.

5. The End of January 1944 on the Rowno–Korosten Road.....

(After-action report by Hauptmann Friedrich Stück)

This report covers (as does the previous one) the operations of the *3. Batterie* at the end of January 1944 while attached to *Korps-Abteilung C*. As far as I know, *Korps-Abteilung C* consisted of the remains of seven shattered infantry divisions and no artillery or armored units. It only had a few units employed as infantry and a few antitank guns and light anti-aircraft guns mounted on self-propelled vehicles. This "hodge-podge" *Kampfgruppe* fought defensively for weeks against clearly superior forces of the 1st Ukrainian Front which was advancing to the west through Korosten and Nowgorod-Wolynsk, south of the Pripjet Marshes.

The *3. Batterie* of *Sturmgeschütz-Brigade 276* (which included my four *Sturmgeschütze* and me) went to *Korps-Abteilung C* in the middle of January. It operated far from the command post of the brigade. The command post was located in the area of Stary-Konstantinow, about 100 kilometers away. We operated in a sector that was about 30 kilometers wide. This strip of land was situated south of the Pripjet Marshes on both sides of the Rowno—Korosten road. The battery was constantly in action, be it defending against enemy tanks, relieving isolated or surrounded elements or even acting as a "reconnaissance" unit. Through these operations the battery was a great contributor to the fact that for several weeks the Russian advance to Rowno in the area of the extremely important road was stopped. Not until the last of the four *Sturmgeschütze* was lost did the intact elements of the battery move from Rowno to the support base of the brigade at Stary-Konstantinow. There we received a few *Sturmgeschütze* the maintenance section had repaired.

But now back to my reminiscences of the Rowno—Korosten road: After the Russian lead attack units, which were accompanied by tanks, had been shattered by the battery immediately on and next to the road from Korec to Goszcza, the Russians changed to a new tactic that was familiar to me from earlier fighting. The Russians infiltrated. That meant they moved west in small groups, widely separated and with low "overhead." They advanced past the forward-deployed elements of *Korps-Abteilung C* which put the German positions in a very precarious situation. After the Russians "hopped" around us, the *Sturmgeschütze* often had to intervene far south of the road in the marshes. In the meantime it had become warmer and the land had become soft. The assault guns frequently had to pull the other *Sturmgeschütze* out of the mud, which was probably the cause of later damage to their motors, among other things. During the fighting southwest of Goszcza a "fire-hissing, flame-spitting dragon" suddenly appeared behind us. What was that, you ask? It was an armored train. Where are there such things, then? We wanted to celebrate the arrival of the dragon's help, but then there was a huge bang.

My assault gun had been hit, but did not suffer great damage. But next to us, our neighboring assault gun (was that Mehner's assault gun?) had also been hit, and with nasty results. The comrades in the train had raked us with the two cm rounds. These had penetrated the rear of the assault gun in the engine compartment and had badly damaged the engine. It was knocked out. The assault gun had to be evacuated. Not until we fired signal flares did the incoming fire from the armored train cease. Quickly thereafter it pulled back. Did the crew fear our revenge? Honestly said, I wanted to get back at them for this mistake! Now we only had two assault guns in operation against enemy forces consisting of infantry with small weapons which were highly mobile in the marshy terrain. When facing strong resistance, these forces would often retreat far north or south, but despite heavy casualties, they constantly advanced to the west.

(In his book "Scorched Earth," Paul Carell wrote, among other things, about the situation in this sector of the front after the fall of Shitomir: "In a makeshift manner, the XIII. Korps blocked the breakthrough. North of there the LIX. Korps along with the 291. Infanterie-Division and Korps-Abteilung C prevented a Soviet breakthrough along the boundaries between the two Heeresgruppen." At another point he wrote: "A cohesive front exist-

ed only from the mouth of the Dnjepr as far as Schepetowka. From there to the Pripjet Marshes there was a gaping hole that was only secured by a single weak army corps, the XIII. Korps (from Nuremberg) under General Hauffe. He was burdened with the responsibility of guarding the strategically decisive land bridge south of the Pripjet Marshes and for blocking the Russians…").

The competent general staff officer, Hauffe, was indeed able to slow down the Russian advance, but not stop it. Now the Russians were standing on the land bridge of Rowno with six armies, right outside the old Polish border. Historians saw later, as perhaps did the general staff officers of *Heeresgruppen "Süd"* and *"Mitte"*, that Hauffe was in an impossible situation.

But how these times were experienced from the standpoint of such a minor battery commander and his men remains only partly in my memory. And perhaps it was just as well not to know everything that was going on around me! While we continued to struggle with the Ivans in the small settlements south of the road, something terrible happened a few kilometers west of Goszcza. The Russians had bypassed the village to the north and during the night had crossed the road. There were a lot of supply trains with supplies and rations, among them 10 field kitchens — all horse drawn — which had moved towards the front without knowing anything about the situation. All of them had fallen into the "trap." The drivers and assistant drivers were all killed. All over the place there were Panje wagons and field kitchens that had been all shot up. There were horses, some still bridled, that were killed or wounded. Some of the ones that were still alive were running around. It was a dreadful sight!

The German troops fighting in and around Goszcza were cut off from their supplies. During this difficult situation the army reserve had to be brought forward and immediately employed. During the next few days a strong *gepanzerte Kampfgruppe* (from the *8. Panzer-Division*, as I recall) counterattacked along the road. From the noise that I heard, I gathered that the *Kampfgruppe* must have advanced eastwards to Korec. The supply route was free once again.

For our two *Sturmgeschütze*, which had used all of their ammunition and barely had any fuel, the counterattack brought a little relief. I pulled them off to the side of the street and into a group of houses. It was a place to rest. The assault gun crews were quite exhausted and dead tired and proceeded to stretch out for a snooze in the two houses. At that point our *Spieß*, *Hauptwachtmeister* Hufnagel, arrived with supplies and warm food. We hadn't had any of that in a long time (…perhaps we had French bean stew with lots of pork?) — first class! Besides that, the *Spieß* brought a lot of paperwork for me which I made a stink about. I can still barely remember the forms with the wide, colored diagonal stripes. Hufnagel had to continually keep me awake while I tried to complete them. I was continually dozing off while signing the forms and my handwriting was more like scribble. At that point I must have landed in bed.

A few hours later unfamiliar *Landser* stormed into the house and said that they had been attacked by Russians in the houses located toward the front. A few of them had been killed and others wounded! There was still a firefight going on in the vicinity, not far from the place where the other assault gun was located. I ordered everyone out and I quickly ran to my assault gun. After pulling away from the cover of the houses, I gave the gunner the "all clear" to fire into the bushes and at the sheds off to the side at the next sign of movement. The first rounds fired at these positions confirmed our suspicions and the results were good: The Russians pulled back from the occupied group of houses to the north and disappeared into the creek bed. The situation in the village remained unclear, however. Presumably some of the attacking enemy had let the counterattacking German troops move right past them while they remained under cover, or they were troops that had infiltrated back to the road. Not a good feeling.

We were in the dark in the groups of houses and without protection. If necessary, we would have to fight in close combat — a disadvantage. In any event, the peace and quiet was over. Consequently, I led the two *Sturmgeschütze* — accompanied by a few *Landser* — on the street on the west edge of Goszcza. (*Hauptwachtmeister* Hufnagel had just moved back to Rowno with the supply vehicles.) I am not sure I can remember for what reason and at what time the second assault gun was put out of action and brought back to Rowno. In any case, only my one assault gun was still at Goszcza. We felt safe the following day. We did not expect an enemy attack or to receive orders to attack as long as the *gepanzerte Kampfgruppe* still operated east of us. There was no doubt that they would come back along the same road and thus pass by us after their relief operation had concluded (which was limited by time and distance). A mistake on my part: They **didn't** come!

To this day I still do not know which route the *Kampfgruppe* took to its new fighting positions or assembly areas. But something else came: Namely, the order for *Korps-Abteilung C* to leave its positions at Goszcza during the following night. By 0200 hours the bridges were to be blown; all mobile weapons and equipment were to be brought to new positions outside of Rowno. The *Pioniere* were to be the last to leave.

And then it happened. During the planned change of positions, the motor began to smoke and then it stopped. There was a huge oil puddle under and behind my assault gun. Oh well, there was still a reserve canister of oil, so we filled it up again. It could only be a leak, since the assault gun had not been damaged during the previous fighting — or maybe? Motor running, we just wanted to get away from the place of the enemy breakthrough. After just a little while we had to stop again! Oil, oil, oil — the entire way, barely 50 meters long — a wide lane. Damn again, it was all over — or maybe not? At any rate, it was still a few hours before it was 2 in the morning. Radio message to the supply trains: Evacuation urgently needed! No answer. Perhaps our transmitter's battery was already too weak. We radioed for help to anyone who might have been on our frequency. It was dark; far and wide there were no more *Landser*. Nearby were the field kitchens and trains that had been destroyed during the Russian breakthrough.

Who was it that had the "great idea" to look for oil — it didn't matter what kind — in the field kitchens? One must have luck, and we did: We indeed found a big container of oil. Whether it was for salad or for a deep fryer, I don't know. We filled the assault gun's engine and, although the oil streamed out the rips in the oil pan, the machine was able to run for a short stretch to the edge of the village. But then it was over, finally over! There was no prime mover or other *Sturmgeschütz* to drag the assault gun any further. The hope that we would be able to save the assault gun and its equipment as well as our gear and personal belongings before the rearguard departed west continued to evaporate.

I had charges placed in the gun, on the radio sets, etc. to have them blown. Then we looked in the vicinity of the shot-up supply trains for Panje horses. The horses would serve as "transportation" since we would no longer have the assault gun to carry us. Soon there were four shaggy-looking horses standing in front of the assault gun. We also found some feed. The feed was scattered on the front slope of the gun so the horses could gather energy for the long trip. A further item was found and dragged forward: A large crate, which, according to the writing on the outside, contained chocolate. Would we soon be able to calm our hunger with candy? Quite a wonderful thought, almost like Christmas. Eight eyes stared at the contents of the crate: "shit, shit, shit!" We were all greatly disappointed, there was no chocolate, no sweets, nothing edible or drinkable, but instead many things from home that would have provided us with great entertainment during the many boring hours on the front. Included were games, among them *Mensch, ärgere Dich nicht!* Then I found something really nice, a harmonica (the only instrument that I used to play really well).

In the meantime it was almost midnight. East of us there was an uncanny stillness, in the south there were a few rounds being fired and loud shouting, presumably from the small settlements. Below the road there were small groups of soldiers silently marching to the west. There were no answers to my calls for information that would have contributed to clarify the situation. Then once again there was the peace and quiet of a pitch-black night. I pulled the harmonica out. Was it disappointment, increasing apathy or gallows humor? Who knows? I played whatever came to me, softly, softly, but not in a sad way. There was still the prospect of escaping this mess with the rearguard (which we expected to eventually appear), even if we didn't have the *Sturmgeschütz* to ride on and had instead to ride "high on the horse."

A while later, after midnight, some more soldiers came out of the village. When I asked them whether they belonged to the rearguard they replied that they were *Pioniere*. They also said their comrades would be blowing the demolition charges shortly, as well as the bridge on the eastern edge of the village.

No one followed the *Pioniere*. Our "rearguard" must have passed by us a long time ago! Deep depression! Was all the waiting and perseverance and all the worries about the last *Sturmgeschütz* for nothing? Well, that was it then, this was the finale for the *Sturmgeschütz* elements and the very successful employment of the *3. Batterie* in the area east of Rowno! We prepared the shaggy little horses for the move in expectation of a grueling, perhaps dangerous trip. Suddenly there were noises to be heard, sounds of tank tracks and motors to the west of us, coming closer. Tanks? Friend or foe? We had to wait to find out, for the time being it was under cover. Then came our answer: A heavy prime mover was supposed to evacuate an 88 mm gun at the bridge. Too late — in the meantime the fuses had been lit. The prime mover crew was no longer able to complete its dangerous mission. Were they greatly disappointed or perhaps a little relieved? Who knows?

For us there was new hope, however. We emphatically tried to persuade the crew to tow our assault gun back so that their mission would not be a complete failure and actually even somewhat successful. I also promised to defend their actions if their superiors were to question them. This promise was what probably finally persuaded them. Seldom had I seen comrades from different branches of service act so quickly and effectively! During the morning hours we arrived with the assault gun — without the horses — in Rowno at the trains. We were tired and hungry. Everyone was seemingly "at the end of his rope" — but definitely a little bit proud!

6. Heavy Defensive Fighting from 23 December 1943 to 21 March 1944…

Sturmgeschütz-Brigade 276 with *Heeresgruppe "Süd"* under *Generalfeldmarschall* von Manstein…
The Pocket at Kamemez-Podolsk from 23 March 1944 until the breakout on 6 April 1944 under *Generaloberst* Hube (After-action report by *Obergefreiter* Heinz Fleischer, *Sturmgeschütz* driver, *3./Sturmgeschütz-Brigade 276*).

From December 1943 until March 1944, *Heeresgruppe "Süd"*, under the leadership of *Generalfeldmarschall* von Manstein, was involved in heavy defensive fighting against large-scale Soviet forces. Enemy offensive movements broke contact between the German armies and once again one of the usual "hold at all cost" orders had led to the final encirclement of the *1. Panzer-Armee* on 23 March 1944. In those fateful days, the surrounded Panzer Army formed a so-called "wandering pocket." It was only due to the skillful and clever leadership of the *Oberbefehlshaber*, *Generaloberst* Hube, that the so-called "wandering pocket" was able to reestablish contact with the *4. Panzer-Armee* at the beginning of April 1944. The breakout operation, which was executed through indescribable hardships, ran a course in which countless German soldiers were to stay behind forever. The encircled *1. Panzer-Armee* consisted of the following units on 10 March 1944:

III. Panzer-Korps

  1. Panzer-Division (5 Battalions, 8 light batteries, 3 heavy batteries, 12 antitank guns, 0 tanks.)

  17. Panzer-Division (10 antitank guns, 5 tanks)

  16. Panzer-Division (9 antitank guns, 11 tanks)

  11. Panzer-Division (4 antitank guns, 9 tanks)

XXIV. Panzer Korps

  Elements of the *25. Panzer-Division*

20. Panzer-Grenadier-Division (10 antitank guns, 0 tanks)

168. Infanterie-Division

208. Infanterie-Division

371. Infanterie-Division

LIX. Korps:

96. Infanterie-Division (6 antitank guns)

291. Infanterie-Division (6 antitank guns)

6. Panzer-Division (4 tanks)

19. Panzer-Division (5 tanks)

2. SS-Panzer-Division "Das Reich" (0 antitank guns, 3 tanks)

XXXXVI. Panzer Korps

1. Infanterie-Division (0 antitank guns, 0 tanks)

82. Infanterie-Division (1 antitank gun)

75. Infanterie-Division (0 antitank guns)

254. Infanterie-Division (2 antitank guns)

101. Jäger-Division (20 antitank guns) with attached elements of the *18. Artillerie-Division*

18. Artillerie-Division (4 light batteries, 8 heavy batteries, 0 antitank guns)

In addition there were various army troops like *Sturmgeschütz-Brigaden*, *Panzerjäger-Abteilungen*, self-propelled artillery battalions, *RAD-Bataillone* (German Worker's Service), combat engineer battalions, artillery observer battalions, headquarters staffs, etc.

The fact that the *Panzer-Divisionen* only had a few or even no tanks proves how weakened the units already were as they were encircled. Against us stood the 1st Ukrainian Front which consisted of the following units:

1st Tank Army:

XI Guards Tank Corps

XXXI Tank Corps

VIII Guards Motorized Mechanized Corps

23rd Guard Tank Army:

VI Guards Tank Corps

VII Guards Tank Corps

IX Motorized Mechanized Corps

4th Tank Army:

X Guards Tank Corps

VI Motorized Mechanized Corps

1st Guards Army: 121st, 99th, 30th, 141st, 304th, 127th, 309th, 395th and 167th Rifle Divisions; 68th Guards Rifle Division

18th Army: 86th, 317th, 71st, 276th, 24th, 271st and 316th Rifle Divisions; 129th Guards Rifle Division

38th Army: 100th, 155th, 211th, 305th, 151st, 135th and 221st Rifle Divisions; 70th Guards Rifle Division; 1st Czech Brigade; 117th Guards Rifle Division; 161st, 183rd and 241st Rifle Divisions

40th Army: 133rd, 240th, 232nd, 74th, 163rd and 38th Rifle Divisions; 42nd Guards Rifle Division

Separate: IV Guards Tank Corps

Also belonging to the 1st Ukrainian Front were the 60th Army and the 13th Army, which were employed against the *4. Panzer-Armee*. The 40th Army and the 6th Tank Army belonged to the 2nd Ukrainian Front. This clarifies the true extent of the superiority of the Soviet forces over the surrounded German 1. Panzer-Armee.

From 23 December 1943 to 22 March 1944, *Sturmgeschütz-Brigade 276* was employed in heavy defensive fighting against vastly superior Soviet forces. There were the Korosten, Shitomir, Schepetowka, Jampol, Proskurow and Schmerinka areas of operation. We only served as the fire brigade; cleaning up breakthroughs and regaining lost positions. During this fighting we had high numbers of losses in both *Sturmgeschütze* and crews. Our infantry was almost at the end of its strength. But if we appeared with our *Sturmgeschütze*, the soldiers would regain their courage and fight like lions. From time to time our ammunition supply vehicles were cut off from us, and we were forced to engage in combat with only a few rounds. As a result, we served mainly as a form of moral support for our infantry. We were always in action; we never got out of our vehicles.

On 17 March 1944 the Russians attacked with such force that the Germans in *Heeresgruppe "Süd"* under the command of *Generalfeldmarschall* von Manstein could barely offer any resistance whatsoever.

The Soviet offensive established a gap between the *1.* and *4. Panzer-Armeen*. Its goal was to break through between the cities of Proskurow and Tarnopol. In addition, an enemy attack on 10 March 1944 broke through the boundary between the *1. Panzer-Armee* and the *8. Armee*, which was on the right flank. *Sturmgeschütz-Brigade 276*, which only had a few combat-ready *Sturmgeschütze*, was engaged in a bitter battle. No one ever even thought of sleep. We were often cut off from our supply vehicles and, at times, we had absolutely nothing to eat. When that happened, we were forced to supply ourselves.

Several Soviet armies advanced through the 15-kilometer gap between the *8. Armee* and the *1.* and *4. Panzer-Armeen*. They advanced over the Bug River and continued to the Dnjestr, reaching it on 18 March 1944 at Jampol and on 19 March 1944 at Mogilew-Podolsk.

The *1. Panzer-Armee* and the *4. Panzer-Armee* were able to regain contact on 17 March 1944 west of Proskurow, but this was quickly broken again, when the enemy attacked with superior forces. He threw the southern wing of the *4. Panzer-Armee* west towards Tarnopol. Strong enemy attack columns pushed on to the west, going around the *1. Panzer-Armee* and moving along the Zbrucz and Soret rivers to the south to the Dnjestr. They reached it north of Horodenka on 24 March 1944. This was the result of Hitler's obstinate leadership, which centered on the unconditional defense of every piece of land and which also placed political considerations before military necessities.

Sturmgeschütz-Brigade 276 was pushed back through Schmerinka in the direction of Kamenez—Podolsk. In the process we lost our last assault gun. The attackers on both flanks pinned the *1. Panzer-Armee* and on 24 March 1944 it was encircled north of the Dnjestr. The divisions of the surrounded army were very much weakened by the fighting during the winter months and only consisted of more or less weak *Kampfgruppen*, which were scarcely in a position to defend themselves. The condition of the troops was poor; they were made up of mixed units and the soldiers were seriously overtaxed by the continuous fighting and hardships. *Sturmgeschütz-Brigade 276* had no more assault guns. All vehicles were blown up, with the exception of the headquarters radio vans as well as two trucks and two staff cars on which *MG 42's* had been mounted. From then on we fought as infantrymen. The fact that the employed *Panzer–Divisionen* had very few tanks proves how weakened the units already were when they were encircled.

On 23 March 1944, *Heeresgruppe "Süd"* issued the following order to the completely surrounded *1. Panzer-Armee*: "...bring the enemy forces advancing to the south on both sides of Zbrucz to a standstill, re-take the lines of communication between Czortkow—Jarmolinzy and make contact with the *4. Panzer-Armee* on the Seret at Trembowija."

The weather conditions caused difficulties for all operations that were to lead the *1. Panzer-Armee* under the command of *Generaloberst* Hube out of the pocket of Kamenez—Podolsk. The temperatures hovered above and below the freezing point. First it would rain, then it would snow, then it would rain again. During the night everything froze and during the day it would thaw once again. The end of March brought colder temperatures, snowstorms and snowdrifts.

On 23 March 1944, all of the details concerning the breakout operation were worked out by the staffs of the *Heeresgruppe* with the staff of the encircled army. The 1. *Panzer-Armee* was consolidated into corps-sized elements. The structure was as follows:

Korpsgruppe "Breith":

    Generalkommando III. Panzerkorps

Generalkommando XXXXVI. Panzerkorps

17. Panzerdivision

Kampfgruppe "Das Reich"

1. Infanterie-Division

82. Infanterie-Division

101. Jägerdivision

168. Infanterie-Division

254. Infanterie-Division

371. Infanterie-Division

Korpsgruppe "Chevallerie":

Generalkommando LIX. Armeekorps

Generalkommando XXIV. Panzerkorps

1. Panzer-Division

6. Panzer-Division

11. Panzer-Division

16. Panzer-Division

19. Panzer-Division

20. Panzer-Grenadier-Division

96. Infanterie-Division

208. Infanterie-Division

291. Infanterie-Division

Gruppe "Gollnick":

75. Infanterie-Division

18. Artillerie-Division

Kommandant Fester Platz Hotin
   (Commander of Strongpoint Hotin)

Other German forces located on the southern bank of the Dnjestr

River included alarm units and security groups.

The Russians were convinced that the *1. Panzer-Armee* would break out to the south. Therefore they established strong troop concentrations south of the Dnjestr River, which would have brought the retreat of the *1. Panzer-Armee* to a standstill. The breakout was directed to the west, however, to the line between Stanislau and Horodenka. There were differing orders given at various times based on the changing situation on the front, until finally the order for the breakout was issued via a radio message. The breakout was ordered for 0150 hours on 23 March 1944.

During the night *Sturmgeschütz-Brigade 276* marched as quietly as possible to the west, one after the other. The soldiers only had the thought, "hopefully we'll get through." In the middle of the formation there were the two leftover vehicles in which we had loaded ammunition and a few belongings. *Ju 52's* flew above us in complete darkness. They were flying into the pocket to pick up as many wounded as possible. Now and then came the order for complete silence and to be ready for action at any moment. We received this order as we sneaked past the Russians who were only a short distance away.

On the vehicles we had placed explosives so that we could blow them up if the Russians surprised us. But it went well for us. For eight days we fought our way to the west. Many soldiers were killed or wounded, but we did not leave a single wounded man behind. The strain was practically more than we could bear. The soldiers were dead. We mostly marched at night; the nights were dark and there was only a few meters visibility. During the day we occupied positions to fend off break-in attempts by the Russians. Snowstorms and snowdrifts made every meter to the west more difficult. The villages we encountered on our way west which were occupied by the enemy had to be recaptured so that we could continue our trek. It was a murderous path — a hellish path — that the *Landser* had to travel.

On 5 April 1944 the relief elements of the *Heeresgruppe*, the *II. SS-Panzer-Korps*, had moved out to the southeast and only had 50 kilometers until it reached the lead elements of the *1. Panzer-Armee*. The *6. Panzer-Division* from *Gruppe "Breith"* had gotten as far as the Strypa.

On 6 April 1944 the division pushed its way into Buczacz. The *10. SS-Panzer-Division* advanced from the northwest to Buczacz and linked up with the lead elements of the encircled army. The breakthrough had been accomplished. The Russians had lost 352 tanks and assault guns during the breakout of the *1. Panzer-Armee* from the pocket and its fight to the west.

After *Sturmgeschütz-Brigade 276* had also managed to break out of the pocket (although with heavy casualties), it was loaded up on rail cars at Lemberg at the end of April 1944. The train took the brigade to Deutsch Eylau, where the brigade was to be reformed.

On 3 May 1944, we arrived at Deutsch Eylau. From there we went on home leave. Thus began a very nice time until 1 August 1944, when we were loaded up and sent back into action at Willkowischken.

7. The Beginning of August 1944 in the Willkowischken Sector…

(After-action report by *Obergefreiter* Willi Wenk, *3./Sturmgeschütz-Brigade 276*, motorcycle messenger and *Sturmgeschütz* loader).

We were set up in a small village, a few kilometers west of Willkowischken, behind a house. There was *Oberleutnant* Friedrich Stück and two motorcycle messengers. About two hundred meters east of the house was a patch of woods, and we knew the Russians were in it. At that moment *Oberleutnant* Stück saw three German self-propelled vehicles stationary on the road outside of the woods. The distance to the woods was about 120 meters. The crews of the self-propelled vehicles did not yet know that the Russians were there.

Oberleutnant Stück immediately recognized the danger that threatened the self-propelled vehicles and their crews. We two motorcycle messengers were asked who wanted to go to the crews and retrieve them. It was about 240 meters from the house to the self-propelled vehicles. I volunteered and then received the order that I was to instruct the leader of the two vehicles to move into a deeper lying meadow.

It was a risk for me since I knew that when I moved away from behind the house the Russians would see me and open fire. What they didn't know was that we were behind the house. I got on my motorcycle and started up the machine, full power. The machine made a powerful leap forward. I had about two thirds of the total distance behind me when the Russians saw me and fired. But they didn't hit me. The Russians probably noticed me too late and that was my salvation. I informed the leader of the guns of the order and they moved into the depression. I moved under cover of the self-propelled vehicles and returned to the house where *Oberleutnant* Stück waited by using a circuitous route and without being seen by the enemy. For my actions *Oberleutnant* Stück awarded me the Iron Cross 2nd Class. I was happy that I had survived it all. We didn't have any casualties.

As a motorcycle messenger I received the order to set up camp for the battery in a village in a rear area a few kilometers behind the front. After travelling a few kilometers I came to the village and thought it was the right one. Also important, the village hadn't been occupied by German troops yet. Along the street stood clay houses with roofs made of straw. I checked them out and wrote on the house doors with a stick of chalk who was to be quartered there. There wasn't a German soldier to be seen.

I had almost gone through the village when I saw seven infantrymen at the last house on the left-hand side of the street. I set up my space in the last house on the right-hand side of the street. Next to that stood another house. It was not in any condition to be lived in. I also put *Unteroffizier* Otto and *Obergefreiter* Erhard in the billets I had chosen. Then the battery arrived and went in their quarters. Everything was going well. Since there were infantrymen in the house across the street, we didn't have any reason to post a guard. We three comrades had a good time with drink and good cheer in our quarters.

It was a dark night and it was already very late when the windowpane was broken and an infantryman from the neighboring house yelled, "The Russians are here and my comrades are all dead!" Since I knew where *Wachtmeister* Köhn was with his crew and assault gun, we ran as fast as we could to the house and sounded the alarm. Within a few minutes we moved to the house with the assault gun, which I had also mounted, and set it alight. We had to do that so that the light from the burning house would illuminate the surrounding area and allow us to see the Russians.

In the meantime everyone in the *3. Batterie* took up positions in the village. We immediately saw many Russians who were moving back; we fired as rapidly as we could. But it was also dangerous for us to follow the Russians in the light of the burning houses. They could have easily knocked us out. It was now clear to us that we were dealing with a Russian patrol. The house burned brightly. The *Sturmgeschütz* was about to move off when, in the light coming from the burning house, I saw a Russian running to the right side of the road to the empty uninhabitable house. With my machine pistol, I jumped off the moving assault gun and started to chase the Russian. He ran into the empty house.

The brightness of the burning house shone on the empty house and lit up the inside as well. I crept along, silently, finger on the trigger of my machine pistol. I approached the house from the rear, careful of my surroundings. I saw how the Russian tried to hide under a wood-slat bed in the room. I jumped inside the room, pointing my gun with my finger on the trigger and yelled, "Rucki-werch!" ("hands up!") and fired my machine pistol over the bed. The Russian immediately put his hands up and tossed his weapon aside. He then had to give me his belt. I indicated to him that he was to walk in front of me.

So away we went into the village, my machine pistol at the ready, using the darkness for cover as long as possible. My comrades then guarded him. *Wachtmeister* Köhn immediately sent a message up the chain of command; the prisoner was then sent to the higher headquarters. I would also like to mention that this Russian received something to eat and also a few cigarettes for the first time in many days. He was hungry. The next day I had to report to a major about what had happened. He congratulated me and turned in a recommendation for the Iron Cross 1st Class, which I never received.

8. Operations on the Schloßberg, Willuhnen, Neustadt–Schirwindt Road on 16 August 1944

(After-action report by *Obergefreiter* Heinz Fleischer, *Sturmgeschütz* Driver, *3./Sturmgeschütz-Brigade 276*).

On 8 August 1944 the *3. Batterie* with all of its assault guns — and without infantry support — was directed to contain a Soviet breakthrough after their offensive northeast of Neustadt/Schirwindt. After this operation, the battery was to prepare for a counterattack with the *227. Infanterie-Division.*

Our five *Sturmgeschütze* started the march south from Bramerhusen. At the same time, the platoon led by *Leutnant* Regeniter — at that time employed at Schirwindt — was supposed to be pulled out of the line and link up with us. With only five *Sturmgeschütze*, a sector of about 10 kilometers could hardly be covered let alone a breakthrough at an unknown sector contained. Radio contact with Regeniter's platoon could not be established. Speed was of the essence! As a result, the battery commander, *Oberleutnant* Stück, my assault gun commander, handed over the leadership of the assault guns to *Leutnant* Sehrt and climbed into the *VW Schwimmwagen* (*Obergefreiter* Naschenweng was the driver).

We set out with the five *Sturmgeschütze*, my assault gun in the lead; the second assault gun was commanded by *Leutnant* Sehrt and had *Obergefreiter* Büdwig as its driver. About 100 meters in front of my assault gun was Oberleutnant Stück in the *VW*, moving in the direction of Schirwindt. His intention was to link up with the other four assault guns as soon as possible. The road and the terrain in the immediate vicinity were apparently free of the enemy. It did not appear to be necessary to be on the alert. Wrong! South of Turcinai came the surprise.

To the right of the road was open terrain (fields and meadows). Left of the road were also fields and meadows about 800 meters deep. Behind the meadows on the left side was a patch of woods. About every 200 meters there was an embankment crossing our path. It was covered with small trees and bushes and extended about 30 meters inward from the sides of the road. What we didn't know was that enemy infantry had already made it as far as the road. Suddenly, *Oberleutnant* Stück's *Schwimmwagen* and our assault guns received small arms fire. I immediately hit the brakes and my assault gun came to a halt. The second assault gun came to a standstill right behind me. Due to the sudden stop, *Leutnant* Sehrt fell into the assault gun.

I then saw how the Russian infantry began to run towards the *Schwimmwagen*. Did they intend to take prisoners? At that moment I began to move towards the *Schwimmwagen* to avoid that from happening. At the same time *Oberleutnant* Stück and *Obergefreiter* Naschenweng jumped out of the vehicle and I moved my assault gun between the *VW* and my two comrades so that they would receive cover. There were rounds being fired from machine pistols and rifles; hand grenades were exploding. Before our comrade Naschenweng reached my assault gun, he was mortally wounded and the amphibious car went up in flames.

After our commander and my assault gun commander reached the *Sturmgeschütz* and were no longer directly in the path of enemy fire, I moved the assault gun to the right and left the road. The other four assault guns had already left the road and taken position. After I had approached the *Schwimmwagen*, the Russians pulled back from the road and back into cover. We could have pursued them, but then our mission would have been endangered. We recovered our dead comrade; later we gave him his final resting place in the vicinity of the trains.

Since Regeniter's platoon could not be brought up, it was now even more difficult to control a wide section of land and, if necessary, contain further enemy advances. The five *Sturmgeschütze* had to remain mobile; in no case were they to be allowed to pin themselves down in a "little war" without infantry support. By the way, 16 Russian "butchers", as we called the IL 2 fighter planes, helped us save ammunition. They dive-bombed their own troops with bombs, rockets and guns, until the Russian infantry were forced from the forest to the road. After five attacks there must have been a lot of casualties.

After everything was over, our assault guns took several routes until

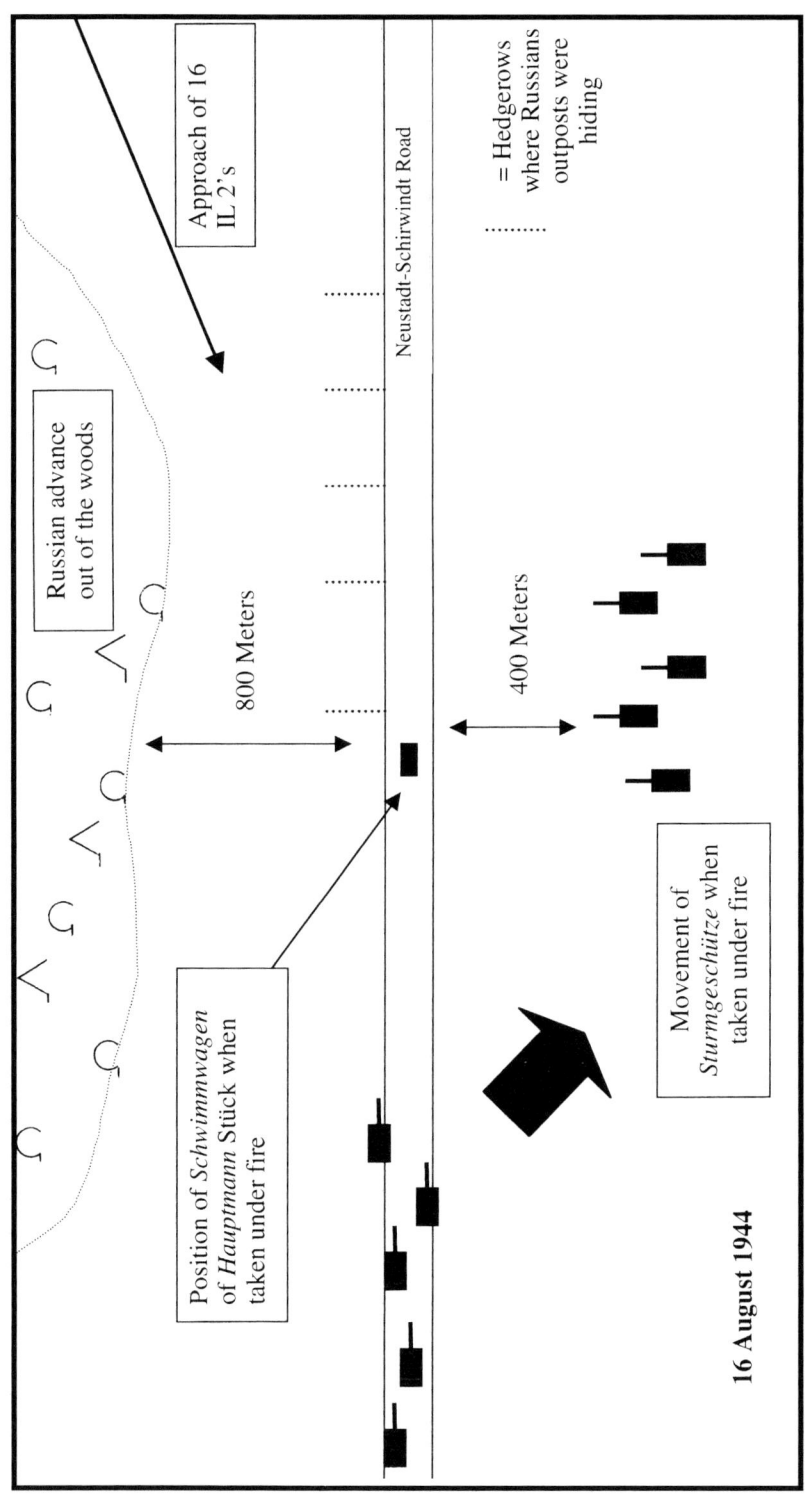

reaching Schirwindt. There was barely a soldier to be seen. We passed a large dairy. In front of the gate there were two German soldiers and a paymaster. They were standing guard, so that none of the cheese there would be stolen. We made it clear to the paymaster that we were the last of the Germans and the Russians would soon be arriving. The three comrades immediately departed. We moved into the courtyard and loaded our assault guns with big round pieces of cheese. After that we continued on.

9. Major Norbert Braun's Last Operation as Commander of Sturmgeschütz-Brigade 276 on 21 August 1944 in the Bramerhusen Section

(After-action report by *Obergefreiter* Heinz Fleischer, *Sturmgeschütz* driver, *3./Sturmgeschütz-Brigade 276*).

On 20 August 1944 it was clear to us assault gun crewmen that an important operation would take place the next morning. We knew that a large bridge was at Bramerhusen and the Russians definitely wanted to take it. The bridge had to be held at all costs, however, because there were still German units that had to cross back over it.

This operation was so important that the brigade commander, *Major* Braun, decided to lead it himself. I was his driver. *Leutnant* Stüwe was the gunner in our assault gun. He also served as the liaison officer to the *1. Infanterie-Division*. This was one of the divisions, along with the *69. Infanterie-Division* and the *349. Volks-Grenadier-Division*, which had yet to cross the bridge. *Obergefreiter* Max Merten was the loader.

It was early, about 0745 hours, when we received the order to move out with our eight assault guns from Turcinai in the direction of Bramerhusen. Due to the fact that *Major* Braun had personally joined us to lead the operation and serve as our assault gun commander, it was clear to us that this would be a difficult operation. Our orders were to secure the large bridge and fend off the enemy (who was approaching the bridge and was only one kilometer away from it) and drive him back. We were the first assault gun and the seven other guns followed me, one after the other.

The terrain was open — meadows and fields — and fell gently into a depression to the left of us. At a distance of about 100 to 200 meters between us and the depression were low vegetation and stands of trees.

After we had driven about four kilometers, I looked off to the left and observed three heavy Stalin tanks (JS 2's) following each other. They were in a field ringed by trees that sloped gently downward away from us, about 1000 meters away. I called out, "To the left — three Stalin tanks — one thousand meters!" *Major* Braun immediately gave the order for assault guns two and three to move ahead two hundred meters and then turn left and go into attack position. Assault guns seven and eight were to immediately turn to the left and also to go into attack position.

The remaining four assault guns also turned immediately to the left and went into attack position. After all assault guns had taken firing positions, our *Major* gave the next order. Should it come to a firefight, the four assault guns in the middle were to open fire and the assault guns to the left and right were to advance four to five hundred meters and then open fire. It was clear to us that at a distance of 1000 meters we could indeed hit the Stalin tanks, but not put them out of action. The JS 2 had a 122 mm cannon, however, which could be very dangerous for us at this distance. Our 75 mm cannon required that we had to advance four or five hundred meters before we could knock out any of the Stalin tanks.

We were in position and waited for the fight to break out. This situation had to be taken care of quickly, since we had a mission that was of great importance. The Russians now saw us and stopped. They didn't take up positions. It was clear to us that we could take out the three JS 2's, but at what price? Besides that, we had our orders, the completion of which could not be endangered. Every assault gun was needed for that mission. My thought was, "Why don't they shoot?" They also didn't move. Suddenly we saw the three JS 2's moving in reverse, not firing a single round. We were all relieved — we would not have been able to survive an engagement such as this without suffering casualties.

We stayed in our positions for a while, just to be sure. We indeed knew that all Russian tanks had the orders to avoid skirmishes with *Sturmgeschütze* whenever they encountered them. After the tense situation had passed, *Major* Braun gave the order to continue our move. Due to this incident we were running short on time. We could not endanger our mission!

We had barely moved one and a half kilometers when there was a jolt and a bang. My first thought was that we had been hit. I reacted immediately and did all the immediate action drills such a situation required of a driver. Since the motor was still running and I couldn't smell any fire, I drove evasively to the left and then to the right. I would speed up and then apply the brakes. My assault gun reacted perfectly to all of these movements. It was at that point that I noticed *Leutnant* Stüwe hit me in the back. I looked around and was shocked. I thought my heart had stopped beating. The sight was horrifying — even though I was used to gory sights already.

Our commander had slid into the interior of the assault gun. Half of his head was gone, blown away by a round from a Russian antitank rifle. It had hit the commander's cupola on the side. His brains and blood shot through the interior of the assault gun and stuck to our uniforms. It was now clear to us that Russian infantry was also in the vicinity. We couldn't make out any of them, however. There were no further rounds fired. The other assault guns were informed immediately of what had happened and received the order to continue to execute the mission.

I broke off from the formation and moved with even greater alertness back to the headquarters. The staff was informed over the radio. Every Russian attack at the bridge was fended off thanks to the *Sturmgeschütze*. The Russians suffered heavy casualties during their attacks. Due to the success of the operation, the *1. Infanterie-Division* was able to cross back over the bridge.

10. An Engagement with four Sturmgeschütze in the Village of Zoliesia, 28 August 1944

After-action report by *Obergefreiter* Heinz Fleischer, *Sturmgeschütz* driver, *3./Sturmgeschütz-Brigade 276*).

Four *Sturmgeschütze* of the *3. Batterie* of *Sturmgeschütz-Brigade 276* received the mission to advance through the villages of Zoliesia, Postvietis and Budziskiai in the direction of the railway between Eydkau and Kowno. This operation was to proceed without infantry protection and our assignment was to seek enemy contact. In the orders it was stated that the village of Zoliesia was clear of the enemy. *Hauptmann* Stück, our battery commander, had gone to a meeting at the regiment staff. I, as driver, received a different officer as the gun commander. He was also responsible for leading the operation.

The village of Zoliesia was situated along a straight road. At the last two houses, the road made a hard left turn. I drove the lead Sturmgeschütz and was the first to approach the left curve. Upon entering the turn I received strong infantry fire from the last two houses as well as from the ditch along the road. My first thought was that they didn't have any heavy weapons that would be dangerous to us. Therefore it could only be a strong Russian patrol that had worked its way forward to this village.

My assault gun commander immediately gave the order to pull back. This order was incomprehensible to me, since I had already determined the Russians did not have any armor-defeating weapons with them. Otherwise, we would not have been able to retreat at all. I said to my assault gun commander not to move back; there was only infantry with light weapons. Just give them some high-explosive rounds.

The result was that the assault gun commander dressed me down; I was to follow his order, otherwise it would be a refusal to follow his orders and he would have me court-martialed. Enraged, I put the assault gun into reverse gear and floored it back in the direction of the left curve. I assume that the assault gun commander lost his nerve and couldn't make the right decision. Further, he failed to order the other three assault guns to also move back. As a result, the other three assault guns remained stationary and I collided right into the assault gun that was behind me.

The motor immediately died and I couldn't get it running again. We stood there with our assault gun, completely unable to move, right in the middle of the road. That was around 1520 hours. The second mistake that my assault gun commander made was to order the other three assault guns to move back, instead of ordering them to go forward and attack the Russians so that we could be evacuated. We began to engage the two houses and destroy them, as much as we could, and held the Russians on the road in check. Since the Russians did not know that we were unable to move, they didn't dare advance further. In the meantime it turned out that the Russians really didn't have any weapons capable of defeating armor. Otherwise they would have knocked us out a long time ago.

The situation became critical for us since we didn't have much more ammunition. It was about 1600 hours when we decided that the assault gun commander should go back to get help. I, as the driver, went up to the commander's cupola with the machine pistol to stop any Russian infantry, if they should decide to try and approach the assault gun. The gunner and the loader remained in their places. The assault gun commander dismounted the assault gun and went for help.

In the meantime, it was 1700 hours and no help came. At that point, we sent the gunner to fetch help. He didn't return either, and no help arrived. In the meantime, I served as gunner. The Russians did not remain passive either. They barraged the village with artillery rounds that sometimes came very close to our assault gun. There were only two of us left in the assault gun and we fired once in a while with our main gun or our machine gun whenever we could make out a target. By this time we both started to feel very uneasy, since it was dark and we assumed that in the meantime the Russians had brought up antitank guns or tanks. But nothing happened.

It was approaching 2140 hours and was completely dark when I said to my comrade, Schwaiger, "C'mon, we're getting out." My comrade got out of the assault gun and disappeared into the ditch on the side of the road. As I was getting out — only my feet were still in the assault gun — there was an impact and I saw flames and sparks before my eyes. That is the last thing I remember. The rest of the story I only know because my comrades told me what happened afterwards.

My comrade Schwaiger, the loader, heard the bang and saw that the *Sturmgeschütz* was engulfed in flames. He saw how I was thrown into the air and landed with a thud about 15 meters away in the road. I was visible in the glow of the burning assault gun. Risking his own life, he fetched me from the road and pulled me into the ditch. He didn't know whether I were dead or alive. My face and my uniform were full of blood.

Since he didn't want the Russians to see him, he couldn't raise his head above the ditch he was in. But since he wanted to take me with him — dead or alive — he bound my feet together with a belt and dragged me about 1200 meters in the ditch to the edge of the village. When we were at the outskirts of the village he saw *Sturmgeschütze*, which were about to turn around and move away. My comrade called to them, he screamed to them, but no one heard anything. He then left me lying there and ran to the *Sturmgeschütze*. They were *Sturmgeschütze* of the *3. Batterie*, which had come to help my assault gun. But since they saw it burning, they gave up and thought that we had been killed.

After my comrade reached the assault guns and told them that I was still lying in the ditch by the side of the road, they came and got me right away. In the meantime a "meat wagon" with a medic was called up to bring me to the nearest dressing station. From there I was sent to the field hospital at Wehlau, northwest of Insterburg. Why no help came, even though the assault gun commander and the gunner made it back all right, is still a mystery to me to this day.

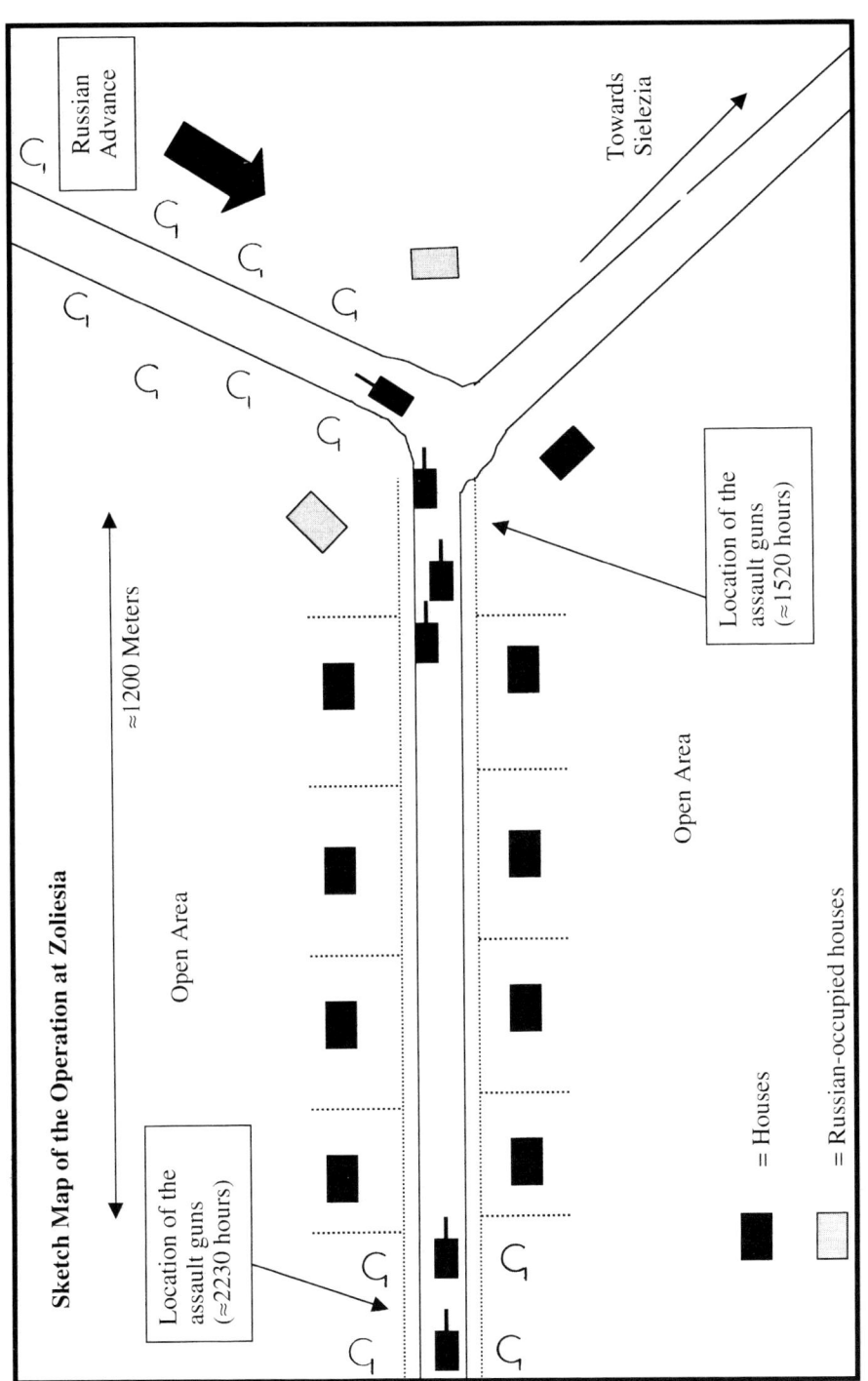

11. The Fighting on 16 October 1944 during the Russian Offensive in East Prussia…

(After-action report by *Obergefreiter* Heinz Fleischer, *Sturmgeschütz* driver, 3./*Sturmgeschütz-Brigade 276*).

Before the large-scale Russian offensive on 16 October 1944, we were located in an estate near Siandiniskiai (Lithuania) with our eight *Sturmgeschütze*. The estate was surrounded by a small forest and was located about 1100 meters south of the Eydkau — Willkowischken — Kowno rail line. The distance from the edge of the woods to the train tracks was about 800 meters. In between there were meadows and fields. In the estate's forest we had built good bunkers and had constructed dug-in positions for our assault guns. They were surrounded with large earthen walls. We cut down trees for the roofs of our bunkers. We placed the thick trunks in two layers onto which we put a thick layer of earth. About 1500 meters from our positions to the north was also a well-camouflaged artillery position.

Every day from 13 to 15 October, there was a Russian reconnaissance plane (they were also called "sewing-machines" or "road terrors") that flew over our sector. The Russian artillery also registered its guns with a few rounds during the day. We could feel it in our bones that something was about to happen. The men at the artillery position could feel it, too. We therefore decided together that we would make dummy artillery guns out of the wooden wagons which were on the estate. At night we brought them to the artillery position. The artillery unit, which had four guns, was relocated to the rear during that same night.

Since my parents had their silver anniversary on 19 October 1944, I received a pass to go on leave. Before I could depart, though, all leaves were cancelled. And that reinforced our opinion that something was in the air and all hell would soon break loose. We also received the order to inspect our *Sturmgeschütze* one more time and make sure they were ready for action. On 16 October 1944 at 0950 hours, we were sitting in our bunkers, eating or playing cards, as the earth began to shake.

At first we did not know what was going on. We heard neither rounds being fired nor incoming rounds. There was only crashing and bursting. The roof of the bunker collapsed slightly on the left. We couldn't get out, since that surely would have meant death. We supported the left side of the roof. The bunker's exit, a stairway that zigzagged its way out, had remained open. We tried to make radio contact. It wasn't possible. What we were worried about was our *Sturmgeschütze*. One thing we were sure of, though, was that as long as the Russians raked our section with their barrage of fire, we didn't have to worry about Russian infantry.

At that point an infantryman staggered in, down the bunker stairs. He was covered in blood. He was completely distraught and bewildered. We pulled him into the bunker, gave him a respectable shot of schnapps and bandaged him. As he pulled himself back together, he reported to us that the Russians were firing a barrage. At exactly 1200 hours the barrage ended. After the barrage ended, we immediately ran to our *Sturmgeschütze* and freed them from the branches and piles of dirt.

After that we immediately moved out in the direction of the railway and out of the forest. We also saw that the artillery position had been shot to pieces. It was a good thing that only the dummy guns had been there. When we got out of the woods, we didn't see a single Russian. In their place was crater after crater, all the way to the rail line. At that point, we took up positions on the edge of the woods. In the meantime, small groups of infantrymen arrived, so that an element in company strength was soon assembled. The wounded, who were also carrying along the dead, were immediately sent to the rear. The infantry took positions on the edge of the woods as a precaution.

Hauptmann Stück discussed the situation with the highest-ranking infantry officer. After that a patrol was sent to the rail line. It was situated on a high embankment. After the infantrymen reached the embankment, a messenger came back. What he reported was not very good news for us. He reported that on the other side of the embankment the Russians were pouring to the west in huge masses. There was a small group of infantrymen with a radioman dispatched to the embankment. They had the mission to report if the Russians were coming over the embankment. If the Russians had done that they would have been in our rear. As a result, it was decided to launch a counterattack about 1200 meters wide with the infantry and our *Sturmgeschütze* in the direction of Boblaukis. The counterattack started.

It was 1240 hours and we knew we would soon encounter Russians. Up to that point, however, not a single Russian had been identified. Along the railway embankment on our side there was a path. An infantry element advanced along this path. I moved my assault gun (with assault gun commander, *Hauptmann* Friedrich Stück) next to the infantrymen. The other assault guns moved to the right of us. Between us were infantry elements and to the far right advanced the strongest infantry group.

After we had advanced about one kilometer, a cornfield that was about 600 meters wide prevented us from advancing further. At this point I have to emphasize what *Hauptmann* Stück did. He was able to sniff out the situation, as he had done so many times before. We were stationary about 100 meters away from the cornfield. He gave the order for everyone to halt. The infantry units were ordered to take position and the *Sturmgeschütze* were to be loaded with high-explosive rounds. Target: Cornfield. Then he gave the order that each assault gun was to fire one round into the cornfield.

When we fired, we couldn't believe our eyes. Hundreds of Russian infantry had wanted to lead us into an ambush and annihilate us in close combat. They had hidden themselves in the cornfield. When we began to fire into the cornfield, the Russians jumped up and began to retreat. Upon seeing that we moved our assault guns forward and fired as rapidly as we could with high-explosive rounds. Our infantry immediately followed and took out every Russian who came in front of their barrels. The few Russians who could still run threw down their weapons so that they could run faster. Then Hauptmann Stück gave the order to everyone: "Forward, comrades!"

We advanced through the cornfield and crushed everything that came under our tracks. The infantry played its part. Mercy was not to

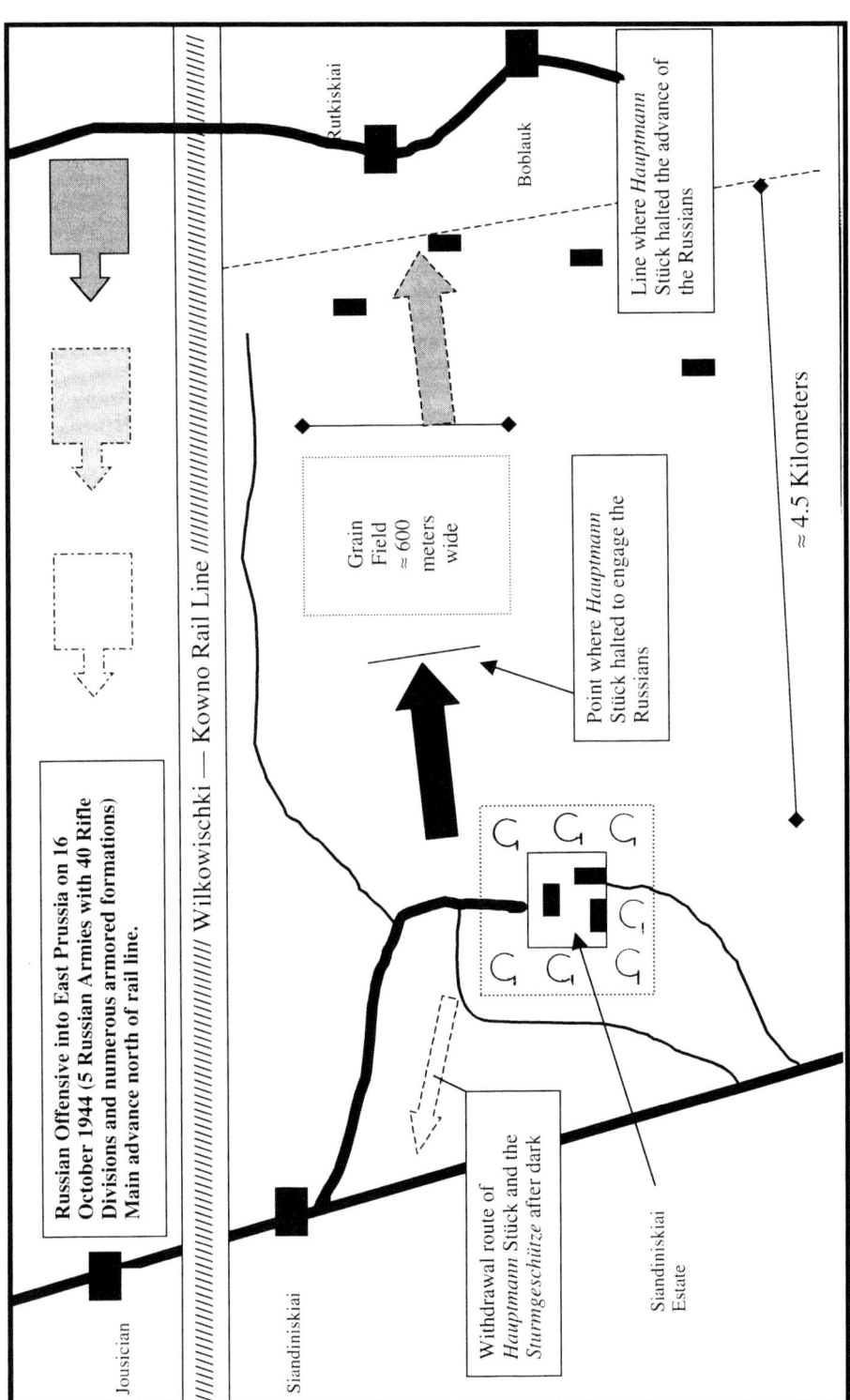

be expected. It was life or death. You or me. After we had crossed through the cornfield, the infantry had advanced even further to the right of our assault gun. I saw a large crater to the left, which I wanted to avoid. At that moment I saw three Russians begin to bring a machine gun into position on the edge of the crater.

I was about thirty meters away from the crater. I immediately turned my *Sturmgeschütz* a bit to the left. Since I often went into action without the driver's protective glass in the driver's vision slit and often kept a loaded machine pistol next to me, I quickly pulled out it out and shot the three Russians through the vision slit. If I had not noticed the Russians, our infantry would have had to deal with heavy casualties.

Now we once again had open land in front of us, with the occasional farmstead and small group of trees. We shot everything that moved to pieces. By this time we had advanced about four and a half kilometers in the direction of Boblaukis. During this time I saw a farmstead slightly to the right at a distance of about 180 meters from us.

A *Sturmgeschütz* had driven into it. The crew had dismounted its assault gun and was involved in a firefight with the Russians who had set up in the farmstead. The crew had dismounted because it believed it had damaged tracks and thought the barn was clear of the enemy. During this firefight, my schoolmate, *Kanonier* Mescher, who was the driver for *Sturmgeschütz 331*, was killed by a hand grenade. His head was ripped off. *Kanoniere* Saunus and Rollin were wounded. I moved as fast as I could into the farmstead — throwing caution to the winds — in order to help my comrades.

When the Russians saw us, they immediately disappeared into the house and fired at us from there. We fired a high-explosive round into the house and seven Russians came out with their hands up. But I saw my schoolmate with his ripped-off head in front of me and that was it for me. I took my machine pistol and shot all seven of the Russians through my vision slit. *Hauptmann* Stück didn't have any idea what was going on as he saw the Russians fall on their faces.

Since it was now dark and we were now in danger of being cut off, it was time to break off our counterattack. We pulled back to our starting point with the infantry and 27 prisoners, as well as a *Sturmgeschütz* in tow. At the jump-off point were two of our guns which were no longer movable as a result of the earlier artillery barrage. The one assault gun, whose driver had been killed, was replaced by another comrade from the battery. By then it was 2200 hours and completely dark. Our withdrawal, with two assault guns in tow, many wounded and dead, as well as 27 prisoners, could only be successful between the villages of Kybartai and Uszkurajcie. The infantrymen covered to the sides, since we could happen upon Russians at any time. Contact with other units was completely lost.

Postscript: As it was mentioned, since it was night, we had to withdraw. Kanonier Mescher was placed in a barn, since the attack continued on. After our withdrawal Obergefreiter Wenk and Obergefreiter Wimmer — both from Austria — went back to the farm with a vehicle and retrieved our comrade Mescher. Even though Hauptwachtmeister Ernst Hufnagel (the Spieß) was against it — since Russians could have returned there — Obergefreiter Wenk and Obergefreiter Wimmer were able to retrieve him.

When they arrived at the barn, there were already rats running all over Kanonier Mescher. Mescher was wrapped in a blanket and put in the vehicle. The two men then moved back as fast as they could. As a result, Kanonier Mescher could be buried humanely and with honor. For this we can all thank Wenk and Wimmer, who made the dangerous move back to pick his body up, without knowing whether they would come back themselves. For that they should have received an award or a promotion.

12. "Front Leave 1945"....

(Report by *Hauptmann* Friedrich Stück).

Next a totally personal affair: "Front Leave 1945". After the brigade had been transferred from East Prussia to the area around Zichenau at the end of 1944, the batteries expected to be reconstituted and re-equipped with new assault guns. It was relatively calm in this section of the front. Therefore, members of the brigade who had been on the front a long time — among them me — could be sent on leave. By this stage of the war the days far away from the front weren't very restful for the majority of the leave takers; frequently they were more depressing than comforting: Bomber attacks day and night, craters everywhere, bad news from the front, many relatives and acquaintances were dead, wounded or missing!

My small family had just gotten a bit larger with our "youngest" — who had been born a few months before during an air raid. He had spent more time in the bomb shelter than in the house. Our house was located just two kilometers away from the airport in Erbenheim.

There were millions of people in the homeland, who were not suffering any less than the soldiers on the front: Fear and concerns, a lack of food, a decreasing desire to fight and, despite all of the propaganda, an increasing sense of hopelessness!

Leave over — Back to the front in the East! But how and where? At the time there was a long stop in the Berlin train stations. There were no more trains taking a direct route to the east. What was wrong? What was the situation on the front? Reports from the Wehrmacht or the local news did not provide much information. Rumors spread. I was led through detours that passed through Wittenberge and then I arrived in Stettin. There I encountered a huge mess. The civilians and the soldiers were very agitated.

Kampfgruppen were being formed from soldiers on leave, lightly wounded soldiers and members of replacement and supply troops. Everyone was urgently looking for more men! Finally we received word from the front lines about the current situation: In the middle of January the Russians had launched a large offensive with strong forces. It had begun in the area around Warsaw and, in the meantime, the Russians had advanced far to the west. Lead attack columns were aimed at East Prussia, West Prussia and Danzig, as well as many positions on the Baltic coast between Stettin and Stolpmünde. Further enemy movements were to separate the above-named areas from the rest of Germany west of the Oder River in one swift move.

The lead tanks elements of the advancing columns on their way to the Baltic coast had almost reached their attack goals in the beginning of February 1945. This had cut off almost all of the contact and railways from Berlin to the eastern areas. At first there was nothing I could do to get further to the east. But then *Kampfgruppen* with armored forces of the army as well as a *Waffen-SS* division counterattacked the lead enemy formations and forced them back. The result was that a few supply lines and railways to the east were passable.

I was then able to travel a distance with supply vehicles of the *Waffen-SS* unit. Then my trip proceeded step by step with the train further. Often I traveled in freight cars. I traveled through Kalberg, Köslin, Stolp, Lauenburg, then to the south to Konitz. On the way there were many forced delays due to damage to the train tracks, which was caused, among other things, by attacks from British heavy bombers (Lancasters). Many of the lines were reduced to one set of tracks. At other times we had to wait in train stations for numerous other trains coming from the east that were packed full with refugees.

In the train stations there were many traumatic scenes. There were older people, women and children, many without warm clothing or blankets, packed into freight trains. There was barely any food. At the train stations there was loud yelling and people searching for relatives and friends from whom they had been separated. Those questioned stated that many had departed weeks ago and that some had been killed while fleeing in boats from the Danzig bay or the Baltic, as the ice thawed or ships sunk as the result of air or submarine attacks.

Many didn't survive the physical strain; their bodies littered the roads and railways. Many remained unburied. An especially sad case: In an open freight train car there was a young woman. In her arms was a small child, dead, frozen. As others wanted to bury the child during a stop, the mother screamed loudly and resisted bitterly, and clung to the child. She was close to going insane from the sorrow and could not grasp that her child was no longer alive nor why strangers would want to take the child from her.

In Konitz the train ride was finally over. In the city there was a lot of turmoil and everything was in complete disarray. There were vehicles of all kinds with soldiers, residents and refugees. Supposedly there were Russian forces only a few kilometers south of the city. I asked about the whereabouts of *Sturmgeschütz-Brigade 276* with the local commander and at other places. If I was not able to reach the brigade, I had orders to form a *Kampfgruppe* for the defense of the city from stragglers, policemen and members of the *Volksturm*. But then again, as chance would have it, I happened upon a truck with the "jumping panther!" Never before or after this incident have I been so happy to run into a "black cat!" A short time later drivers and crewmen from the headquarters battery arrived, who happily took me to Heiderode. On the way they told me some of the things that had happened while I was away. If I remember correctly, I must have arrived at the *3. Batterie* sometime between 12 and 16 February. *Finally!*

13. Fighting on 19 January 1945 with five Sturmgeschütze about 30 kilometers northwest of Ciechanow and 9 kilometers south of the Soldau–Lautenburg road

(After-action report by *Obergefreiter* Heinz Fleischer, *Sturmgeschütz* driver, *3./Sturmgeschütz-Brigade 276*).

It was 19 January 1945 and we were on the march to Gorzno. There was a lot of snow, snowdrifts and frost. At 0840 hours we received orders to move northeast in the direction of Kurkau and then again south to the village of Bursch with 45 infantrymen who were mounted on our vehicles. Outside the village of Bursch we were to take up positions.

The Russians were trying to advance so that they could cut the road between Soldau and Lautenburg. The road was full of military vehicles that were pulling back in the direction of Lautenburg, Strasburg and Kulmsee. The village of Bursch was located about nine kilometers south of the road between Soldau and Hohendorf. We departed from Kurkau and were travelling in the direction of Bursch. We had traveled about three and a half kilometers over open terrain deeply covered by snow and large snowdrifts. There was still about another 1200 meters to move until we arrived in Bursch. About 800 meters from us to the left was the road from Wiersbau to Kurkau.

Suddenly we were fired upon from the road. We immediately took position facing left and opened fire with our five tubes. We counted seven Russian tanks on the road and many trucks, two of which were loaded with ammunition and fuel. We realized that only after our rounds hit them. Besides that, there were two prime movers with limbered antitank guns. The Russians were moving in the direction of Kurkau. It was to our advantage that the Russians could only move on the road, which was as flat as a pancake.

The terrain was full of snowdrifts. Immediately after the first rounds hit the trucks that were loaded with ammunition and fuel, the detonations caused the Russians to take flight. The job of taking care of the Russian infantry was handed over to our infantry. There was a real fireworks display. We quickly knocked out four T 34's, six Russian assault guns as well as all of their trucks and the two prime movers with the antitank guns.

What we didn't know during this engagement was that the Russians already occupied the village of Konigshagen, which was about 1800 meters behind us to the southwest. The Russians also had tanks there. While we were still oriented to the left, that is, towards the road, Russian tanks advanced out of Konigshagen and into our rear. When they were at a distance of about 900 meters they opened fire. We only noticed they were there when four of our assault guns with mounted infantry were hit.

The rounds landed among our infantry who were sitting on the back of the assault guns. They were ripped to shreds. There were body parts flying all over the place. The four *Sturmgeschütze* burned. What I saw next — I also had to get out of there with my assault gun — was horrifying. The snow was not white, but red. And everywhere there were body parts lying around. My assault gun was the only one that was still able to fight and move. The infantrymen that were on my assault gun had jumped off and tried to somehow get out of the danger zone. When I finally decided to get out of there with my assault gun, there was not a single German soldier to be seen.

Since I was still at a distance of about 200 meters from the road between Kurkau and Nielterhof, I tried to reach the road at a left curve. During my flight I continually changed direction, because the Russian tanks were firing at me. The clouds of smoke coming from the burning guns came to my rescue. The only thing I thought about was reaching the road. At the edge of the road were poplar trees and, if I could cross the road, then I would be out of the danger zone.

As previously mentioned, there was deep snow and large snowdrifts. Therefore, during my flight from the scene, I overlooked an antitank ditch that stretched around from the road from Wiersbau—Nielterhof to Kurkau. The ditch was completely snowed-in and flat with the other terrain. During my flight toward the road — I was still about 80 meters away and was making another change of direction — my assault gun suddenly slid into the ditch. At that time I thought to myself, "Now it's over." I'm sure someone reading this story would believe the same thing.

I tried for a few minutes to get my assault gun on firm ground again. But I achieved the complete opposite. My assault gun sank deeper and deeper and was at a significant cant. I yelled to my comrades, "Get out! I'm going to blow the assault gun!" No one answered. And when I looked around, I saw that there was no one there. I set a shaped charge in the fighting compartment and got out. I had to get to the upper edge of the ditch as fast as possible so shrapnel wouldn't hit me when the assault gun blew up.

When I reached the edge, I saw that the Russians were still in the same place, about 1000 meters away. I knew that I had to run, so that shrapnel from the detonation wouldn't hit me. But I also knew that Russians would fire at me as soon as I got over the edge. I ran and the Russians started firing with their cannons and their machine guns. After a few meters I threw myself on the ground, since the assault gun blew. Then I saw I still had another 60 meters before I would reach the road. I also saw that if I ran any further along the edge of the ditch, that I would be shot at.

Therefore I slid into the antitank ditch, snow up to my chest. I worked my way somewhat out of the snow and then lay on my stomach, since that way I would cover more surface area and not sink so deeply. Then I began to work my way to the road. The Russians fired a few more rounds that missed their target.

When I reached the road, I lay down behind a poplar tree. I was totally exhausted. I couldn't go another meter. Even though it was -18 degrees Celsius, and even though I was wearing only my boots, socks, underwear, cotton pants and a shirt, sweat was pouring from my body. I still had my pistol, a few magazines and four egg hand grenades. Far and wide I could not see a single German soldier. After I managed to regain some strength, I ran about six and a half kilometers over open terrain to the road running between Soldau and Lautenburg. There was about thirty centimeters of snow. And when there was firm land under the snow, I spent the majority of the time on my face instead of running. When I reached the road — completely exhausted — I saw that it was full of military vehicles.

I thought to myself, "something is going to be happening here," since seven kilometers away Russian tanks were approaching. A minute later a *VW Schwimmwagen* came with a *Major*, two *Hauptleute* [the plural of *Hauptmann*] and a noncommissioned officer who was driving. I stopped the car and made my report, as best as I could given my condition. I could tell by looking at the officers that they hadn't a clue what to make of me. The reader must understand that I looked a fright! After I was able to convince the officers that only seven kilometers away Russian tanks were coming to cut the road, they immediately formed *Kampfgruppen*.

Only drivers were allowed to move on with their vehicles. Then two 88 mm antiaircraft guns and a 75 mm antitank gun arrived. Positions were taken about three and a half kilometers from the road. I set off in the direction of Hohendorf. Shortly outside the village I encountered SS and field policemen who were collecting all of the straggling soldiers. The stragglers were brought to houses and formed into *Kampfgruppen*. In front of every house was a guard. When a group reached a certain strength, it received the necessary weapons and ammunition and was sent into action as infantry.

That didn't please me at all. I wanted to get back to my unit. I looked around the house and found a window that was about three meters from the ground. Then I jumped out and ran through a garden and down to the road. I had barely made it to the road when I saw an officer from my unit in a *VW Schwimmwagen*. There was a panther on the door. He had a driver with him. When he saw me, he shook my hand and said, "Thank God I have found the first one." My battery had heard over the radio that the last five assault guns had been lost. As a result, he had come forward to look for members of the unit. It was crucial for our unit to show that we had full crews, so that we could get new *Sturmgeschütze*. Otherwise we would have been put into action as infantry. A short time later we were able to pick up new *Sturmgeschütze* at Marienburg. From that time on we were only employed as the fire brigade in the Weichsel sector.

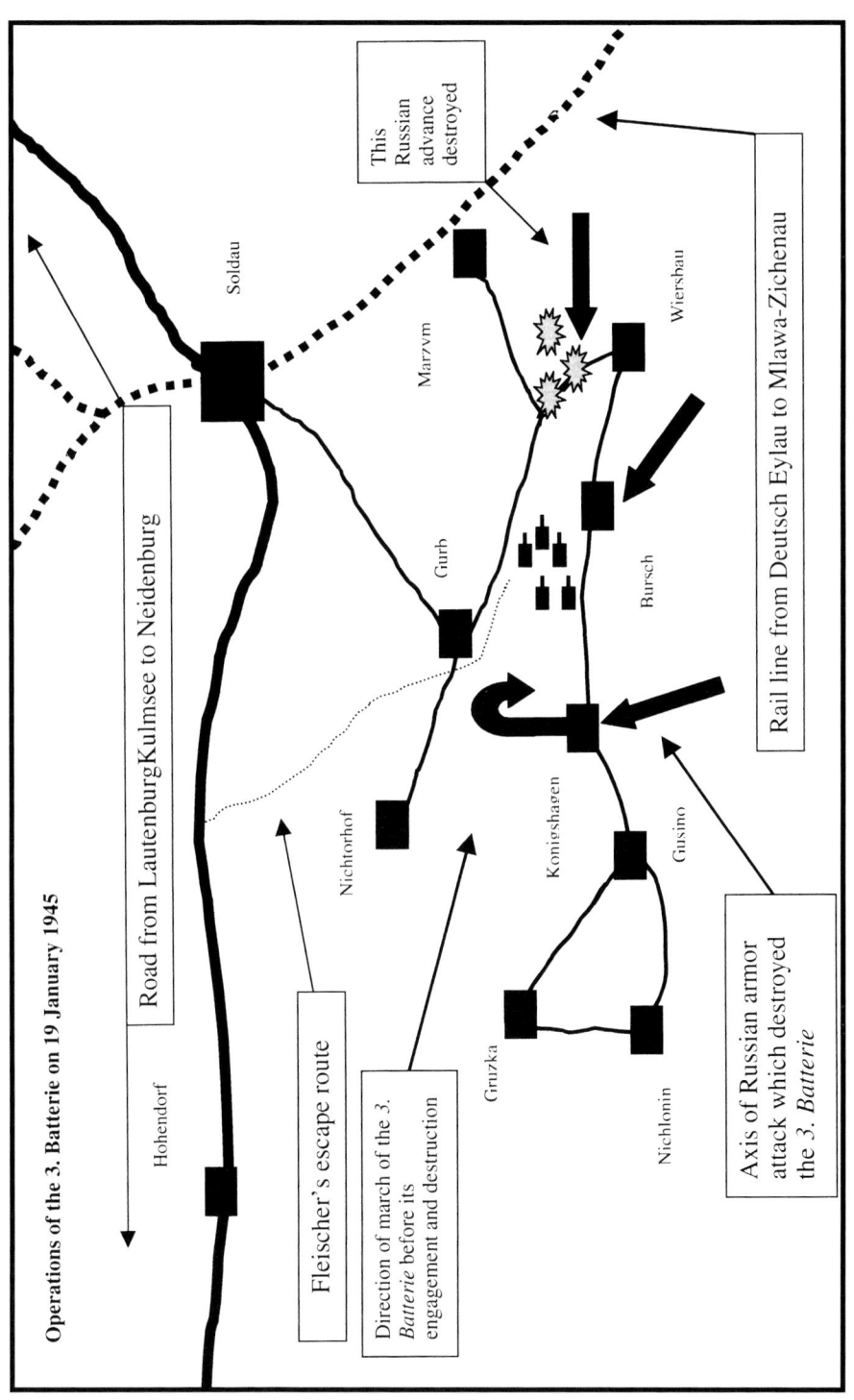

14. After-action report from 2-12 February 1945 in the Area of Operations of Schwetz, Julienhof, Belino, Bislau and Tuchel...

(After-action report by from *Obergefreiter* Heinz Fleischer, *Sturmgeschütz* driver, *3./Sturmgeschütz-Brigade 276*).

At the beginning of 1945 the Russians were west of Schwetz and had managed a breakthrough between the *251. Infanterie-Division* and the *337. Volks-Grenadier-Division*, advancing in the direction of Oscha. There was a lot of snow and the temperatures were below freezing.

The *3. Batterie* received the order to advance with six *Sturmgeschütze* in the direction of Schlewitz on the Weichsel River, in order to stop the Russians that had broken through there. The Russians were already firing on the village of Schlewitz. We moved until reaching the Weichsel and saw Russian tanks on the other side of the river. The Russians were not prepared for our sudden appearance. Due to the surprise, we were able to quickly knock out two T 34's. At that point the Russians pulled back.

The next day we were ordered to attack Julienhof near Schlewitz and throw out the Russians. We weren't successful, however. The Russians were superior in both infantry and equipment. We knocked out a few Russian tanks and anti-aircraft guns during this engagement. We did not pull back, but remained there during the night, securing the position. *Oberwachtmeister* Kampmann remained on radio watch. The other assault guns turned off their radios so that the Russians could not determine where we were located. *Oberwachtmeister* Kampmann was informed during the night that all assault guns were to return to Schlewitz. The loader from Kampmann's crew was to inform the other assault guns of the order, since he knew where the individual guns were located. But he didn't show up at any assault gun and we also never saw him again. When that happened, Kampmann sent another comrade who brought us the order. Our departure was therefore delayed by about three hours, which could have proven disastrous for us.

The next day we were to defend the Schlewitz train station with three assault guns, since Russian tanks had apparently advanced there. The train station was about 500 meters away from the village. The assault gun commanded by *Wachtmeister* Richter, in which *Obergefreiter* Willi Wenk was loader, moved as the last assault gun. When we reached the train station, seven T 34's advanced over a rise from the left. They were still about four hundred meters away from us.

The first two *Sturmgeschütze* had turned in the direction of the Russian tanks and initiated the engagement. When Richter's assault gun turned in the direction of the enemy tanks, he received a direct hit to the front. All of the crew were able to escape without a scratch. At that point the other two assault guns turned around and pulled back. At a distance we noticed the Russians standing on the knocked-out assault gun. Since Richter's crew was without an assault gun, O*bergefreiter* Wenk once again became a motorcycle messenger.

On 10 February 1945, *Obergefreiter* Wenk went into action as the radio operator and loader for *Leutnant* Regeniter's (Knight's Cross Winner) crew. On the same day *Leutnant* Regeniter's assault gun was knocked out, the result of a direct hit. *Leutnant* Reginiter was badly wounded and *Obergefreiter* Wenk risked his life to bring him to safety. The driver, *Obergefreiter* Tischler, and the gunner, *Unteroffizier* Strobach, were killed during the incident.

On 12 February 1945 our assault guns captured a Russian anti-aircraft gun with a lot of ammunition. *Unteroffizier* Morawitz, *Stabsgefreiter* Warken and *Obergefreiter* Wenk took over the anti-aircraft gun. They received the order to occupy a position on a hill about 18 kilometers outside of Danzig. The Russians tried twice to take this hill. Their attacks failed thanks to the anti-aircraft gun we had "acquired". A few days later the front line was pulled back.

Obergefreiter Wenk got a horse-drawn cart from a farmer so that the anti-aircraft gun and all of the remaining ammunition could be brought to the new position. It was there that the last of the ammunition was used up. The anti-aircraft gun was then evacuated to Danzig where it was destroyed. *Unteroffizier* Morawitz, *Stabsgefreiter* Warken and *Obergefreiter* Wenk took up with the trains at Danzig—Langfuhr. *(Author's note: Leutnant Regeniter published his personal experiences with the Sturmgeschütz-Brigade 276 in December 1996.)*

15. Tuchler Heide: Mid-February 1945….

(After-action report by *Hauptmann* Friedrich Stück).

After my previously mentioned "Front Leave 1945" and the long, wandering journey during the search for my unit, I found my way back to *Sturmgeschütz-Brigade 276* in the middle of February 1945. About 25 kilometers from Tuchel, where the headquarters and parts of the assault gun batteries were, it was reported to me what had happened while I was away. As previously mentioned, the brigade was transferred from East Prussia to the area around Zichenau in December and was waiting for new equipment and personnel and also to be re-equipped with new *Sturmgeschütze*. The assault guns that were still in working order at the time that the brigade was transferred were handed over to another brigade.

In the middle of January, the Russians initiated a large-scale offensive from the Narew salient. The Russians were successful in breaking through the weakly held German lines and thereafter they quickly advanced with tank and motorized forces. While all of this was going on, the brigade still did not possess a single *Sturmgeschütz*. The batteries were forced to move in a northwesterly direction and set up new quarters in the area of Danzig. The remaining elements and trains of the brigade made this journey in order to escape encirclement and annihilation by the Russian advance.

Hauptmann Sewera and other officers of the brigade's staff made urgent requests to higher headquarters; new *Sturmgeschütze* finally arrived on 26 January 1945. The assault guns were immediately given to the batteries and employed just three days later, on 29 January 1945, along the Weichsel River between Schwetz and Mewe. Comrades of the brigade have reported elsewhere in this book about the great successes of the batteries during the hard defensive fighting against greatly superior enemy forces, but also about the painful losses suffered in the first weeks of February.

Immediately after my return I was informed of the sad events that happened shortly before my arrival. *Unteroffizier* Strohbach and *Obergefreiter* Tischler had been killed and *Leutnant* Regeniter, who had temporarily commanded the battery in the meantime, was also badly wounded when their assault gun was knocked out. In February, the brigade had only a few assault guns at its disposal; these had been employed southeast of Heiderode. Under most difficult conditions, the maintenance personnel tried to bring the damaged vehicles back into running condition.

I intended — with the agreement of the brigade commander — on taking over one or more of the repaired *Sturmgeschütze* and to find the *Kampfgruppe* that the *3. Batterie* was fighting with at that time. But first there were a number of administrative affairs to take care of: Meetings with the *Spieß*, the section leaders and the brigade staff, among others, as well as the not-to-be-forgotten pile of paperwork that had to be done.

I can still remember a certain "disturbance": There was a meeting in the "orderly room" in a schoolroom. Then there was a bang; bombs had landed behind the building. Everyone was on their stomachs on the floor, lying in dust, dirt and shards of glass. Probably a welcome-back greeting from the Russians!

I would gladly have forgotten one memory, if that were only possible! It is as follows: A short time after I returned, our "medicine man", Dr. Cordes, who still had a fair amount of reserves in alcohol in his possession, also included me in his invitation for a get-together in his quarters. At a later hour, I was entrusted with the details of a certain operation by one of those present: Upon orders from above, a unit under the command of an officer which was located in Heiderode was to conduct an operation which was certainly not in accordance with a fighting unit's "sense of honor". It was feared that because of the local situation, the order would be given to the brigade which, in turn, would have to select one of those officers present at the gathering to execute it. *[Translator's Note: Stück is referring to the execution of soldiers for desertion and the establishment of summary courts-martial by field units to adjudge and carry out sentences against alleged deserters.]*

This "disclosure" had the effect of a strong shock! Just a few days earlier I had to observe the suffering, concerns and sadness of many people in the homeland and those fleeing for their lives. Their concerns were not only for themselves, but also for loved ones on the various fronts. Still greatly affected by these memories, the thought of such an operation was unbearable; even worse was the thought of becoming a tool of an institution which, "far away from the place where things happened", made decisions about the life and death of frontline soldiers (…and, as later proven, those soldiers were frequently judged harshly and illegally in military courts only in order to be made an example of; the result of which was unutterable suffering for both those directly affected and the next-of-kin!).

Note: I would like to explicitly state that then, and at no time later, did I have a negative opinion about comrades of our unit or other units, who were forced to obey orders in this case. Further events, dates, names, etc. are scarcely known to me anyway and were never inquired about later.

Back to the aforementioned evening: I immediately withdrew from the gathering and searched for a way to clear my conscience during a sleepless night. The next day my decision had been made: "escape to the front!" Unfortunately, there was not a single combat-ready *Sturmgeschütz* at the maintenance facility. Despite that: Take care of the most urgent matters within the battery and report my departure to the headquarters.

The next night it began. Alone with my driver in the *VW* with the windshield lowered, machine pistol and hand grenades ready for action, the lights turned off, we moved under the diffused moonlight through the meadows and wooded terrain in a southerly direction. Our destination was village X. From the last reports we had received our three assault guns were employed there. I barely knew anything about the friendly or enemy situation.

There was no continuous defensive line due to the very weakened German troops. Instead, there were only individual strong points that were occupied and held. We had to keep a watch for enemy troops that had broken through the lines and also for partisans. We had luck, although we had not run into any of our own troops during the move that had lasted many hours, we also had not run into any enemy troops either. As morning approached we found our comrades with the *Sturmgeschütze* and ammunition vehicles at the northern outskirts of the long and narrow village that ran along the main road.

Note: I have no records of the situation or the name of the localities, but the approximate layout of the village is still in my memory. The village could have been Groß Schliewitz — about 20 kilometers southeast of Czersk (Heiderode).

The platoon leader, who had taken over the leadership of the three assault guns after *Leutnant* Regeniter had been wounded, reported the local situation to me. Then I contacted officers of the *"Kampfgruppe"* that had prepared defensive positions in and around the village. As far as I remember, the infantry troops present came from decimated units. They appeared to be worn down and exhausted. The *Kampfgruppe* hardly had any heavy infantry weapons. As far as I know, they also did not possess any artillery pieces or armor-defeating weapons; this task was to be assumed by the *Sturmgeschütze*.

On the first day after my arrival there was only little activity. Occasionally, the southern portion of the village was covered with fairly heavy mortar and artillery fire (the latter presumably from heavy antitank guns). This fire was coming from the edge of the forest on the other side of a meadow, against which our forces there could do nothing. We therefore moved the *Sturmgeschütze* into position southwest of the village and fired at the positions we could make out through movement and muzzle fire. There were detonations, flames, smoke, and men were fleeing…proof of the effect of our operations — this time acting as "artillery". In spite of this, the local situation gave us no pause.

As previously mentioned, here, as elsewhere, only a small settlement and a small sector of land could be defended in strong-point fashion; there was no contact with neighboring troops and, with our weak forces, we could not even carry out combat reconnaissance. We feared that at any time the Russians would advance with massive troop concentrations into the large gaps, bypassing strong resistance or knocking out threats to their flanks with far superior forces. (According to later documentation, on this front the Russians had a 4:1 to 5:1 advantage in tanks, artillery and infantry and a 7:1 to 8:1 advantage in the air).

On the next day nothing out of the ordinary happened! But at night something did: From the rear there were the sounds of tank tracks. It actually turned out to be reinforcements for us; *Leutnant* Koch brought up a repaired *Sturmgeschütz* (was it also an "escape to the front?"). How important this would prove to be — especially for my assault gun crew — was revealed that night.

During the night there were loud sounds of fighting east of the extended village: Incoming artillery rounds, the sounds of tank tracks, tank and infantry fire. Alarm in our quarters! Assault guns 1 and 2 immediately departed. The other two assault guns followed close behind. The four assault guns departed from the northern outskirts of the village into the open field on the east side. Here two barns offered concealment for the forward two assault guns. A halt enabled an overview of the actual situation, which would have scared anyone!

To the left oblique of us on a hill, the west edge of which sloped gently towards the village, there were tanks, tanks and more tanks. They appeared as ghost images under the weak moonlight but soon came into focus with the scissors scope. It was a group of T 34's in extended formation advancing and firing on the village! Behind them on top of the hill there were more tanks and armored vehicles which could not be identified well at first. Coming from the east slope there were rounds of large caliber. Were they from Stalin tanks or artillery?

A lucky situation for us: All the T 34's were "oriented" on the village and offered us their broadsides. Then it started, round after round: Assault guns 1 and 2, which had moved into position backwards some 25 meters away, opened fire at the same time at the T 34 that had almost reached the outskirts of the village. At this short of a distance and thanks to our first-rate optics, the targets were not to be missed. In short order four T 34's were knocked out, one right after the other!

But then the situation became really hot: While the first two assault guns fired, assault guns 3 and 4, moved up to the left and echeloned themselves to the rear. Suddenly there was yelling and warnings coming over the radio! What was going on? A look back to the other assault guns: Where did the large number of *"Landser"* come from who appeared behind us? I didn't know we had such reserves!

When these "reserves" ran between assault guns 3 and 4, the assault guns moved around in wild fashion and fired! It was a big mistake on our part: Those weren't *Landser*, they were Russian infantrymen! In retrospect I can only assume that they were intended to support the right flank of the nighttime tank attack but had veered too far off course and had probably also lost their orientation. It appeared to me that they mistook our assault guns for their own tanks. At any rate, they fled back to the southeast while being fired upon by assault guns 3 and 4. In the meantime, the Russians had "become fully enlightened" about the situation. If the Russians had planned their attack better and had taken us between the pincers of their assault guns and their infantry, this operation could have had a very nasty outcome for us!

During all this the situation on the hill became dramatically different. The greater portion of the remaining enemy tanks — mostly T 34's — turned in our direction. At the same time, we were taken under fire by Russian artillery. The large barn, in the vicinity of which assault gun 2 was located, was shot alight. The high flames forced a change in position.

On the other hand, the entire area where the attackers were located was well lit up. *Sturmgeschütze* 1 and 2 were able to cover themselves from the light in the dark shadows of the second barn and use this to their advantage. While assault gun 2 was still moving, two T 34's attacked from the front. They approached, alternating firing and moving. The first tank had approached to a distance of about 100 meters before assault gun 1 was able to engage it effectively. But the tank continued to move, made a strange swing to the left and, after being hit again, made a complete turn and remained positioned right in front of the burning barn, its cannon "devoutly" pointing to the ground, as if it were praying.

It went quicker with the second Russian tank; after just a few rounds it stood still and began smoking. Then there was a horrible sight: A man dismounted, his clothes burning. He ran up the hill like a human torch, screaming, wildly beating himself and rolling numerous times on the ground. But it was all for nothing, he couldn't put out the flames! (What soldier was capable of viewing others "over there, on the other side" as their enemies in such situations?)

Shortly thereafter came a warning call from *Leutnant* Koch: "*Achtung!* Tank on the right!" How did that happen? No enemy tanks could come from the village! Think again! The T 34 in front of the burning barn had "come back to life" (my round had presumably not put the entire crew out of action; there was at least one man still able to put the tank back in motion). He roared out of the flank in the direction of my command assault gun, obviously with the intention of ramming it. Our assault gun could indeed go back a few meters, but it definitely could not be brought into the right position. Then there was a horrible crack! *Leutnant* Koch had moved quickly and had given the Russian tank its final blow while it was only at a very short distance from us. (An old lesson was confirmed: Not every "kill" was "deadly". A healthy skepticism about "verifiable" information was and is not forbidden!)

Sturmgeschütze 3 and 4 had rejoined the fray after their "close combat" with the Russian infantry. They aggressively engaged targets that were on the east side of the hill, as well as the far side of the woods. They were also able to knock out the "big boys" which had previously covered us with heavy heaps of metal. These were no "Stalins" — in contrast to our earlier fears — but just self-prepared guns mounted on KW I or II chassis.

As a consequence of the heavy casualties, the enemy attack on the village lost more and more steam. For unknown reasons, the attack had only been carried out very hesitantly, despite the great superiority in equipment and men. The *Sturmgeschütze* were barely ever attacked head-on again. The armored vehicles then tried to press forward from behind the hill to the southern part of the village, placing themselves at a greater distance from us. They continued to provide us with worthwhile targets. In the dusk we were able to observe that only a few heavy tanks and a conglomeration of armored vehicles were carrying out this "second wave attack". (I remember that I could identify reconnaissance vehicles, among them the so-called "bed pan", and other light tanks of older construction.)

Later in the night, the enemy tried to recover damaged but not completely destroyed vehicles. Despite that, very many destroyed vehicles remained on the "battlefield" and served as proof of the successful operation that was conducted by our *Sturmgeschütze*. *(Note: I didn't count the number of "bodies." Perhaps other comrades can make an approximation as to how many there were.)*

Net result: The Russians were only able to push back our infantry in the southern part of the village. Our men were able to hold in the middle and northern parts. Our assault gun and vehicle crews did not suffer a single casualty! During the morning there was no activity in this area, but to the left and right of us serious situations obviously must have developed due to enemy advances. Our *Kampfgruppe* was in danger of becoming outflanked on both sides.

Next there was a meeting with the leaders of the *Kampfgruppe*. Result: The units were to prepare an immediate, but well-planned and unnoticed withdrawal! Direction: North.

Soon the men and vehicles were resupplied and ready for the march. The order to withdraw was awaited. But something else happened. An order for the Batterie arrived: The *Sturmgeschütze* (accompanied by an infantry element in roughly platoon strength) were to make an advance on the southern, occupied part of the village while the other troops were to withdraw.

A senseless order? Not at all! According to "the fundamental rules of tactics", every conscientious troop leader must make arrangements before a withdrawal which provide the bulk of his forces with adequate time and space for an ordered departure for the heavy weapons and equipment, trains, staffs, etc.! Means to an end can be the "final actions" of a rearguard. For example, harassing or interdictory artillery fire by individual guns (if available!) or delaying actions based on time or space. Or, offensive operations made by the rearguard — as was planned in this case!

But the intent of this operation was difficult to convey to the *Landser* who were assigned to conduct it. There was a *Major* in a leather coat who — at the top of his lungs and while waving his arms furiously — was trying to convince the few stubborn ones. It was almost a small mutiny! (By the way, I could understand the position of the soldiers. After many such operations during the past few years — most which went well — I was not able to rid myself of the feeling that we were being fired up for a suicide mission.) But as our assault guns assembled west of the village, about 25 men followed us…and everything went well!

A few rounds were fired at more or less readily identifiable targets; actually more to "impress" than anything else. ("Pay attention over there! We are still here and very strong!") There was barely any return fire. The the rear guard was informed: "Forward comrades, let the retreat begin!"

Soon we had caught up to the march column, the pace of which was determined by horse-drawn carriages and men travelling on foot. We had to split up the *Sturmgeschütze*, even though we would have preferred not to. The "stimulating effect" our assault guns had on the *Landser* was definitely just as important as the protection our assault guns received from the infantry while travelling through the wooded terrain. The column reached the area around Heiderode without incident and there it was dissolved.

If I remember correctly, the fighting that I just described was the last successful operation of *Sturmgeschütz-Brigade 276* where the unit as a whole was involved and we were very successful. We fought according to the doctrine of the *Sturmartillerie*!

In the meantime, the brigade was transferred to Berent. The remaining assault guns were given to another unit. Supposedly the brigade was to be "pulled out" and re-equipped into a newly planned *Sturmartillerie-Brigade* in Denmark. By then such plans had few prospects of fruition, but hopes and rumors continued to circulate. In fact, the brigade's leadership made numerous requests to the field army command and the *Oberkommando des Heeres* (Supreme Command of the Army).

Several visits and personal discussions by *Leutnant* Walter Schmitt resulted in the fact that the brigade was to receive 42 brand-new

"Hetzer" Panzerjäger instead of the *Sturmgeschütz G*. They were to be staged at Pasewalk for the brigade. *Leutnant* Schmitt, who later described the situation, waited for the arrival of the brigade or at least the brigade's assault gun crews. But he waited in vain; West Prussia, Danzig and East Prussia were cut off. *Sturmgeschütz-Brigade 276* went without *Sturmgeschütze* and sat there together in the trap with units of the Army, the *Luftwaffe* and the *Kriegsmarine* — and many civilians! That was the beginning of the bitter end!

16. Operations on 18/19 February 1945 in the Tuchler Heath and the Village of Altfliess...

(After-action report by *Obergefreiter* Heinz Fleischer, *Sturmgeschütz* driver, *3./Sturmgeschütz-Brigade 276*).

It was about 0720 hours. We were in the village of Altfliess and had two *Sturmgeschütze*. At that time a regimental command post of the *252. Infanterie-Division*, as well as a strong element of the division, was also in Altfliess. We received the mission to advance in the direction of the villages of Klinger and Oscha together with 60 infantrymen. Our task was to head off Russian units that had broken through and destroy them. This operation was very difficult, since we had to move through woods with narrow trails and no one knew where the Russians were. We were happy to have 60 infantrymen with us. They provided us protection against the possibility of Russian infantry which had penetrated.

After moving three and a half kilometers in the direction of Klinger we still had not encountered any enemy forces. But we felt that we would soon run into the Russians. For that reason and in consultation with the infantry we decided it would be better not to advance any further and to take up positions where we were. The assault guns took up positions where they could see each other, each assault gun on one of the forest trails. By doing that we had good firing positions. Escorting each assault gun were 30 infantrymen.

After we had occupied positions, both infantry elements sent three patrols in different directions to look for signs of the enemy. They were not to get engaged with the enemy, however. The other infantrymen occupied positions around our assault guns. The patrols were to send a messenger back as soon as they came upon enemy troops. The messenger was to report how strong the enemy units were, what weapons they possessed and on which trail they were advancing. We would then post our assault guns and infantry on the appropriate trail.

It was about 0910 hours when the first messenger came back. He

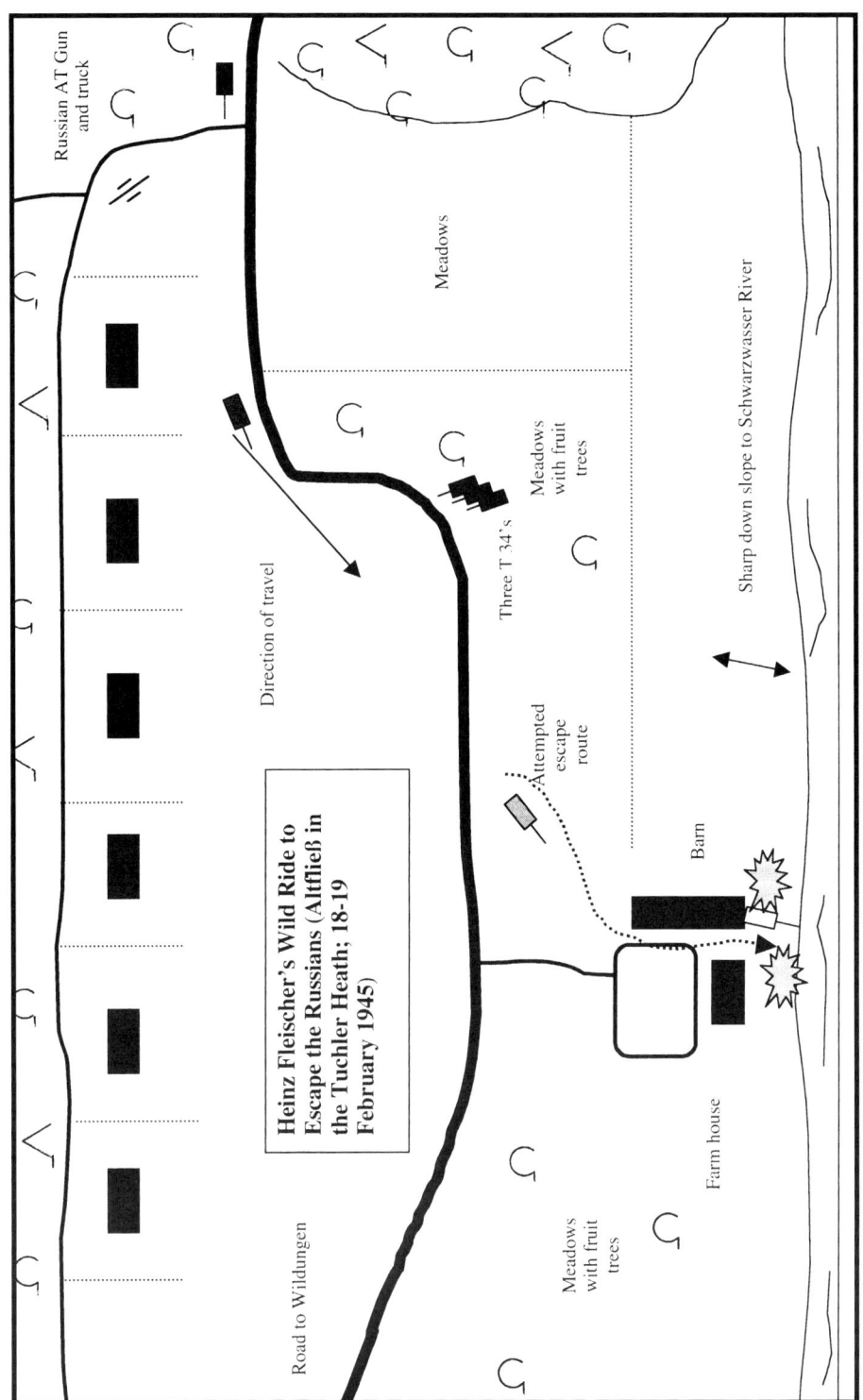

reported to us where the Russians were advancing with trucks towing antitank guns. We immediately moved to the reported position with our *Sturmgeschütze* and the infantry took position to the right and left of the trail. The infantry positioned themselves so that they would not be noticed by the Russians. The Russians would move into their trap as if advancing down a hose.

Our infantry had the task to maintain absolute silence and only to open fire after the *Sturmgeschütze* fired their first rounds. An additional task of the infantry was to engage the Russian infantry who might have the opportunity to dismount the trucks and withdraw into the woods after the initial fire trap was sprung by our guns. Using this method we were able to knock out five Russian trucks with limbered antitank guns as well as two T 34's and all their infantry. After the results of our attack made a further Russian advance impossible, we moved back one and a half kilometers. We were lucky the Russians had been completely careless. They were confident and never expected that we would be there. There were no main lines any more.

Our trains were in the village of Ofen, about 27 kilometers from where we were. We, as well as the infantry, had no casualties to report up to that point. After we had moved back the one and half kilometers, we turned off on a road to Altfliess. The village was about two kilometers away. We drove past a meadow that was about 500 x 400 meters in dimension. When we had reached the end of the meadow, the infantry reported that they heard the engine noise. We immediately moved to the left at the end of the meadow land and onto a trail. Between the meadow and the trail were medium-sized bushes. We took up positions there with the infantry.

The engine noises grew stronger and then we saw two Russian trucks towing antitank guns, accompanied by infantry that they were carrying on their vehicles. They were travelling on the trail and coming out of the woods. The Russians had not seen us. We could take our time getting them in our sights. They were then on the other side of the meadow and without cover. And then, in a very short time, we shot everything to pieces. The ammunition they had loaded onto the trucks exploded and everything burned.

After this short engagement was over, the infantry was supposed to go with us to the village of Altfliess, since we believed that the regimental command post of the *252. Infanterie-Division* was still located there. But the infantry didn't want to go and took off in the direction of the Schwarzwasser River. The infantry's decision was to have serious consequences for our *Sturmgeschütze*.

We then moved alone in the direction of Altfliess. It was around 1250 hours when we headed in that direction. I was the lead assault gun. The second followed shortly behind me. The assault gun commanders as well as the gunners sat on top of the assault guns as if there were nothing untoward going on. They were of the belief that the regimental command post was still in the village and there was no immediate danger.

The village was laid-out as follows: Running through the middle of the village was a straight road about 800 meters long. The road then made a strong S-curve. Behind the first curve was a small village square. To the right of the road were gardens that climbed up to houses. The houses formed a row that bordered the edge of a patch of woods. Between the houses and the woods was a path. The main road was on a small decline. To the left of the road was a meadow, then there was a fence and then again another meadow, upon which fruit trees were standing. After the S-curve there was a path about 160 meters long which led to a farm. To the left there was the barn with stalls and to the right was the farmhouse. Between them was a path about four meters wide. Behind that was a meadow, which sloped sharply down to the Schwarzwasser River. The distance from the river to the farm was about 200 meters.

As I moved out of the woods with the *Sturmgeschütz*, I saw a Russian antitank gun to the right at a distance of about 30 meters. It was located between the first house and the woods. When the Russians saw us, they stood there as if made of stone. They were shocked to see us! I immediately yelled, "*Achtung!* Russian antitank gun to the right at 30 meters!" At that moment the assault gun commander and the gunner both jumped off the assault gun and ran into the woods. My loader jumped over the empty casings holder and crouched behind me. I then saw that the Russians had overcome their shock and had swung the barrel of their antitank gun in my direction.

I thought to myself, lightning fast, "Two men in the assault gun — no round in the barrel — there isn't enough time to roll over the antitank gun!" They would have knocked us out at a distance of two meters. Since I was broadside to the antitank gun and behind me was the second *Sturmgeschütz* — which I would have hit if I had reversed while still being in the kill zone of the antitank gun — there was only one option for me: Move into the village.

As a soldier you didn't rule out any possibility to stay alive. For me, in this situation, it was the only possibility. Russian infantrymen, who were on the road, cleared off to the side and let me move by without a fuss. We were amazed why they did that and also why the antitank gun was not firing. Every second passed as if our last hour had come. I was so wound up I practically exploded.

I could not attempt to flee to the left over the first meadow, since the antitank gun could reach me there. At that point the road made a sharp left-hand turn. There were three T 34's in the small village square. The crews stood outside. Some of them ran up to the houses. The other Russians stood there like stone statues and didn't know for sure what was going on. I could have halted and took over as the gunner. But the antitank gun to my rear forced me to keep my thoughts moving along. Now it was clear why the antitank gun did not fire. The crew knew that the three T 34's would take care of me.

In the meantime I came upon the meadow with the fruit trees. Here I saw a chance to flee since the trees would offer me some protection from the antitank gun. I moved right by the three T 34's. When I passed the last T 34, I moved my assault gun to the left and floored it over the meadow. We heard numerous rounds being fired from the antitank gun, but none hit us. Driving further to the left, so that we could pass to the left of the barn, was not a possibility, since there was another wall there and I would have been in the firing range of the antitank gun — without cover. The only thing left was to flee between the barn and the farmhouse. But it was not to be.

In the meantime the crews of the three T 34's had overcome their shock and had driven to the path that led to the farm. By then, I had already passed between the farmhouse and the barn and moved to the steep slope that led to the river. We had just managed to regain hope that we had once more escaped a deadly situation when there was a horrible bang. It was not a direct hit and ricocheted off our assault gun. At that moment we thought, "Guardian angel, don't abandon us!" We had not finished thinking this thought when there was a second horrible bang. Sparks flew. I smelled smoke and we knew the assault gun was burning. The round had hit the superstructure squarely.

I yelled, "We're hit!" My comrade, *Gefreiter* Schwaiger (loader), immediately bailed out. He was sitting directly behind me. After he managed to get outside, I got out as well. While dismounting, flames rose towards me. We ran to the river. Our only thought was that we had to get out of there. There was still about 180 to 200 meters until we would reach the river. When we got there, we jumped in the river. The water reached up to our chest. After we had gotten to the other side, we ran another 60 meters over a meadow, where we finally reached the woods. For weapons we still had our P 38's and three egg hand grenades.

We were completely exhausted. Besides that we didn't look like humans any more. Our faces were black, smeared with oil, and we were soaked to the skin. We were still deathly afraid. After we were able to gather some strength in the protection of the trees, we tried to figure out where we were and in which direction we should go. We didn't know whether there were Russians here as well. We stalked slowly and silently through the forest until reaching the road that connected the villages of Klein Schliewitz and Laski.

When we reached the road and ran next to it in the woods, we heard the sounds of motors. We hid ourselves behind the trees because we didn't know if it were Russians or Germans. Then we saw them coming. They were Germans with sidecars, motorcycles mounted with machine guns and a number of personnel carriers with infantry. It was a unit of the *227. Infanterie-Division*.

We were happy to have German soldiers in front of us. We stood on the road and indicated they should stop. They stopped, but weren't so happy to see us. They disarmed us. It was now clear that it was due to the way we looked. We tried to explain to them what happened, who we were — but without success. Guards took us to their unit's command post. Luckily we knew where our trains were located. They were indeed in the village of Ofen. The command post contacted our trains and the officer was told that we belonged to the 276. Forty minutes later our *Spieß, Hauptwachtmeister* Hufnagel, picked us up personally. Were we ever happy to rejoin our comrades.

As mentioned previously, the second assault gun moved back into the forest and tried to ford the river. But it sunk. Only the radios were removed. My assault gun commander and the gunner had arrived with the other four comrades of the sunken assault gun at the trains a long time before we had and reported that we were either dead or had been taken prisoner.

July 1943: *Sturmgeschütz-Brigade 276* shortly before rail loading to the Eastern Front.

The officer corps of *Sturmgeschütz-Brigade 276* in June 1943. Sitting, from left to right: *Oberleutnant* Schaubs, *Oberleutnant* Hippler, *Oberleutnant* Tobler, *Hauptmann* Rünger (Commander), *Oberleutnant* Schulte, *Oberleutnant* Ertel, *Oberleutnant* Fratt and *Oberleutnant* Lötsch. Standing, from left to right: *Leutnant* Ulps, *Zahlmeister* Müller, *technischer Inspektor* Müller, *Leutnant* Albert, *Leutnant* Erdweg, *Leutnant* Basten, *Leutnant* Kany, *technischer Ingenieur* Pöhlmann, *Leutnant* Winkelmann, *Leutnant* Niemietz, *Leutnant* Beckmann and *Leutnant* Nippes.

July 1943: *Sturmgeschütz-Brigade 276* shortly before rail loading to the Eastern front.

August 1943: Operations at Labutky.

September 1943: Knocked out SU 85 assault guns in the Korosten area of operations.

September 1943: Another view of the knocked out SU 85 assault guns seen on the previous page.

October 1943: Captured T 70 in the Korosten sector.

Crossing the Desna River using ferries in 1943.

The crossing appears to have been uneventful...

...and to have allowed the trains elements a rare opportunity for rest and skinny-dipping!

Some final views of the unopposed river-crossing operation.

Assault gun of *Sturmgeschütz-Brigade 276* after knocking out a T 34 in the area around Sihaletni-Vahnlitz.

This was the view the gunner got through the *Sturmgeschütz* optics.

October 1943: Assault guns awaiting a Russian attack.

Leutnant Albert with his crew.

The funeral of *Gefreiter* Rudolf Fröhlich, killed in action on 16 October 1943.

Burial service for *Oberleutnant* Tobler, killed in action...

...in November 1943 at Oranoje on the Dnjepr.

Two additional views of the burial service for *Oberleutnant* Tobler, as seen on the previous two pages.

Oberleutnant Tobler in the middle.

Burial and field grave of *Leutnant* Kurt Nippes, platoon leader in the *1. Batterie*, killed in action on 10 December 1943. He received the Knight's Cross posthumously on 29 January 1944 and was promoted to *Oberleutnant*.

December 1943: An assault gun and infantry await a Russian attack in the Schitomir-Starokonstandino sector.

Opposite page: Three additional views of the burial and field grave of *Leutnant* Kurt Nippes.

December 1943: Assault guns of *Sturmgeschütz-Brigade 276* move out for a new operation in the Schitomir-Starokonstandino sector.

January 1944: After close combat with 5 T 34's on the road from Korec to Mosza. Score: 4-0. One of the kills was credited to the *Sturmgeschütz* of *Leutnant* Kany.

January-February 1944: Employment in the Schepetowka area of operations.

January 1944: Comrades of *Sturmgeschütz-Brigade 276* at a celebration in the Rowno—Goszcza—Korec sector. Another view of the celebration. Standing to the left is *Obergefreiter* Fleischer.

January 1944: Comrades of *Sturmgeschütz-Brigade 276* at a celebration in the Rowno—Goszcza—Korec sector. **Opposite page:** Another view of the celebration. Standing to the left is *Obergefreiter* Fleischer.

March 1944: Knocked out T 70 in the area around Winniza.

Knocked out T 70 with a carbonized Russian tanker.

March 1944, Proskerov-Schmerinka sector: Assault guns attempting to get firm ground under their tracks. Front right: *Obergefreiter* Fleischer (Driver).

Another view of the tough going as seen on the previous page.

Beginning of March 1944: Comrades of *Sturmgeschütz-Brigade 276* in the Schepetowka Proskurov sector.

Additional views of soldiers of *Sturmgeschütz-Brigade 276*...

...in the Schepetoka Proskurov sector.

Additional views of soldiers of *Sturmgeschütz-Brigade 276*...

...in the Schepetoka Proskurov sector.

Final views of soldiers of *Sturmgeschütz-Brigade 276* in the Schepetoka Proskurov sector.

Departure of the *3. Batterie* out of the city of Proskurov. Note the *Panzer V Panther* in the background.

March 1944 on the road from Tschertkow to Butschatsch: Comrades of the *3. Batterie*.

Additional views of the March 1944 road march from Tschertkow to Butschatsch: Comrades of the *3. Batterie*.

Above; Sturmgeschütze of 3./276 travel along a supply road in March 1944 in the Schmirinka sector.

Sturmgeschütz-Brigade 276 taking a village near Kamenez-Podolsk.

Beginning of April 1944: An assault gun on a collapsed bridge at Kamenez-Podolsk. **Below:** *Obergefreiter* Fleischer sitting on his *Sturmgeschütz*. **Opposite page, top:** Another view of the accident.

Opposite page, bottom: April 1944 in the Kamenez-Podolsk pocket: *Sturmgeschütz-Brigade 276* is employed as infantry. First in the row is *Unteroffizier* Strobbach, killed in action on 10 February 1945 in East Prussia; second is *Obergefreiter* Fleischer. On the outside left is *Oberleutnant* Stück, the battery commander.

Above, fourth from the left: *Obergefreiter* Fleischer. **Below:** Alternate means of transportaion is found.

Comrades of *Sturmgeschütz-Brigade 276* after breaking out of the pocket. They were relieved by the *10. SS-Panzerdivision* at Buczacz on 6 April 1944.

Additional views of soldiers of *Sturmgeschütz-Brigade 276* after breaking out of the pocket. They were relieved by the *10. SS-Panzerdivision* at Buczacz on 6 April

The village of Buczacz, then and on 6 April 1966.

The assault gun of the *3. Batterie* commander, *Oberleutnant* Stück.

Assault guns with mounted infantry.

Sturmgeschütz-Brigade 276 on the move from Lemberg to Deutsch Eylau (East Prussia) for reorganization.

May 1944: Officers of *Sturmgeschütz-Brigade 276*. From left to right: *Leutnant* Schmitt, *Leutnant* Sehrt, *Oberleutnant* Lötsch and *Oberleutnant* Semke.

May 1944: Officers of *Sturmgeschütz-Brigade 276*. From left to right: *Oberleutnant* Schäfer, *Oberleutnant* Erdweg, *Leutnant* Regeniter, *Ingenieur* Pöhlmann, *Hauptmann* Sewera, *Oberleutnant* Lötsch, *Hauptmann* Stück, *Zahlmeister* Müller, *Leutnant* Schmitt and *Leutnant* Pflaum.

Although not positively identified, the pictures on this and the next two pages were probably taken by a member of *Sturmgeschütz-Brigade 276* at Deutsch-Eylau during the reorganization. **Above**: An early model Pz.Kpfw. V *Panther* Ausf. D. **Below**: An early model Pz.Kpfw. VI *Tiger* on transport tracks, possibly undergoing engine maintenance.

This page and left: Two fine views of the experimental 12.8cm *Panzerjäger* on the *Vk 30.01 (P)* chassis. Two vehicles saw action with *3./schwere Panzer-Abteilung 521* in Russia, one was subsequently captured intact and is on display at Kubinka.

Above: More views of the reorganization at Deutsch Eylau (East Prussia). Standing to the right of the 10.5 cm *Sturmhaubitze* is *Obergefreiter* Fleischer. **Left:** Assault guns lines up in a motor pool. It is believed these may have been *Sturmgeschütze* used for training by the brigade while it was at Deutsch-Eylasu.

July 1944 at Deutsch Eylau: Obergefreiter Fleischer next to the barrel; Gefreiter Walter Budwig standing on the track on the right.

Above and next page: 30 July 1944: *Sturmgeschütz-Brigade 276* loads up its assault guns in preparation for new employment in Lithuania.

A final view of the rail-loading operation.

Sturmgeschütze of *3./Sturmgeschütz-Brigade 276* with accompanying infantry form up for an operation.

Assault guns of *3./Sturmgeschütz-Brigade 276* in an assembly position. Some attempt has been made to camouflage the vehicles.

Sturmgeschütze in an ambush position.

Above and Below: August 1944 in the Willkowischken (Lithuania) sector: Villages taken back by the brigade.

Knocked out T 34/76: *Obergefreiter* Fleischer next to the barrel. Next to him is *Gefreiter* Schwaiger, who was killed in action in December 1944 in the Willkowischken (Lithuania) sector.

Opposite page, top: 12 August 1944: Following an early-morning attack at Pranskatudis (Lithuania). Shown is Knight's Cross recipient *Leutnant* Regeniter. In the background is the assault gun driver, *Obergefreiter* Fleischer.

Opposite page, bottom, from left to right: *Leutnant* Regeniter, *Hauptmann* Stück, *Leutnant* Sehrt and *Hauptfeldwebel* Hufnagel.

August 1944 in Lithuania: *3. Batterie* with mounted infantry on the move to a new operation.

Officers of *Sturmgeschütz-Brigade 276*: Hauptmann Stück, *Oberleutnant* Lötsch, Dr. Cordes, *Oberleutnant* Doetsch, *Leutnant* Schmitt, *Leutnant* Regeniter, *Zahlmeister* Müller, *Oberleutnant* Erdweg, *Ingenieur* Pöhlmann and *Leutnant* Pflaum.

August 1944, from left to right: Naschenweng, Doß, Wimmer, Dollkopf, Buck, Budwig, Fleischer, Wenk, Rollin.

Above and next page: August 1944: *Major* Braun, commander of *Sturmgeschütz-Brigade 276*. He was killed in action by an antitank rifle on 21 August 1944 at Wolfshof. He was buried at Ebenrode (East Prussia).

Above. 1944: Comrades of the *3. Batterie* with a Russian.

Left and below: Buial of *Major* Braun at Ebenrode (East Prussia).

August 1944 in the Willkowischken sector. The gun crew of *Sturmgeschütz 313*, from left to right: *Unteroffizier* Dienst, *Obergefreiter* Fleischer, *Gefreiter* Schwaiger.

August 1944 at Willkowischken: In the *Schwimmwagen* are *Hauptmann* Stück and his driver, Alfred Naschenweng. Standing to the left is *Leutnant* Regeniter. Behind him to the right is *Leutnant* Rudi Sehrt. Notice the brigade symbol on the side of the *Schwimmwagen*.

August 1944: Standing to the right of the 10.5 cm *Sturmhaubitze* is *Obergefreiter* Fleischer.

The gravesites of *Obergefreiter* Rudolf Bauer (top of page) and *Unteroffizier* Hans Kreil. Both men were killed on 4 August 1944 in Bilderweiten (East Prussia).

The grave site of *Obergefreiter* Alfred Naschenweng. He was killed in action on the Neustadt to Schirrwind road on 16 August 1944.

August 1944: 22-ton lowboy with a *Sturmgeschütz III* of the *3. Batterie*.

August 1944: Knocked-out assault gun. Russian soldiers can be seen on the left.

August 1944 at Willkowischken: A T 34/76 which has just been knocked out by *Hauptmann* Stück and his crew.

August 1944: Three Russian T70 light tanks knocked out by *Sturmgeschütz-Brigade 276*.

August 1944: *Sturmgeschütze* in an assembly area awaiting an attack.

1944 in Lithuania: The band of the *3. Batterie*. Standing on the left is *Wachtmeister* Hans Richter; sitting on the right is *Obergefreiter* Fleischer.

August 1944: A crew member delouses

Leutnant Sehrt (left) and *Leutnant* Regeniter.

Motorcycle messenger Willi Wenk and *Leutnant* Regeniter.

September 1944: *Sturmgeschütz* in a camouflaged position.

September 1944: A *Sturmgeschütz* awaits an order to attack.

September 1944: Comrades of *Sturmgeschütz-Brigade 276*. From left to right: *Gefreiter* Scheuren, *Wachtmeister* Kohn, *Leutnant* Ertel, *Obergefreiter* Nehmann und *Obergefreiter* Riese.

Preparations are made for a company fest.

End of September 1944: *Sturmgeschütz* with clutch damage being towed by two 18t "Famo". Sitting on the barrel: *Obergefreiter* Fleischer.

Sturmgeschütz with antitank rifle hit. *Major* Braun was killed in this assault gun. *Obergefreiter* Fleischer was the driver.

October 1944: *Obergefreiter* Fleischer paints a kill ring on the barrel.

October 1944: Assault gun and comrades of the *3. Batterie* await new orders.

December 1944: *Sturmgeschütz 333* of the *3. Batterie* in an assembly area.

December 1944 in East Prussia: An assault gun is dragged out of a river.

Hauptmann Friedrich Stück. From December 1943 to December 1944 he was the commander of the *3. Batterie*; effective January 1945 he was the commander of *Sturmgeschütz-Brigade 276*.

A *Sturmgeschütz* of the *3. Batterie* with its crew. From left to right: *Obergefreiter* Nehmann, *Obergefreiter* Riese, *Wachtmeister* Kohn and *Gefreiter* Scheuren.

Obergefreiter Helmut Zararias, motorcycle messenger for the 3rd Batterie. The time period for the photographs on this page and the next cannot be fixed with any certainty.

Members of the command group outside a burning village.

Two more photographs of *Sturmgeschütz-Brigade 276* which cannot be fixed in time or location.

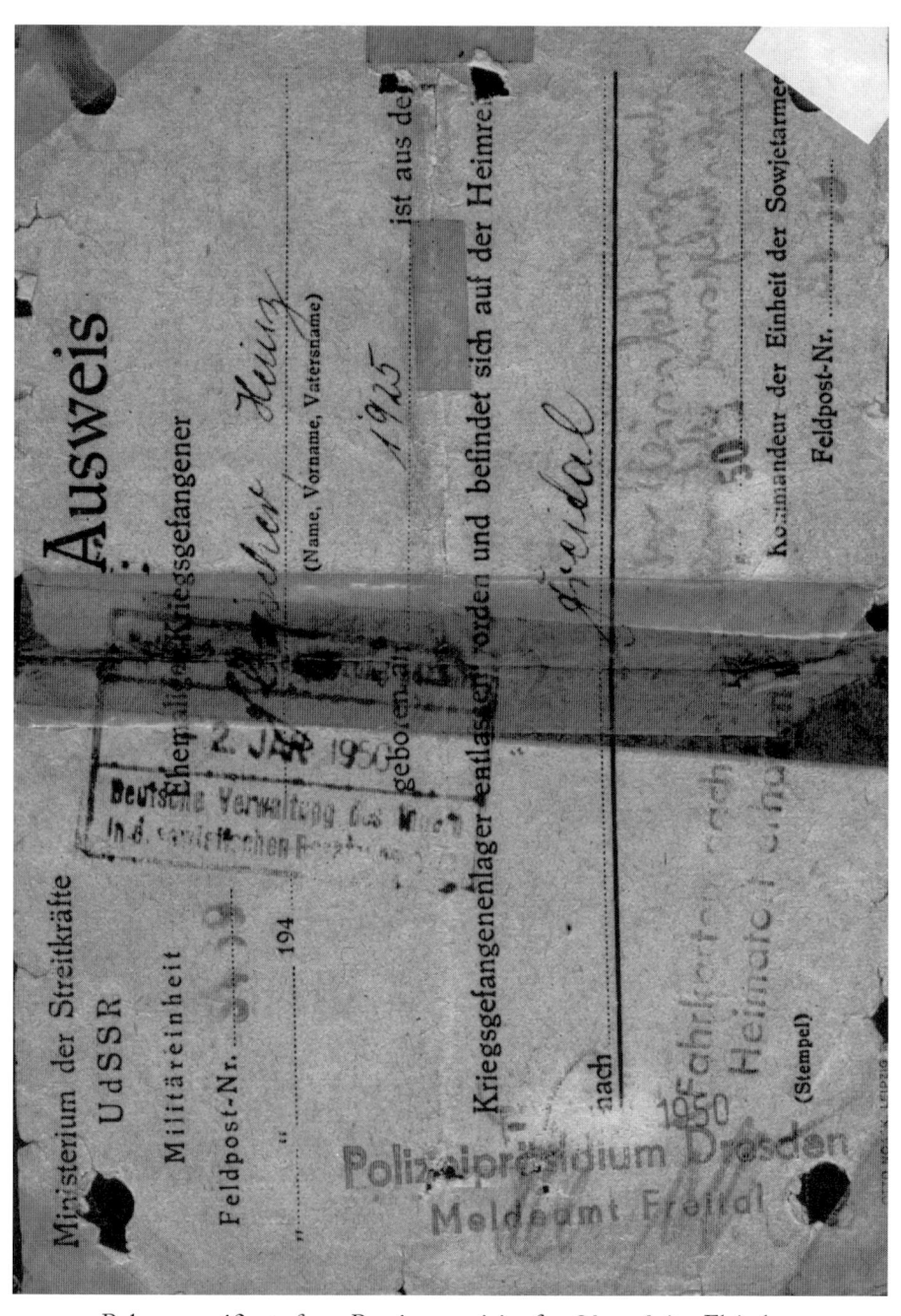

Release certificate from Russian captivity for *Obergefreiter* Fleischer.

The *Strumartillerie* memorial at Radstadt (Austria).

Former *Obergefreiter* Fleischer at a meeting of Knight's Cross recipients. Radstadt (Austria).

September 1999: *Obergefreiter* Fleischer at a meeting of former *Sturmartilleristen* at Radstadt (Austria).

Former *Leutnant* Regeniter dons his *Sturmartillerie* tunic ater learning of his award of the Knight's Cross in the early 1970's.

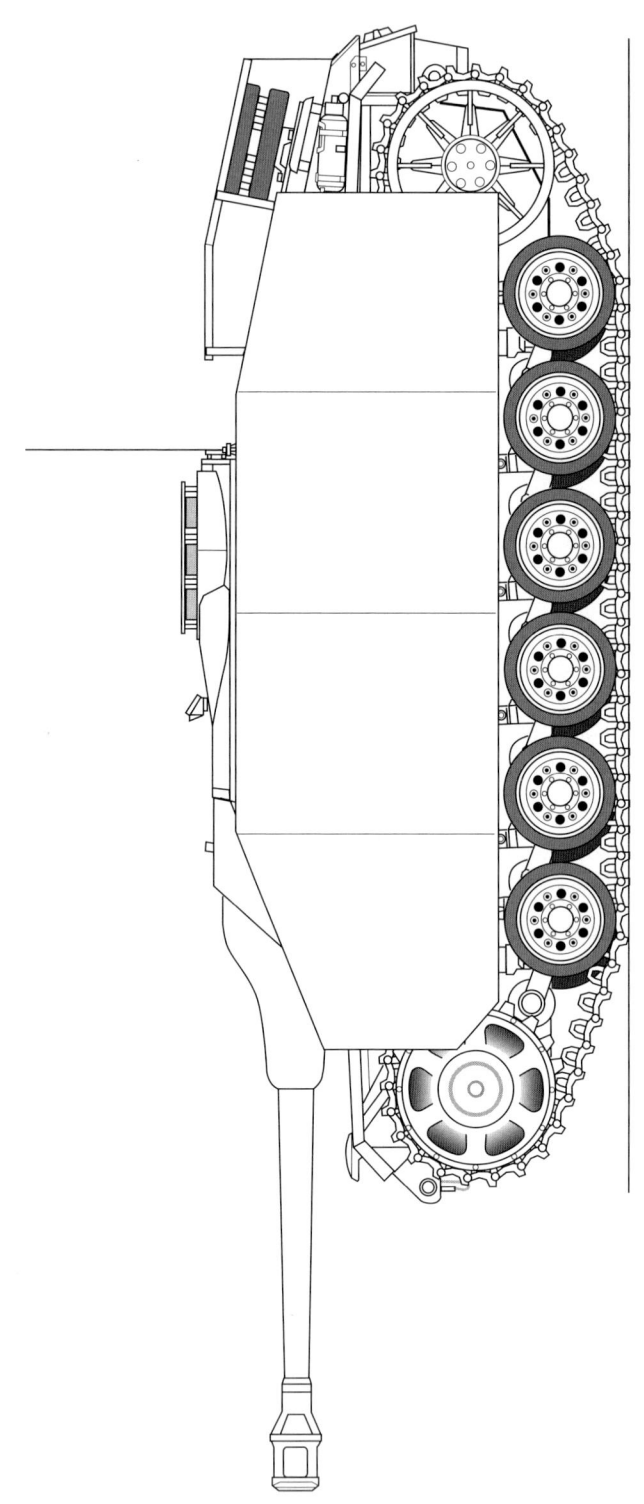

Sturmgeschütz III, Ausführung G (late model)
(courtesy of George Bradford)

17. Operations at Mewe from 27 February until 5 March 1945….

(After-action report by *Obergefreiter* Heinz Fleischer, *Sturmgeschütz* driver, *3./Sturmgeschütz-Brigade 276*).

The area of operations for *Sturmgeschütz-Brigade 276* from 13 to 26 February 1945 was north of the Tuchler Heath in the area of Lubichow, Bobau and Wolenthal. The Russians tried to advance north to Preußisch Stargard with strong forces. We were engaged in heavy defensive fighting, clearing up penetrations and pressing our opponent back to where he had started from. After that it became quieter in this area. The enemy had suffered such heavy casualties that he could no longer afford to attempt a further advance.

Our trains and supply section were initially located in the village of Ofen and then moved to the village of Lipinken, southeast of Preußisch Stargard. On 27 February 1945, the combat elements of *Sturmgeschütz-Brigade 276* received orders to move to Mewe with nine assault guns. They were under the command of *Hauptmann* Stück. I was Stück's driver. We knew that the Russians had planned an attack on Mewe, jumping off from the villages of Marienwerder, Riesenburgh and Stuhm. On 27 February 1945, at about 1100 hours, we arrived in Mewe. During the days before our arrival the Russians had started to attack Mewe from the air. They had also fired harassing fire with artillery. A good 70% of the population had already fled the city. When we arrived in Mewe, we positioned our assault guns in the town square.

Hauptmann Stück immediately went to the divisional staffs of the *542. Volksgrenadier* and the *337. Infanterie-Divisionen* to get briefed on the situation and receive further orders. We received the order to inspect our assault guns, fill up our gas tanks and upload the assault guns with ammunition. Furthermore, we were to stay in the vicinity of our assault guns. Located around Mewe were also units of the *542. Volksgrenadier-Division* and the *337. Infanterie-Division*. After we had prepared our assault guns for operations, I jumped from my vehicle. I was completely dirty and covered with oil from the assault gun.

What I didn't notice when I jumped from the gun was that there was a girl with long blonde hair passing by. I landed at her feet. We were both so shocked, that neither of us said a word. She was probably also afraid, due to the way I looked. And for me it was as if my assault gun had received a direct hit and Christmas and Easter had fallen on the same day. I was so taken with this girl! For me the war had been forgotten for a moment, until reality came back to me. I apologized and introduced myself. I also asked her right away where I could wash up. She said to me that her name was Liesbeth and that I could come with her.

I told my comrades in which house I would be, since there was the possibility that orders would arrive. Liesbeth led me to a house on the marketplace and introduced me to an older couple. Then she brought me a large bowl of warm water and some soap. After I had finished washing, I was given an invitation to lunch, which I thankfully accepted. During the conversation, I found out this blonde child was named Liesbeth Pahl, she was 18 years old and she was also on the run. She didn't know whether her parents were still alive or where they might be. After the meal, Liesbeth came with me back to the assault guns.

Shortly after that, our *Hauptmann* came back from a meeting and we moved to the edge of the village, to the road between Mewe and Sprauden. I received permission from our *Hauptmann* that Liesbeth could go with us there. When we arrived, we received the order to position an assault gun at every house and camouflage them well. The population had already abandoned the houses. The contents were still intact and food was available in abundance. Left of the road was a park and there were large Linden trees on the sides of the street.

Liesbeth and I agreed to see each other again the next day, 28 February 1945, at 0900 hours. We occupied the houses and, for the first time in a long time, we slept in a real bed. Except for the Russian harassing fire, which didn't bother us much at all, the night was calm. The next day Liesbeth came at about nine o'clock, which made me very happy. She was there for about 40 minutes when we received orders to move out. According to the order, six T 34's had broken through on the road south of Mewe at Rakowitz — Pehsken — Nichtsfelde and were attempting to reach the edge of Mewe.

Liesbeth began to cry, hugged me and told me to take care of myself. Then she ran away. Within a few minutes we were ready and we took off in the direction of the village of Nichtsfelde, which was located about 2000 meters south of Mewe. According to the last report we had received, the Russians were about 5000 meters away. Arriving at the village outskirts of Nichtsfelde, we immediately occupied well-camouflaged positions with our nine assault guns. In the meantime, 40 infantrymen from the *542. Volksgrenadier-Division* arrived.

The infantrymen took position between 400 and 600 meters in front of us in the woods to the left and right of the road. Next to the road on both sides was a patch of woods of tall pine trees, so the T 34's were only able to move on the road. As previously mentioned, the comrades from the infantry took position about 400 to 600 meters away to the left and right of the road, so that they could take care of any Russian infantry that were possibly accompanying the tanks or tank crews who were trying to escape after they had been hit. In the meantime, a messenger notified us that there was no Russian infantry accompanying the tanks.

According to our orders, we were to remain quiet, unless we were discovered by accident. Not a round was to be fired until all 6 T 34's had rounded the corner on the road about 600 meters from us. Next, every assault gun received orders as to which Russian tank it was to shoot at. The last two tanks were to be knocked out first, then the others. The infantry also received the order to remain quiet and only to shoot at Russian tank crews trying to escape their burning coffins.

Then came the moment when we could see the first two T 34's. They felt their way on both sides of the road. The lead tanks were within a distance of 400 meters when the last ones turned the corner. We started to sweat in our assault guns. We didn't know if they had discovered us or not. We were relieved when we realized that they had not. Then our *Hauptmann* gave the order to fire, and within a good minute, all six T 34's were burning. We saw how a few Russian tank crewmen tried to escape. But they were immediately taken under fire by our infantry and killed. The others burned up in their coffins. After this successful, casualty-free operation had concluded, we returned to Mewe.

As we moved up the road to the marketplace, I saw Liesbeth standing on the sidewalk. My *Hauptmann*, comrade Stück, said to me that Liesbeth was standing there and that I should stop. He didn't know that I had already seen her. I spoke a few words with her and she cried with relief that I was back. I told her that we were setting up in a new location. It would be on the road to Gogolew, in the last houses in Mewe.

After about an hour Liesbeth was again with me. In the meantime, our supply elements had arrived with ammunition and fuel. We got our assault guns operationally ready once again. The change in position was made for security reasons. There was some peace and quiet again, except for the increased Russian artillery fire. I also had somewhat more time to spend with Liesbeth.

During the night of 28 February/1 March 1945, the Russians established a bridgehead over the Weichsal between the localities of Neu-Liebenau and Aussendeich about 2000 meters southeast of Mewe. The Germans did not notice the crossing which was done without heavy weapons and in the strength of two companies. The bridgehead was about 1000 meters wide and 800 meters deep. At the point where the Russians had crossed there were meadows and fields bordering the river. Then there was a steep slope to a forest, where there were newly-planted pine trees and sawed-off branches. The Russians quietly occupied this clearing all the way to the edge of the forest during the night.

On 1 March 1945, at about 0500 hours, we received an order that we were to carry out immediately. We moved on the road in the direction of Nichtsfelde. During the move to the area of operations we received notice that a company of infantry from the *337. Infanterie-Division* had been attached to us. It was waiting for us at the marketplace in Mewe. The infantry sat on our assault guns and there was barely any room left to sit or stand. When we arrived in the village of

Nichtsfelde, the infantrymen dismounted and turned off to the left of the road.

We spread out in attack formation — as far as the terrain would allow that for our *Sturmgeschütze* — and immediately launched a surprise attack on the Russians. After about 700 meters the clearing became wider and the Russians opened fire. We quickly determined that the Russians did not have any armor-defeating weapons with them. Their defensive fire was so strong, however, that our infantry was hard pressed for a while and had to take cover. A further advance by our infantry was not possible at the moment, so we moved our nine assault guns forward about 150 meters. We then fired on the slope with high-explosive rounds at a distance of about 200 meters.

We used field-expedient proximity fuses. What this means is that the rounds were aimed at the ground about two meters in front of their target. They then ricocheted up and exploded in the air so that the Russians located behind the slope were rained on by shrapnel and were forced to pay a high price in blood. This enabled our infantry to make a further advance. This fire proved successful. The Russian defensive fire was scattered, since most of them were dead or fleeing to the river.

When our infantry started to advance again and were even with us, we moved to the edge of the slope. During the advance I had a traumatic experience. About four meters in front and to the right of my assault gun a *Leutnant* from the infantry assaulted the edge of the slope with his machine pistol firing. Suddenly I saw how he raised both his arms high and his MP slid out of his hands. He fell on his face on the ground. He had been shot dead. After we had advanced to the edge of the slope with the infantry, there was only isolated resistance on the part of the Russians.

Six assault guns remained on the edge and provided fire for our infantrymen who were pursuing the Russians down the slope. A forest path ran down to the Weichsel left of the clearing. The path demanded expertise from a driver. I drove the assault gun with our *Hauptmann* and moved with two other assault guns and a group of infantrymen down to the Weichsel so that we could attack the fleeing Russians from their flank. When we arrived at the bottom, we immediately attacked.

Some of the Russians surrendered while others stood up to their chests in the water. We also took them prisoner. After the fighting had ended and our infantry had combed through everything, we had 63 prisoners. Then came the individual situation reports. The Russians had 170 dead. Our infantry had 14 killed and several wounded. We didn't lose a single assault gun. We did the same thing with the Russian wounded they had done with our wounded since the beginning of the war — they were shot.

Among the Russians that were taken prisoner were two officers. *Hauptmann* Stück and an infantry officer interrogated them. Among other things, the officers were asked why they intended to build a bridgehead here and why they didn't go back to their own people on the other side of the river when they were attacked. To the first question: On 5 March 1945 a feint was to be launched from the Rohhof Forest. They had the mission to attack German units from this bridgehead or stymie the attempts of German units to break out of Mewe. This was to support the main Russian advance coming from the Tuchler Heath with the objective of reaching the city of Preußisch Stargard. The city of Mewe was to be encircled and all German troops there were to be wiped out.

With regard to the second question: They had an order from their political officers to hold the bridgehead. And whoever came back over the Weichsel would be shot. That's why the Russians preferred to surrender. They said they were dead either way. Due to the important statements of the two officers, we handed them over to the divisional staff. The other prisoners were handed over to our infantry. The infantry company was then relieved by a unit from the *542. Volksgrenadier-Division*, which occupied positions there. The fate of the Russian prisoners remains unknown to us.

On 5 March 1945, we found out that the statements made by the two Russian officers were true.

During the afternoon, at about 1400 hours, we moved back to Mewe to the point where we had departed. There I met Liesbeth again. She was very scared and didn't know what to do. Since I could not send a message to her earlier, she didn't know if I had left Mewe forever or was fighting somewhere. She was happy to see me in one piece. After arriving at our jump-off point, the assault guns were again made operationally ready. We cooked warm food and caught up on our sleep.

The Second of March 1945 was, by our standards, a calm day, even though there were two air raids in Mewe and the Russian artillery fired increasingly on the city. Of the remaining residents and refugees, a great portion fled in the direction of Danzig. Liesbeth did not want to go, but I encouraged her to leave.

On 3 March 1945, we had just prepared macaroni and cheese with lots of ham. The comrades had just begun to eat when orders to move out arrived. We packed our mess kits full and climbed into the assault guns. As the driver, I was once again left holding the bag since my other comrades could eat during the move. We received the order to move in the direction of Rakowitz, since tanks had broken through there once again. The infantry had the task of letting the Russian tanks move through and only holding up Russian infantry.

We did not know the number of Russian tanks that had broken through. We encountered them in the Rakowitz Forest. We almost drove into an ambush, since they saw us first and immediately opened fire. Their mistake was opening fire from too great a distance. We identified five tanks: Three T 34's and two T 70's. Six of our assault guns opened fire and three assault guns snuck around the flank. The battle lasted about 50 minutes until we had finished them off with direct hits. We moved back to Mewe after this engagement. Since we were to go back to our original position of 27 February 1945, I informed Liesbeth about it and told her that she should go there.

From 3 March until the morning of 5 March 1945 there was no more fighting. Except for a few Russian artillery barrages, there was calm. Our assault guns were once again replenished and overhauled.

It was 5 March 1945. We were just eating breakfast. Our assault guns stood ready and were well camouflaged near some houses in the village. At that point a heavy barrage of Russian artillery fire, as well as air raids from the Russian air force, hit the city of Mewe.

The residents and refugees who had remained, as well as the

German units and their vehicles, fled from the city. We grabbed our personal weapons and ran to our assault guns. We moved them immediately across the road and into the park, which was thick with trees and provided better concealment from the air. We took cover next to the assault guns since many of the incoming rounds were very close and shrapnel crackled against them.

As previously mentioned, we were located at the outskirts of Mewe, west of the road between Mewe and Deutsch Brodden. There was neither a civilian nor a soldier to be seen as we waited for our orders. About 20 minutes had gone by. The Russians were continuing their barrage, round after round, when I saw a woman on the road who was running towards us. Upon closer examination, I thought I had been hit by lightning. It was Liesbeth.

Despite the warnings from my comrades, and throwing caution to the winds, I ran to Liesbeth and brought her from the road. She was completely distraught, speaking nonsense and crying bitterly. I brought her into cover behind my assault gun and covered her with my person. My first thought was that nothing should be allowed to happen to her. My second thought was, what should happen to her when we received our orders? I had to find a solution so that she wouldn't fall into the hands of the Russians.

Then a thought came to me. I wrote on a piece of paper the name and address of my parents in Dresden and gave her 360 Marks that I had hidden away. I told her that she should try to get to Danzig as soon as possible and from there she should try to get to my parents in Dresden as soon as possible. But how was I to get this girl out of here? Still no orders had arrived and the Russians continued to fire on Mewe. After about six minutes I saw a *Wehrmacht* truck with three soldiers driving as fast as the crater-filled road would allow. They were driving towards us. I realized that the truck was Liesbeth's rescue.

I jumped out into the road and tried to get the truck to stop. But they wouldn't think of stopping. Only after I fired my machine pistol into the road did they brake hard. A soldier asked me what was going on. I told him to take the girl and take good care of her so that nothing would happen to her. Liesbeth got in the truck with the soldiers and the vehicle moved away as fast as it could. That was the last time I saw Liesbeth. The Russians continued to barrage the city unabated.

After about 35minutes our orders arrived. We were to move northwest from Mewe to the area around Rosenthal and Grabowitz. There we were to try to hold up the Russian advance. The Russians were fielding strong forces accompanied by tanks and were advancing in the direction of Preußisch Stargard. We were to meet up with a few *Panthers* from *Panzer-Regiment 35*. We reached our supply section by radio and gave it directions to go to the village of Lipinken, which was about 3.2 kilometers south of Preußisch Stargard. It was to await further orders there.

When we moved from the village of Rosenthal in a westerly direction towards the village of Grabowitz, we came upon individual *Kampfgruppen* which wanted to pull back in the direction of Preußisch Stargard. There was no longer a continuous main line. When we appeared with our assault guns, the German troops gathered some courage and accompanied us for the counterattack. They told us where Russian tanks had broken through and where individual *Kampfgruppen* had been surrounded.

In Klein-Jablau the four *Panthers* from *Panzer-Regiment 35* linked up with us. We immediately launched the counterattack with the infantry. Shortly after we began our counterattack, we came upon a large number of Russian tanks that had broken through. Within a short time we had knocked out 17 Russian tanks. On our side, an assault gun received numerous hits and burst into flames. All four comrades were killed.

Our counterattack managed to push back the Russians about four kilometers to the village of Bobau. This had the effect of freeing three *Kampfgruppen* that had been cut off by the Russians. During those engagements we managed to knock out an additional five Russian tanks. Another one of our assault guns received a hit to the tracks and remained immobile. We tried to contact our headquarters by radio and get two prime movers so the assault gun could be recovered. But in this mess that wasn't possible.

Since we didn't have much more fuel or ammunition, four of the assault guns secured the area, so the other assault guns could recover the fuel and ammunition from the immobile vehicle. Then it was blown up. We continued to send urgent messages since we were low on fuel and ammunition. Our supply section promised to send two vehicles. But when they showed up at the agreed meeting point, either the Russians were already there, or we were already employed somewhere else. Finally, the two vehicles reached us at Klein-Jablau. We were happy to finally have fuel and ammunition. In the meantime it had become dark and the fighting died down in our area. After refueling and loading up ammunition, we moved back to the point from where we had departed and linked up with the four *Panthers*. In the meantime we heard on the radio that the Russians had taken the city of Mewe.

At dusk on 6 March 1945, Russian tanks renewed their attack to recapture the area they had lost the previous day. During the night the German infantry had built up their positions somewhat and was able to pin down the Russian infantry. Between the Russian tanks and us began an regular firefight. The Russians had a 3:1 advantage. With six *Sturmgeschütze* and four *Panthers* we were able to bring the Russian advance to a halt. We knocked out 21 Russian tanks; the others turned back. We lost a further three assault guns and had dead and wounded comrades to report. Since the Russians had gained territory in the southwest and were advancing from the area of Mewe, we had to pull back in the direction of Danzig with our four remaining assault guns until we were behind Preußisch Stargard.

A new defensive line had been established there. The Russians took Preußisch Stargard on 7 March 1945. We lost our last four assault guns north of Dirschau between 20 and 24 March 1945.

(Note: After I had been released from Russian captivity I found out from my parents that Liesbeth had actually arrived at my parents' residence and had lived there until 1948. Liesbeth found out from the Red Cross that she had relatives living in Lübeck and she traveled there. In 1955 I fled to West Germany. In 1986 my wife and I asked the authorities to search for Liesbeth and we found out that she was living in Siegen. We contacted her and we were very excited to see each other once again. Since that time we have remained in contact.)

18. The 3. Batterie of Sturmgeschütz-Brigade 276 Employed as Infantry and in the Heavy Defensive Fighting around the City of Danzig...

(After-action report by *Obergefreiter* Heinz Fleischer, *Sturmgeschütz* driver, *3./Sturmgeschütz-Brigade 276*).

Between 26 and 29 March 1945, the Russians broke through the positions around Danzig and fired upon Danzig-Langfuhr with heavy weapons. The German units resisted fiercely against the Russian army which was vastly superior in terms of equipment, weaponry and number of soldiers. Our brigade hadn't had any assault guns for a long time. The trains were waiting at Schiewenhorst, not far from the arm of the Tote Weichsel. The comrades, who shortly before had been in their assault guns and tried to stop the enemy, were now "infantrymen", armed with machine pistols and *Panzerfäuste*.

After the heavy bombardment of Danzig-Langfuhr, we pulled back to the Heubuder Forest. There we received orders to dig in. We had barely begun when new orders arrived. In small elements, mostly on their own and with no other support, we were set off on a march to Danzig. Without any concept of the operation, we moved through the streets of the Danzig suburbs. Since Russian tanks had been reported, we were very careful. We were always on the lookout for where Russian tanks could appear. It was a questionable undertaking.

At that point *Stabswachtmeister* Schwarzbach, *Unteroffizier* Buck and *Unteroffizier* Doß as well as *Stabsgefreiter* Warken and *Obergefreiter* Wenk received the order to immediately depart on foot for Danzig-Langfuhr and report to the Hussar's Barracks. The barracks were located on a road that led to Oliva and consisted of old brick buildings, empty and abandoned. There were only a few infantrymen standing at the official entrance gate. They had already prepared for close combat by hammering out holes about the size of a child's head in the walls located on the south side of the barracks, about five meters from the stalls. The holes were spaced just a few meters apart from each other.

Between the walls and the stalls there were trenches dug in a zigzag formation.

We reported for duty there on 27 March 1945 and were immediately sent to the holes in the walls. We looked through the holes and saw a hill close by and right in front of us was a street. Shortly thereafter we saw four Stalin tanks approaching the wall through a defile. For a moment we lost all sense of reality and thought of home, because for us it was a hopeless situation. But once again we were lucky.

Lined up along the wall, they left their motors running and remained stationary. Their barrels were pointed down the street and they fired a few rounds into the city. The Stalin tanks were directly in front of the holes in the wall. They were close enough to touch. It was reported there were another 17 Russian tanks accompanied by infantry about 800 meters away. The motors of the Stalin tanks droned on dully, black clouds of smoke rose along the wall. Some of the exhaust went through the holes and right up our noses.

A tank commander opened his hatch, looked forward, and appeared terrifying with his protective helmet and headset. We were lucky, because the Russians didn't think there were German soldiers behind the wall. We thought, "now or never." That was our only thought. *Stabswachtmeister* Schwarzbach whispered orders to us. We divided ourselves up among three of the Stalin tanks and pointed our *Panzerfäuste* through the holes in the wall, directly at the drive sprockets.

Then the signal! We pulled the triggers. There was a huge detonation, scraps of iron flew through the air, black clouds climbed into the sky. Three of the tanks were no longer capable of fighting. But the fourth one had an idea where the attack had come from. It moved backwards to the opposite side of the barracks. We stood in a corner in the drill field. Then something flew into the field. Like a broom, a small mine swept from the sky and detonated; it was probably sprung from a catapult. We knew, though, what would come next. There was a crackling noise coming from the barracks' gate, which surely had not been used for many years.

The fourth Stalin tank pushed itself in; its barrel pointed to the rear. At that point we were in danger. We thought about what would happen

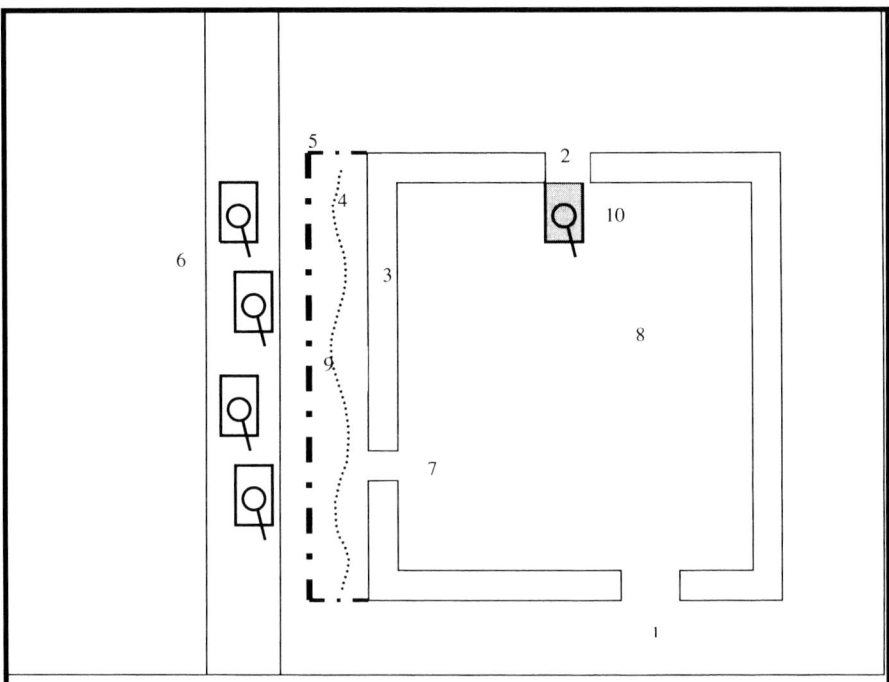

Husaren Base at Danzig-Langfuhr: 1. Main gate. 2. Unused rear gate. 3. Stalls. 4. Ditch. 5. Wall with firing ports. 6. Road with 4 Stalin tanks. 7. Passageway. 8. Parade field. 9. Positions occupied by soldiers after knocking out the third Stalin tank. 10. Location of 4th knocked out Stalin.

if he managed to fire. Then *Obergefreiter* Willi Wenk jumped forward, stood before the monster and squeezed the trigger of his *Panzerfaust*. Hurray! He hit it! The tank could no longer hurt us. By then we had run out of *Panzerfäuste* and we took off for the Heubuder Forest.

Stabswachtmeister Schwarzbach was badly wounded. He had burned himself badly while firing his *Panzerfaust*. He had not held it high enough. The jet of flame came back and burned him when the weapon was fired and his uniform caught fire. After we reached the Heubuder Forest his wounds were dressed. Comrades Schwarzbach, Warken and Wenk then crossed over to the Hela Isthmus on a boat. Due to *Obergefreiter* Willi Wenk's presence of mind and courage, we were saved from a disaster. He did not receive any award for this. The war was almost over. Everyone was thinking about surviving. In our memories Willi Wenk lives on as a brave soldier. That is his award.

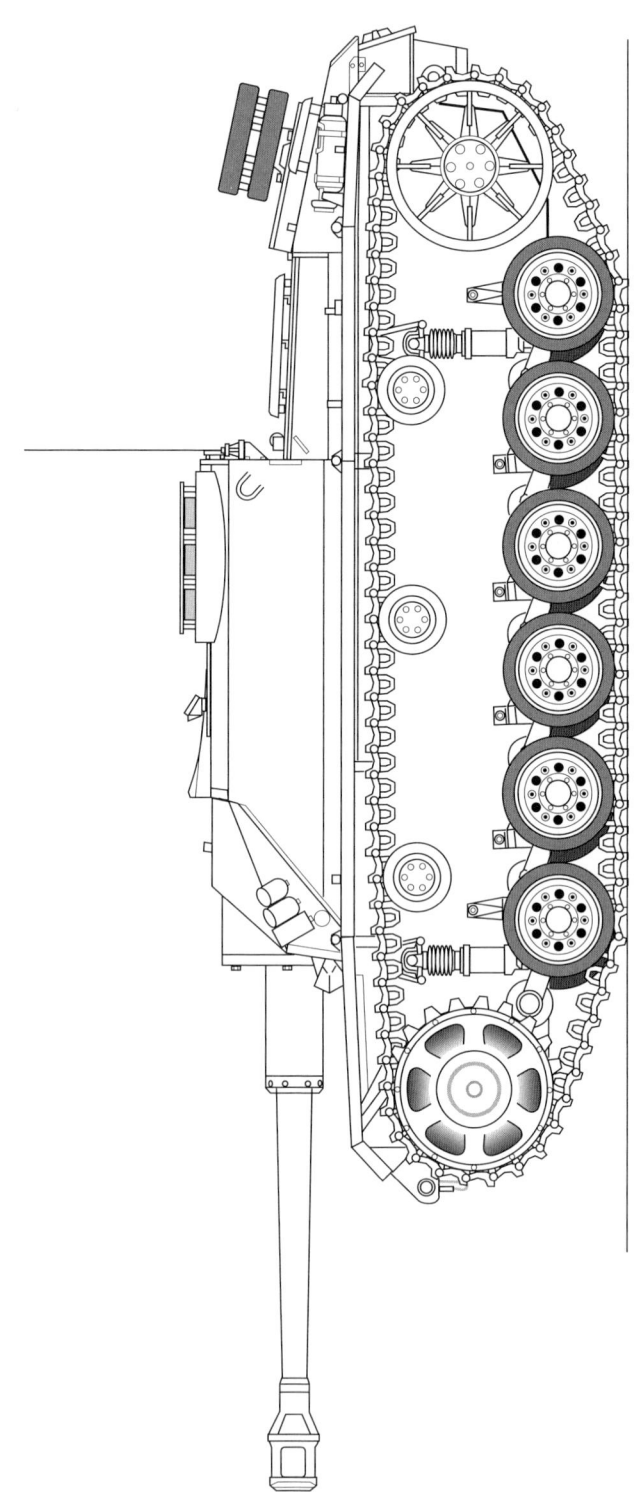

Sturmgeschütz III, Ausführung G (early model)
(courtesy of George Bradford)

19. Sturmartilleristen of Sturmgeschütz-Brigade 276 Employed as Infantrymen from 2-15 April 1945 in the Landau, Scharfenberg, Wotzloff and Gottsfalde Sectors…

(After-action report by *Obergefreiter* Heinz Fleischer, *Sturmgeschütz* driver, *3./Sturmgeschütz-Brigade 276*).

There was fighting from 10 to 11 April 1945 in Gottswalde-Wotzloff. It was 10 April 1945 when we received the order to set up a position near a small estate that was about three and a half kilometers away from our position in the direction of Wotzloff. Wotzloff was southwest of Gottswalde and we were to fight as infantry with 18 men of the brigade. South of the estate was a meadow about 300 meters wide which lay in a depression that ran in an easterly direction and bordered on a forest. About 800 meters west of the estate ran the road between Wotzloff and Schönau. In between the estate and this road were meadows and fields spotted with bushes and small groups of trees. About 600 meters east of the estate on our side was once again a forest.

The estate consisted of a house, a barn and stalls. We had 18 men. There were two *MG 42's*. Every soldier had a *Sturmgewehr*, a pistol, hand grenades and two to three *Panzerfäuste*. We had more than enough ammunition. Since we had to take care of our own rations and up until that time it wasn't difficult to find enough food and drink in every abandoned house, we didn't bring along any rations. Before I begin this report, I would like to say that there was no longer a main line, but only smaller or larger *Kampfgruppen*. In addition, there wasn't a single German soldier for two kilometers.

When reports were received that Russian units were advancing here or there, local *Kampfgruppen* or units thrown together from what was available were called into action. Due to this style of tactics and the tenacity with which the *Kampfgruppen* fought, the Russians were dealt very heavy casualties. Often these *Kampfgruppen* would show up where the Russians never thought there could be German units. The *Kampfgruppen* were completely reliant upon themselves. It often occurred that we would suddenly identify a Russian unit and then we would ready ourselves for an ambush. The Russian unit was then wiped out.

Frequently the *Kampfgruppen* would wind up between Russian elements, so you had to make sure whether it was Russians or Germans. Even though we knew that the war was about to end, the *Kampfgruppen* fought with great tenacity to stop the Russian advance and wipe out as many Russians as possible. We had to win time, so that as many women, children and wounded as possible could escape to sea. German artillery pieces, tanks, antitank guns or other heavy weapons were virtually non-existent.

When it was dark, 17 other comrades and I traveled towards the aforementioned estate that was about three and a half kilometers away. We traveled through fields and meadows, interspersed with vegetation. We marched in column with the appropriate distance between us and with our *Sturmgewehre* at the ready under our arms. We sent two soldiers about 150 meters ahead to determine whether the vegetation or the 2 individual houses on our way were clear of the enemy or not. We didn't want to fall into a trap. We had to go to ground many times, so we could provide our two comrades with cover. But there wasn't a Russian to be seen.

Only the harassing fire of the Russian artillery made us somewhat nervous. In the meantime it was almost 2350 hours as we had approached the estate where we were to set up. We were about 100 meters away from it. We discussed the situation for a short time and then I left with five other comrades. We made our way to the estate, walking softly, always taking advantage of cover. It had to be determined whether or not the enemy was there. It seemed it was clear of the enemy, but that was a mistake on our part.

Suddenly, out of the darkness, an elderly German couple quietly appeared. The estate belonged to them. They were trembling and put their fingers to their mouths. They indicated we should not speak and should be very quiet. They took us into the house and pointed in the basement with their finger. That meant extreme danger for us. We crept down the stairs with our *Sturmgewehre* at the ready. We saw two men in civilian clothes laying on straw and sleeping. Next to them was a radio. We also immediately smelled that the two were full of booze. It smelled like a bar. That was also the reason why the two were sleeping so soundly.

We placed the barrels of our rifles on their heads, woke them and said "rucki-werch!" (hands up). When they realized that they had German soldiers in front of them, they were completely shocked. We searched them and found a pistol on each of them as well as Russian army identification. For us it was now clear that they were Russian soldiers who had the assignment of passing along information concerning German troop movements. For us it was also clear that every soldier wearing civilian clothes was also a partisan and therefore doomed to die.

In the meantime other comrades came to the estate and we discussed the situation briefly. We agreed that we could not send the Russians back as prisoners, since we needed every soldier. It was also clear to us that we didn't know where or how we would take care of the two, because there still existed the possibility that the village that we had left that evening could already once again be in Russian hands. We were also in agreement that we had to be completely quiet, since the Russians were located 300 meters away on the other side of the meadow in a forest. If we shot the two Russians, then they would have noticed that German soldiers occupied the estate. With that we would have had to count on a Russian patrol troop and then our plan to wipe out the Russians while they were crossing the meadow at dawn would have been ruined.

Therefore we decided to hang the both of them. In the meantime, of course, we had posted guards, who were to guard us from any surprises. We pushed away a pile of wood and dug a ditch. After that we hanged the Russians. We then buried them in the ditch and piled the wood on top of it again. It was a measure we took to ensure that the German couple would not be endangered if the Russians were to take the estate intact. We also told the couple that they should immediately abandon the estate, but they didn't want to. They told us that their two sons had been soldiers, one had been married. His wife had already left the estate with the child and was trying to escape.

We then began to take up positions in an area that was 200 meters wide. Small walls of dirt were constructed and we reinforced them with wood and camouflaged them with branches. We posted one of the machine guns to the left of the house. There was still a small wall and several fruit trees there. An ideal position for a machine gun.

The second machine gun was positioned 200 meters to the right of the barn. This machine gun had the additional task of guarding against enemy forces that could come from the forest about 400 meters away. Two comrades established themselves in the house and the others dug holes outside and strengthened them with wood. They then camouflaged them with branches. All of this had to take place in complete silence so the enemy would not notice anything.

After we had finished, every comrade was spoken to and reminded what the success of the operation depended on: 1. Remaining completely quiet and hidden. 2. Keeping one's eyes open and not losing one's nerves when the Russians attacked from the forest. 3. Letting the Russians approach to a distance of about 70 meters and not firing until ordered to do so. 4. Don't fire the *Panzerfäuste* except at short distances.

The goal was to confuse the Russians and make them think they were dealing with a very large unit which also had heavy weapons — breaking through here was impossible. This was to be accomplished by a massive and fiery surprise attack. It was also our intention to prevent any Russian from penetrating and inflict the heaviest casualties possible. After the firefight was over everyone was to move back as fast as possible about 1000 meters to the rear, using the available cover. We knew from experience the Russians would shell this sector very soon after the attack was repulsed. We therefore had to be out of the danger zone.

We then had the mission to re-occupy our position after the artillery barrage was over, since we knew the Russians would attack again after the artillery barrage was over. We had an advantage: Because the Russians were so sure that they had victory already in their grasp they didn't take any precautions in most cases. Because we had taken our positions during the night and in complete silence, they believed that there were no more German troops in this area. We also knew that the Russians were celebrating their victory with lots of booze and that they often attacked when drunk. That was a factor why the Russians suffered such heavy casualties in East and West Prussia. It was to be the same for this operation.

It was 0545 hours when we heard the sounds of shooting coming from the sector to the right of us. As a result, we figured that the "excitement" would soon begin. I reminded all my comrades once again they should remain calm and wait until the Russians had approached to a distance of about 70 meters, at which time the order would be given to begin firing. It was exactly 0605 hours when the Russians came out of the woods 300 meters away. We had guessed right. The Russians believed no Germans were in front of them. Otherwise, they would have saturated our position with artillery before advancing.

We couldn't believe our eyes. They were coming in masses, but not like we were used to during previous Russian attacks. No, some of them advanced in groups and were talking with one another. Our calculations had turned out to be right. They ignored any and all precautionary measures. We let the Russians approach to a distance of 70 meters, as our orders had dictated, and then began firing from every barrel. We also fired antitank rounds. After this massive bombardment of fire, the Russians were so surprised, and already had taken such high casualties, that the ones who could still run threw their weapons away and tried to reach their jump-off position. We fired with everything we had. Then we fired low to the ground, so the Russians who had thrown themselves down to avoid getting hit would also be shot. Based on what we saw, only a few of them reached the forest.

The meadow was filled with dead and wounded Russians. We heard the screams. It was horrifying. After we had cut off the Russian advance without having any casualties of our own, we quickly pulled back unseen about 1000 meters. There we took up a new position. And, as we knew from our experiences, the Russians covered our previous position with artillery fire. At times some of the incoming rounds came close to our new position. The first rounds fired by the Russian artillery were too short and landed in the meadow where the wounded who had survived our attack were then killed. We also saw that the estate received several rounds and went up in flames. The old couple was killed during the artillery barrage.

After the artillery fire was over, we advanced around 800 meters towards our old positions. We couldn't get as far as the estate because it was in flames. So, we set up to the right and left of it and somewhat further back. But we were still able to view the meadow.

It was about 0940 hours when the Russians moved out from the woods to attack. This time they were more careful. We took them under fire from two sides but didn't have much success. The Russians only took light casualties. A few minutes after we had opened fire, they covered us with mortar fire and we had to pull back. We were lucky once again. Only a few of our comrades were slightly wounded. We took off in the direction of Gottswalde.

20. From the End of February until the End of the War in May 1945....
(Report by *Hauptmann* Friedrich Stück).

In my previous report I mentioned, among other things, the very successful operation of four *Sturmgeschütze* of the *3. Batterie* which took place around 20 February 1945, southeast of Heiderode (Czersk?).

(Note: After my return home I found out that a report was made on the radio about these engagements, during which "the white lions from the Weichsel" had knocked out 30 enemy tanks under my leadership. The reference to the "white lions" is explained by the circumstance that the Sturmgeschütze still had their dirty white winter camouflage. Apparently the reporter saw our emblem — the jumping Panther — and mistook it for a lion. I will forgive him the mistake after the fact!)

Because I did not know the situation in the neighboring sectors at the time, I couldn't understand why the *Kampfgruppe* (*227.* or *251. Infanterie-Division?*) pulled back to the north despite our defensive success. From later publications about the fighting — among them those of the *4.* and *7. Panzer-Divisionen* which were employed as the "fire brigade" in the area around the villages of Konitz, Tuchel and Mewe — it became clear that at this time the important railway and road junctions in Konitz were already in enemy hands. Further, strong enemy formations had already crossed the road and rail line from Konitz to Preußisch Stargard about 10 kilometers west of Heiderode at Schöndorf. Finally, they had almost reached Schwarzwasser, about 10 kilometers northeast of Heiderode.

The *Kampfgruppe* and its rearward services sat in a long narrow "hose" which the Soviets could have easily pinched off on either end. That is, they could have done it, if our four assault guns had not made the decisive contribution in spoiling that idea. While our *Sturmgeschütze* were being pulled out of this area, other *Kampfgruppen* were able to iron out the dangerous enemy breakthroughs. These *Kampfgruppen* were assisted by the *4. Panzer-Division* which had received new *Panthers* in the meantime. For the time being they were able to establish a new front line on both sides of Heiderode.

But only a few days later, the leading Russian armored spearheads (70th, 49th, and 65th Armies of the 2nd White Russian Front under the leadership of Rokossowski) were able to break through with their massive superiority. They attacked the weakened and worn-down German *Infanterie-Divisionen* which occupied the thinly held "front". Although the Germans inflicted heavy casualties, the fighting shifted to the areas south of Berent and Preußisch Stargard.

As I recall, only the headquarters battery (that is, a few of its sections) was still at Berent. After I arrived, I requested information on the situation but received nothing that shed any light on it, especially with regard to future operations of the brigade. I remember that at that time, and until just weeks before the end of the war, rumors continued to circulate that the brigade was to be shipped to Denmark and be re-equipped there. As stated: Rumors! They aroused hopes that were never fulfilled.

More realistic were the plans to pull the assault gun batteries out of the line, turn over the remaining assault guns to other brigades and then re-equip *Sturmgeschütz-Brigade 276* with new assault guns (possibly new models). In fact, the brigade's leadership (*Hauptmann* Sewera and a few officers in the staff) pursued this plan aggressively. It was later found out that *Leutnant* Walter Schmitt was successful in obtaining 42 brand-new *"Hetzer"* for the brigade at Pasewalk. This was only accomplished after numerous and somewhat "adventurous" trips to the *OKH* and other staffs. The intention was to send all *Sturmgeschütz* drivers and maintenance personnel to pick up the vehicles and move them to Danzig for transfer to the brigade. But the fighting that took place foiled this plan!

During the course of their advances through West Prussia and Pomerania, numerous armies of the 2nd White Russian Front swung to the north to the coast. The goal was to capture the Baltic seaports and the railway and road junctions that were so important to the Germans.

On 5 March 1945, the Soviet troops reached the Pomeranian coast. On 8 March they captured Stolp and Stolpmünde. With that, all ties between East Danzig and West Prussia and the northern German areas were cut off. By the middle of March, the majority of Pomeranian seaports were in the enemy's hands.

The lead attack units of the three armies previously mentioned and the 2nd Tank Army then swung to the northeast towards the west coast of the Danzig Bay. They reached Neustadt on 12 March and soon thereafter Putzig Wiek and the west end of the Putzig land spit. By the end of February the Soviets had built bridgeheads over the Weichsel between Mewe and Dirschau and then attacked the Danzig area from the south and southeast.

That's the abridged overview of the general situation in the increasingly constricted Danzig pocket. I find it difficult to describe individual details of the military situation. The Soviets were constantly breaking through many positions on the German "lines" which, in actuality, were not lines at all. Worn down and decimated infantry units, most of which did not possess any heavy weapons, and which were barely supplied with rations or supplies, clung firmly to their strongpoints, fighting heroically, as long as they could. They hung on until they were steamrolled or bypassed.

They were in constant danger of being cut off, surrounded, and then being snuffed out. The most combat capable formations of the *Panzer-Divisionen*, the *Panzerjäger* units and the *Sturmartillerie* had to fight in contravention of the employment doctrine of those weapons. They were split up into the tiniest of units and constantly played the role of "fire brigade". They suffered numerous casualties, not only due to fighting with the enemy, but also because of the lack of fuel, ammunition, supplies and maintenance.

However, the worst thing was how the civilian populace was affected. Many of them had been trying to escape for weeks and were cut off from all paths to the west. They were being pushed back and forth by enemy tanks or pushed off from the roads and into trackless terrain. There was hunger, sickness and death of all kinds. The only thing left was the possible escape to Danzig and the hope of being saved by a ship of the *Kriegsmarine* or the merchant marine!

Now back to the events at the end of February 1945 in which the brigade was directly involved. The assault guns of the three gun batteries were assembled and employed in mass at Mewe on the Weichsel. Up to that point they had been employed in different areas of operation south of the important transportation nodes between Heiderode, Preußisch Stargard and Dirschau. The crews of the nine assault guns were able to inflict very heavy casualties on the attacking Russian units — the 65th Army and 2nd Shock Army — and thus play a role in preventing a "walk in the park" for these powerful forces on their way to Danzig. The assault guns operated at times with *Jagdpanthers* and *Panthers* of *Panzer-Regiment 35* as well as smaller *Kampfgruppen* from the *337.* and *542. Volksgrenadier-Divisionen*. The Soviets were attacking simultaneously at several points from the south and across the Weichsel from the east.

The section of the front between Mewe and Preußisch Stargard was held until about 5 March, although with a very high number of casualties. This enabled streams of refugees of the harried population to flee to the Bay of Danzig without everything ending in complete chaos. Preußisch Stargard had to be abandoned on 7 March 1945. The last assault guns were able to escape to the area northwest of Dirschau, but only under the most difficult of circumstances and the hardest of fighting. It was there that the brigade finally lost its ability to fight as *Sturmartillerie*!

(Note: Comrade Heinz Fleischer, who took part in the fighting as a Sturmgeschütz driver, reported in detail about the operations of our Sturmgeschütze in the time period from the end of February until the middle of March. He was able — from his point of view — not only to report about the fighting in detail, but also to impressively reflect on the human, the very human, experiences in an "inhumane time.")

What happened during the early days of March with the headquarters and the batteries that didn't have any more *Sturmgeschütze*? I remember a move to Karthaus where I linked up with other elements of the brigade. The headquarters and the majority of the sections had already been moved to Danzig or were in the process of preparing all mobile vehicles to move there with minimal manning. The situation in and around Karthaus was extremely volatile; for the leadership there was no sense of the "big picture" and for the local civilian populace it was chaotic! What had happened?

The flanking maneuvers of the Soviets mentioned at the beginning of this section could be disturbed but not stopped by the German formations that were still mobile and possessed some combat power. This included, among others, the *4. and 7. Panzer-Divisionen*. They were tossed about, however, by the Soviet formation advancing to the north and, later, from the northeast out of the area around Konitz. As a result, the Russian spearheads were able to penetrate again and again and advance deep into the "rear areas" of the German forces. They caused confusion and, in some places, panic — just like at Karthaus on 7 March!

In the meantime, the order to form tank hunter/killer teams was issued to the brigade. These were to engage enemy tanks which had broken through in close combat. These orders were primarily intended for the assault gun crews that were "sitting out" the fighting due to a lack of *Sturmgeschütze*, but they also affected the comrades within the supply sections and the trains.

These tank hunter/killer teams were the smallest of elements and operated by themselves under the leadership of platoon leaders, assault gun commanders or section leaders. They operated in various places and frequently without contact with their own batteries. They were also always in danger of running into other units that would impress them into their service or accuse them of desertion! Their weapons: Machine pistols, pistols, hand grenades and *Panzerfäuste* — that was it!

The operations of the *"Panzerjäger"* of *Sturmgeschütz-Brigade 276* on foot did honor to their branch. Their operations, their successes — and especially their sacrifices — made them deserving of suitable recognition, even though they never received it. Just as their later operations deserved recognition when the batteries were hastily assembled as infantry and employed in the area around Zuckau (more about that later!).

However, under the circumstances, there was barely any "competent authority" which awarded medals or decorations or offered public recognition for bravery or special deeds or was even prepared to receive such recommendations and pass them along. Due to this, many heroic deeds remained unnoticed and unrewarded. What remained, perhaps, was the "proud knowledge of having loyally fulfilled one's duty", as it is so glibly called. Probably more meaningful, however, was knowing that one had passed muster in the eyes of his other comrades and had completely fulfilled his duty — no payment could be expected for that.

Why did our comrades continue to fight? The situation with the war could not be changed to our favor, the pocket around Danzig became increasingly smaller, the number of casualties continued to increase and personal hopes and expectations shrank even more. Hardly any soldier was fighting for a "Greater German Empire" or a National-Socialist regime with all their might at this time! However, there was still a "must", a duty to hold out, when we saw the continually increasing suffering, predicament and despair of the German people that stood before one's eyes. Hundreds of thousands of women, children, old people and many, many soldiers placed their hope on an evacuation via the Baltic. Thus, they only had a chance if German soldiers of all branches of service, ranks and duty positions were ready to deny the Soviets access to the last open seaports and German ships for as long as possible.

If certain circles presume to curse the persevering units of the army, the *Luftwaffe* and the self-sacrificing *Kriegsmarine* and their leaders as "war mongers", they should let the civilians and soldiers who were saved be heard! (From the end of January until the end of the war about three million people were evacuated across the Baltic Sea!)

But on with the events that remain in my memory: On 12 March, Karthaus had to be abandoned. During the following days a small group from the brigade and I were "impressed" into an infantry division and employed between Karthaus and Zuckau. We were reinforced with some stragglers. Our "grab-bag" forces were as incapable of withstanding the massive pressure on the frontlines along Rheinfeld — Zuckau — Ramkau as were the regular formations (*12. Luftwaffen-Felddivision, 252. Infanterie-Division, 389. Infanterie-Division* and elements of the *4. Panzer-Division*). The situation was marked by the fact that retreating stragglers were constantly joining our unit in the defense. Was it for fear of being impressed into other units or of a court-martial?

One day a large unit of policemen and auxiliaries from Königsberg wanted to join us. They also did not have any heavy weapons. How was I supposed to lead such an element — with a strength of about two to three companies — devoid of any signals equipment, suitable subordinate leaders or supply and logistics capabilities? But I was relieved of the decision; before the mostly older men could be brought up and put into position on the neighboring hills, enemy tanks and infantry steamrolled over them. A tragedy!

One day, as we "dug-in" on a hill west of Zuckau, a member of our brigade from "way to the rear" reported for duty. It was the medic noncommissioned officer from the headquarters battery who, as an officer candidate, had requested to be transferred to a gun battery. As hard as it may be to believe, that still occurred in the waning months of the war!

He had barely arrived when he received his baptism of fire. There was massive mortar and artillery fire on the entire top of the hill. A direct hit in the angled dugout next to us: One man dead, the second had his buttocks and his hips ripped wide open. Another round hit the edge of our dugout and the newcomer and I escaped with small scratches. He had to help the many wounded after the barrage; it was indeed fortunate that we had a veteran medic with us!

A few days later I was hit two more times, but in each case only wounded slightly. I was treated and bandaged right where we were. Despite that I remember the second wounding very well: On the previous day we were able to hold a small patch of woods against infantry attacks, but in the afternoon it was covered uninterruptedly with small-caliber rounds that exploded in the trees. The barrage brought us high casualties in a short amount of time. The number of casualties was more than we had experienced in the open.

During the night we pulled back about 500 meters to a farmstead. Next, we slept, slept, slept…The next morning we had a rude awakening: A few hundred meters to the right of the farmstead there were enemy tanks, about five or so, that were out-and-out hunting retreating German infantrymen looking for cover. Our handful at the farmstead remained unscathed, but then three tanks came out of the woods. The tanks were widely dispersed and came directly at us. Right away there were loud bangs everywhere in the vicinity. When I sneaked between the residence and the walled-off stalls so that I could observe what was happening, there was a spark, a bang and a scream…and it came from me, myself. Suddenly it was dark and there was blood all over my face. I ran behind the house screaming. What had happened?

After the tanks left us to rest in peace — literally — and simply departed to the left and bypassed us, I determined that the round had not hit the corner of "my" house. Instead, it had hit the stalls. What had happened was that a few small pieces of shrapnel and a lot of red brick and dust had flown all around me. There was blood mixed with dust smeared all over my face and, naturally, I couldn't see for a while. But then I was relieved to find out that my eyes were OK, the "scratches" from the shrapnel meaningless — the fright it had caused was the worst part. During the night we crept into field trenches and small depressions and continued through groups of trees and bushes. We remained unseen by enemy tanks and continued to the rear until we met up with some *Landser*.

During those days the brigade staff and a large part of the trains were located in the sand dunes at Oliva. At some point in time, I heard that that an incoming round had hit the command post and there were numerous wounded. *Hauptmann* Sewera was one of those who had been badly wounded. In the meantime he had been brought either to a field hospital or to a ship.

After I had reported my departure to the staff of the division to which my small group of men was attached — was it the *12. Luftwaffenfelddivision?* — I went to Oliva. There was only a small group of us from the brigade. It was a horrid sight on the way from Langfuhr to Oliva: The bodies of German soldiers hung from many telephone poles on both sides of the road. The cardboard signs posted with the majority of them stated they had been hanged for desertion! It was reported this had happened on the orders of the person who had "complete command authority" in the pocket, the *Gauleiter*. (Was it Koch or Forster?) Those sentenced by a court weren't even given the benefit of "death by the bullet," instead, they were hanged "as a deterrent". Mercilessness even in death!

After taking temporary command of the brigade, it appeared necessary to take a few especially important and urgent measures. These were caused by the enemy situation and the increasingly critical friendly situation. The Soviets had apparently already reached the Danzig coast near Putzig (based on our gap-filled knowledge of the situation). The next thrust would be aimed at Gdingen (Gotenhafen) followed by the coastal strip north of Danzig. This move meant that the villages of Zoppot, Oliva and the northern suburbs would be extremely endangered.

Immediate measures had to be taken. As a minimum, all of the trains and supply vehicles — inasmuch as they were still west and north of the city center of Danzig — had to be moved to an area east of the mouth of the Weichsel and the harbor. The soldiers who were fighting as infantry or as antitank hunter/killer teams should return to the brigade as soon as possible. Some of them were fighting under other commands and they were spread out over a wide area. It was intended for them to fight together only under the command of the unit leaders of the brigade.

The battery commanders, the officers of the staff, the platoon and section leaders — and especially the leaders of the trains — were only able to carry out these measures under the most difficult of circumstances. It proved once again how important the trains' positions were in critical situations since they also acted as collection and rallying points.

During the increasingly critical situation on the "fronts," the commanders mobilized all available forces and committed them. Staffs, administration and supply sections, trains and other elements were "combed" and personnel strengths reduced to a minimum or eliminated entirely. Military police were used to round up stragglers. Whoever made himself scarce or left his unit without orders or identification lived very dangerously!

It was inevitable that the brigade would once again be issued orders. This time the brigade was attached to one of the divisions that operated north and south of the road between Zuckau and Nenkau (*4. Panzer-Division, 389.* and *252. Infanterie-Divisionen, 12. Luftwaffen-Felddivision*). After reporting to the command post, we were assigned to a sector of the "main lines". *(Note: Places and dates cannot be ascertained with any exactness. It can be assumed, however, that the attachment took place on or about 20 March south of Kokoschken, halfway between Leesen and Nenkau.)*

Next there were a lot of problems: How many men were needed to complete the mission; how many were available; how should the transport of supplies and rations from the far-away trains be arranged over roads which were already sporadically under fire; how could our weaponry be improved; and so on and so on...I cannot claim whether my measures were optimal solutions, but at any rate, they were able to be accomplished.

I told the division that a maximum of two platoons would be able to be put in the front lines for the time being. As a result of insufficient clothing and deficient resupply capacity, they would have to be relieved at short intervals. I wasn't "cheating" when I told the division this information. The widely dispersed batteries hadn't even been collected yet. Later on, the relief among the units — conducted under cover — could take place between three units instead of two! (Of course, a few may have shook their heads about the constant "back and forth" — perhaps even have cursed me — but everything was well thought out and I stand by my decision!)

The batteries occupied forward support positions from which the relief of the units and supplies were "steered" to the right places. The men were armed with hand weapons, hand grenades, and Panzerfäuste. That weaponry was complemented considerably by light machine guns. They had been intended as crew-served weapons for the *Sturmgeschütze* but had not been mounted due to the absence of the proper fittings. In most cases they had been stored somewhere and still in their shipping containers. The previously mentioned measures taken reduced the burden placed on the assault gun crewmen when they had to fight as infantry. Despite this, there were many casualties and dead. In those trying times, they often had to forego proper words of thanks and praise!

During those days, even elements of the *Kriegsmarine* supported the ground fighting. One day I was called on to make radio contact with the heavy cruiser *"Prinz Eugen"* from one of our radio sets with longer range. I was supposed to observe fire and report. Those efforts were soon called off; they were taken over by a radio unit from the *4. Panzer-Division*, since the heavy and effective fire of the ship's guns was to be shifted to their area of operations.

From about the time between 19 and 25 March, several hundred American "Flying Fortresses" and heavy English and Russian bombers repeatedly attacked the inner city of Danzig. There were sheets of fire in all districts of the city and the beautiful old city with all of its irreplaceable historic buildings sank in ruin and ashes. The number of dead civilians and soldiers could not be counted. The lines of communication for the troops fighting west of the city were buried under debris or barely passable for vehicles. For the brigade it was advantageous, the majority of the heavy vehicles had previously been able to move to the area around Heubude. As it would prove later, that was of extreme importance.

Dogged resistance while suffering a high number of casualties west of Danzig could not stop the advance of Soviet tanks, heavy artillery and infantry supported by fighter planes, but only slow them down in some places. On or about 26 March, they were near Nenkau. Oliva was lost and Langfuhr was given up on 28 March.

(Note: Comrade Fleischer reported about the operations of an antitank hunter/killer team under the leadership of Stabswachtmeister Schwarzbach on 27 March in Danzig-Langfuhr. There all of the members of this team were able to contribute to the knocking out of four Stalin tanks in close combat with Panzerfäuste in the area of the Hussar barracks. Not until the unit had used all its ammunition, did it pull back to Heubude with the wounded Stabswachtmeister Schwarzbach).

As the Soviets inexorably continued to advance through Nenkau to Emaus and to the side of the main road, it seemed senseless to me to start a long engagement with our battered *Sturmartillerie* men who didn't possess much in the way of ammunition! Elements that had been relieved fought their way back to Heubude along tiny paths. Along with a small group of men, only *Leutnant* Koch and I remained on the west edge of Emaus, near the church.

Emaus was a suburb of Danzig with long streets. Along the main road there were multi-story houses. In the western part of the city there was an open square with a small church. The church had dark red brickwork, a pointed tower and was surrounded by some high trees. Along the road to Nenkau there were small groups of houses. South of the road there was a narrow meadow with groups of bushes. That is how I remember the village.

There was also a reason for that. After pulling out of Nenkau, my small group of men was extremely exhausted and burnt out. We established "billets" in a partly burned-out four-story building along the main road, about 100 meters from the church square. We crawled into the basement and hurled ourselves to the ground wherever we could find a place. The basement was full of soldiers and civilians — mostly women. My bed was a half-filled sack of coal; it made no difference to me! There were others with even less comfortable accommodations. Just get some sleep, sleep, sleep!

We couldn't care less what was going on with the fighting, at least not at that moment! Outside there was hell to pay! There was heavy artillery fire, bomber and fighter attacks, Stalin organ barrages — but almost everything was landing in the cities east of Emaus. Our area was only sporadically hit by heavy mortars and light artillery. After waking up after a long sleep, I realized I was hungry, so out I went to find something to eat.

We struck it rich! There was a dairy across the street. The delicacies had already been plundered, but there were still some things; hard cheese, skim milk and even a few cans of condensed milk. We brought it all over to our "billets"; and oh, what a wonder, soon we were spooning some great, wobbly pudding. Some of the women had rummaged through the floors above us, without regard for the incoming artillery rounds and the danger of the building's collapse, and had found home-made items as well as pudding powder.

Our skim milk, a little fire, utensils from the kitchen…Ladies and gentlemen, Dinner is served! Something sweet (well, half-sweet, a bit watery perhaps) which we covered with condensed milk. On top of that there was a spoonful of berries from the jar…Was there anything better?

Our "pleasure" did not last very long. There was yelling on the streets and at the entrance to the house. A few younger women plunged into the basement — completely frantic, crying, their clothes were torn and dirty! After a while they were able to report what had happened to them: Many people had searched for protection in the basement of the church during the Russian barrage. When Russian tanks and infantrymen took the western group of houses, it was obvious they were more concerned with more than fighting the pockets of German resistance. Many of the intruders stormed into the church and attacked the many frightened women. (How did the call to arms from Ilja Ehrenburg go: "Soldiers of the Red Army! Kill the Germans! Kill all of the Germans! Kill! Kill! Kill!"…They had carte blanche from Stalin; they killed and did more than kill!)

Some of the women were able to rip themselves free — pursued by drunk Russians — and flee into houses along the main road. They were in a state of shock and, as they hesitantly told of their experiences, the women, especially the younger women and girls, became very pensive. Many of them had previously mentioned their feelings of apathy and fatalism. They said it wouldn't be all that bad. They would get used to it. Dancing on the volcano? Some of the German soldiers who had taken positions in the forward houses along the square and who had been relieved reported that the Russians were barely attacking any more. Now we knew why!

Leutnant Koch, a third man and I crept along the houses edging the square when we again heard loud screaming. A middle-aged woman ran across the square towards the corner of the house. Reeling closely behind her was a Russian, his hands stretched out, trying to catch the woman. We didn't need to say much. As the woman approached close enough, Koch and I jumped in front of her and pulled her behind the corner of the house in cover. There were a few burps from the machine pistol of the third man, and it was over, the Russian's "last wish" was not to be fulfilled.

After the woman had been brought into the basement, we decided to advance to the end of the road, this time through back yards and gardens on the other side of the street. We wanted to see for ourselves what had occurred at the church.

In fact, there was a T 34/85 stationary on the street not far west of the church square. It was probably located next to an obstacle or a road crater. It was covered a bit by the trees and vegetation on the sidewalk. It was obvious that only a couple of soldiers from the crew had remained behind to guard the tank while the others were pursuing other activities (in the church?). From the last house we could easily make out a row of tanks and two to three Russians who must have felt very sure of themselves. We talked over the situation. What could we do with a few machine pistols and *Panzerfäuste*? We really didn't have any prospects of success, and every advance against the tanks would bring the prospects of casualties.

But suddenly *Leutnant* Koch said: "I'll try it." He gave us his machine pistol and ammo pouches, took three *Panzerfäuste* and took off. He went through the gardens in the dip to the side of the street to the next group of houses located behind the tanks. Soon we were unable to see the approach he had taken. We could only guess where he was based on the terrain and the vegetation which offered concealment. We would have only been able to provide him cover with the machine pistols.

Time passed by and nothing happened. Thank God there were no shots fired or yelling near the tank. Then there were detonations, one, two, right after another. After a while there was a third. There was bright smoke, then flames, then clouds of dark smoke. There was nothing to be seen of the "guards," but brown figures stormed from the church, across the square and to the tanks. But the tanks were no longer quite ready for combat!

My dear Koch — it was now time to run like the wind. Then he appeared, crept slowly to us and we pulled him through the bushes into cover behind the house. However, his head looked strange. Was he badly wounded? His entire face and his hair were filled with soft white-gray lumps; it looked like chunks of brain! But that was a bunch of crap, because how could he have crept to us? After he wiped his face we saw there were no wounds, only powder mixed with grease! Well done, *Leutnant* Koch, bravo!

The day after the next we had to evacuate our "positions" in Danzig for the last time. I can't really say nowadays which paths (or, better said, detours) our last handful of men followed to make it to Heubude. We moved through the burning, smoking, abandoned inner city, over high craters, and past wrecked vessels in the waterways. What remains is the impression of a destroyed, dead city, burned out ruins and vehicles, dead people whom no one buried, animals staggering around, bloated corpses and, between them all, soldiers in small groups, who were looking for ways through the field of craters.

(Picture this: A group of three to four men trying to take an abandoned VW Kübelwagen over a mountain of rubble, all for nothing. Their strength was no longer there. The vehicle remained hanging over the heap of rocks. The soldiers resumed their hike with sunken heads.)

Danzig was lost. On 30 March 1945 it was vacated by German "rearguard units" with the exception of small areas in the east. The civilian population had, for the most part, already been evacuated and was now fleeing to the east with the masses. Others had escaped to the west by taking cargo ships, ferries and naval vessels to Hela or directly to the west. The remaining population sought protection and shelter in basements, bunkers and shelters until the city was occupied by the Soviets and the fighting was over.

When I reached the area of Heubude on 30 March, where our trains were supposed to be located, a true chaos reigned. On all streets and roads there were streams of people and vehicles. But the streams of people could no longer do anything, since all escape paths were completely jammed. Bombs fell into this pandemonium and fighter planes attacked everything. Heavy artillery also rained down and there was no defense. There were dead and wounded on the sides of the road and in the fields. "Sandwiched-in" were medical vehicles, horse-drawn vehicles, civilian and military vehicles, and between all of them were fighting vehicles of all kinds — intact or shot up!

In the middle of all this were also vehicles from our brigade, which had departed earlier. I looked and found stragglers in the dunes who were able to give me information where the other units of the brigade could be found. Continue to march!

In the meantime, the order was issued that all vehicles, except for medical ones and certain types of combat vehicles, were to clear the roads immediately, especially the road from Bohnsack to Schiewenhorst. If necessary, they were to be pushed off the embankments. The horse-drawn wagons were sometimes able to move out cross-country, but the non-cross-country vehicles were tied to the improved roads. The order was partly followed and actually managed to give everyone some breathing room.

Anyway, I was successful in reaching the Weichsel Channel, moving step by step. I wanted to see what the possibilities of crossing were. While proceeding there I was happy to finally be able to link up with many of the vehicles of the brigade. Among them were the heavy trucks of the headquarters battery as well as ammunition and supply vehicles. As part of the long column they were only able to move ahead from traffic jam to traffic jam.

I instructed the acting battery commanders and the senior non-commissioned officers of my intention of getting all of the vehicles across the Weichsel Channel as far as the village of Steegen. So far, so good.

That's what you think! On the trip back to Bohnsack I waited for the vehicles at a position about two kilometers outside of the village. They never showed up. There was a commotion on the street. In front of me and driving in the same direction was a *VW Kübelwagen*, occupied by an army *Oberst* and a *Hauptmann* of the *Luftwaffe*. Both were highly decorated.

Occasionally they would stop and order column leaders or drivers of vehicles report to them. The two officers then gave orders in a very loud and energetic fashion and informed them they were to move all the vehicles off the road embankment immediately and without exception (that is, into the very soft cultivated fields and meadows). They gave their orders emphasis with a drawn pistol.

And, in fact, these orders were followed by many, especially since a similar but considerably less drastic directive had already been issued. Even a half-track ended up in the morass. A few drivers still hesitated…and then there was a confrontation. A column leader pulled out a machine pistol and pointed it directly at the man "in field gray." The *Oberst* stepped back to his companion and quickly moved on in the direction of Bohnsack. They returned rather quickly, without stopping this time.

Undecided as to which order to follow, most of the drivers moved to the right and let medical vehicles with wounded and other "privileged" and command vehicles pass by. Then I was amazed — later, I laughed out loud: The trucks of the ammunition section and of the trains of the *3. Batterie* approached with *Hauptwachtmeister* Hufnagel. But according to the aforementioned order they weren't supposed to! But no, they really were allowed to: They were obviously ambulances or transport vehicles for the wounded. That was recognizable from the "red cross on the white background" over the radiator.

So, why did I have to laugh? Well, the *Spieß* had really departed from following the rules this time and made the internationally recognized Red Cross symbols with white towels and our beloved "soldier's lard" (civilians called it red marmalade), which served its purpose completely. It must also be mentioned, however, that the markings were actually not being misused, since many sick and wounded civilians and soldiers were being transported in the vehicles to care facilities. Were it not for the transport, many of them would have probably been forced to stay in the abandoned areas, helpless and without a doctor's care.

So, gradually all the vehicles of the brigade made it to the Weichsel Channel and crossed over on ferries. They continued on until reaching Steegen. There the batteries "crumbled" into the wooded dunes — until other instructions received!

We had experienced yet another "special incident" previously that should be noted: The surprising reunion with the previously mentioned gentlemen "in field gray and air force blue," who had so energetically made sure that all vehicles were driven into the morass on the side of the road. We encountered them again on the ramp to the ferry dock. They carried their heads even higher this time, but they weren't as loud and energetic. Neither were they decorated with medals nor were they wearing their boots. The fact was that they were hanging next to each other high on a lamppost — executed! Someone had recognized the two supposed officers who had presumed too much authority as being from the "National Committee for a Free Germany." They had put a timely end to their doings. *[Translator's Note: The Nationalkomitee Freies Deutschland was a Soviet front organization that attempted to act as a fifth column movement. It was composed of traitorous officers of the German armed forces who had been captured on the Eastern Front.]*

The situation in the pocket at the mouth of the Weichsel had critically worsened for the civil population and the troop elements after the fall of Danzig, Zoppot, Gotenhafen and Putzig. After the Soviets had advanced east of Danzig through Heubude and Krakau as far west as Neufahr, no more large ships which could be used for evacuation or resupply of the units could approach the sea ports in the western part of the Bay of Danzig. Hela was the last large seaport in this area that was still in German hands. As a result, small ports such as Schiewenhorst gained considerably in importance.

Between the Weichsel Channels and Hela, the *Kriegsmarine* organized a regular shuttle service with all of the available "military ferries" (flat ferry barges). These took refugees as well as wounded and sick soldiers to Hela or to the ships lying at anchor there. These ran continuously and at high tempo. Not to be forgotten are also the small merchant marine ships that could dock at the small port of Schiewenhorst. These also performed magnificently and with great dedication. In total there were supposedly more than a 100,000 people evacuated by ships of all kinds and sizes from the pockets *along* the Baltic Sea during the last weeks of the war! The performance of the *Kriegsmarine* and the merchant marine and all their sacrifices will never be forgotten!

In the beginning of April the military leadership was able to stabilize to a certain extent the considerably shrunken area that was still in

German hands. Split-up units were brought back together and reinforced as much as possible with replacements and supplies. They were then inserted into sectors along a newly built front line.

The previously executed destruction of the Weichsel dikes led to flooding which, in some areas, considerably simplified the defense against attacks by armor. Although the shortened front lines could then be occupied by the heavily attrited combat units, it was necessary to strengthen their combat power as much as possible. Newly formed units had to be created out of units which hadn't been employed yet, the small *Kampfgruppen* of decimated divisions, stragglers, etc. In some cases, these had to be held as a reserve. These measures had to be so the evacuation of many thousands could continue and be completed under the protection of the army!

After a few days of quiet in the wooded dunes, all unit leaders of the brigade realized that in no case would we be able to "play dead" for much longer. With that there was the danger that our assault gun men would be impressed into service with some other unit, spread out along the lines or picked up by some military police unit somewhere and treated accordingly! What was to be done?

After discussing it with the commanders, the other officers and the senior noncommissioned officers, I came to the conclusion that a meeting at a higher headquarters — as far up as possible — would be the most advantageous for us. I had found out that not far from us in the vicinity was the Artillery Commander of an Army Corps (General?) who was located in the abandoned barracks buildings near Stutthof. Accompanied by my adjutant, *Leutnant* Stüwe, I reported in to the commander and informed him of our condition, strength and equipment and requested further instructions. We were promised to be given a mission, but it hadn't been formulated yet. With that we were "out of the woods." No one could consider us as a straggling unit and deal with us accordingly. We were "officially reported." That was very important during those days!

A few days later came the order for me to report immediately to the *XXIII. Armee-Korps* command post. It was in the dunes about two and a half kilometers west of Schiewenhorst. As ordered, I reported to the chief of the general staff, an *Oberst im Generalstab* (signature unreadable!). Report about the brigade: see the above passage. Orders: Get the brigade ready to move. Take all elements back across the Weichsel Channel to the area of the dunes around Schiewenhorst. Once there, we were to wait for further orders. The orders were carried out.

A short while later I was able to brief the corps commanding general and his chief of staff and personally report to him in detail about our unit. *Leutnant* Stüwe accompanied me. I stressed our good equipping with vehicles, radio equipment, technical equipment from the maintenance section, etc. and our resultant mobility.

There were a few anxious minutes awaiting orders! The chief of staff had already half-decided that the units of the brigade that were capable of being employed as infantry would be attached to a division and the technical portions of the brigade would be directed to support a *Panzer-Division*. The general hadn't decided yet, however. *Leutnant* Stüwe and I both talked as eloquently as possible so the threatening disaster would be avoided — with success! The general suddenly asked me how I thought the brigade should be employed. Such a question from a high-level commander was new to me and very surprising. Dear fantasy and calculation, don't abandon me!

With the energetic help of *Leutnant* Stüwe we submitted the following plan: The brigade should not be split up and stay in its current organization. If an allocation of *Sturmgeschütze* were absolutely out of the question and only employment as infantry possible, then, in addition to its current weaponry, the brigade should be supplied with heavy machine guns, mortars, and light antitank guns. Straggling groups of infantry, *Sturmgeschütz* men waiting for equipment, and so on, could be integrated into the brigade's batteries. Available signals equipment would be employed commensurate with the operation; missing equipment could be brought forward. The first-rate radio equipment and vehicles would be used and smaller equipment would be altered so it could be transported on sleds, wagons or vehicles.

The intact light vehicles and trucks — which were available in sufficient quantities — were to remain with the brigade. They would be available for rapid employment, even to remote localities. They could function as either the "fire brigade" or a mobile reserve. The excellent and valuable technical equipment — in some cases mounted in our large trucks — and our highly qualified maintenance personnel could be used by other units, as needed.

The recommendations obviously must have pleased the General and his chief of staff. Immediately orders were given to equip our units with heavy infantry weapons (which we actually later received) and officers and enlisted men were directed to the brigade. And the main point: The brigade remained together and was not employed on the new lines. It remained as a corps reserve unit; now called *Korps-Füsilier-Bataillon Nr. ?*. It stayed in the direct vicinity of the corps command post and was attached directly to the corps!

More was really not to be expected or achieved. The batteries set up and dug-in in the dunes and the area around them. The kitchen was able to obtain the required amount of meat for the most part "off the land" (enough "orphaned" cattle were roaming around). The supplies were sufficient. So far, so good.

But then came the training! Were the brigade and battery commanders totally crazy? In actual fact, they arranged for strenuous training as infantry, especially on the light and heavy infantry weapons. There were even maneuvers and firing exercises (the latter were carried out in a "combined arms" fashion with live ammunition engaging targets at sea, that is, firing at floating targets). What was all that intended to accomplish? Incomprehensible…

Those who thought about it understood, however. The "concessions" made by the corps were not based solely on charity. Considering the situation, it was important for the commander and his staff to have a large, well-trained and functioning troop element at their disposal. I was sure that as long as we could maintain this impression upon the corps leadership, we would not be committed carelessly!

But then the bitter end approached. The fact it was coming once and for all and in the not-to-distant future was obvious to everyone. Not even the higher headquarters of the elements in the pocket could begin to determine when it would happen and what would lead up to it, however.

Anyone who listened to the *Wehrmacht* reports on the radio or the news in general was able to paint the "big picture" for themselves of what was happening on the different fronts and in the homeland. At least as long as one was able to listen or was permitted to listen to the radio. One day it was all over with that as well. The high command of the *Wehrmacht* ordered that reports were only allowed to be heard by the highest-level command posts in the Danzig pocket. Perhaps that order went to other places as well. All radios capable of receiving more than local stations were to be destroyed immediately. As far as I know, that meant even the radio equipment at divisional staffs. Unfortunately, that was also the end for our radio equipment which had been modified with much effort. Those radios were able to receive signals over a very large area.

During the first days of May 1945 I received the order to prepare all the equipment to be destroyed. This included all vehicles and everything that could not be carried on one's person, with the exception of light weapons.

The brigade was to ready to move on short notice and be prepared to be shipped to Hela. It could be employed there, attached to a *Panzer-* or *Infanterie-Division*. Area of operations: a new front line along the Putzig land spit. The troops were to be liberally supplied with ammunition and rations. An advanced party under my leadership was to depart for Hela at the earliest possible opportunity. Once there, we were to report to the harbor captain so that he could direct us to the headquarters located on the Putzig spit.

Everything went very quickly. The demolitions were executed; the field kitchen slaughtered cattle and cooked enough meat so everyone could take a full mess tin along with him. Upon receiving further orders, the batteries set out to the ferry dock at Schiewenhorst. In anticipation of the ferries, they set up camp along and behind the long dike on the west side. The ferries usually came at night, loaded quickly and sailed to Hela during darkness due to enemy air attacks.

When the batteries arrived, the advanced party had still not departed. All discussions with the loading officer, a major, to include the high priority of the orders issued the previous evening, were in vain. A

Landesschützen unit [Translator's Note: a home guard force], which was pretty much made up of older men with an even older Major as commander, was placed ahead of us. The elderly major urgently beseeched me to forgive him. I could only look on and watch along with the men of my advanced party!

(Personal note: Among these Landesschützen was my older brother Walter. I did not know he was there. He was captured on the Putzig spit, went to Russia and, after two years, returned to Germany, deathly ill. He died shortly after his return.)

The advance party's attempt to start transporting it and the batteries at the same time to Hela the next evening also failed. Only three barges came, others were to arrive shortly. But they never arrived!

As the first barge departed, I noticed that members of a divisional staff booted off some of our people who were on the second barge. This was shortly before it and the third barge departed. We yelled over to *Oberleutnant* Poldi Schäfer and *Oberleutnant* Loetsch where to meet us in Hela. A lot of comrades were waiting on the dike for the next ferry. Among the others was also *Hauptwachtmeister* Hufnagel. Many called back to us, some waved. After all, we were supposed to see each other again, or so all of us believed. Besides, very few of us — including me, to be honest — were in a hurry to get to Hela and then be employed a few hours later in a sector of the front on the Nehrung spit.

The barges sailed in the darkness; the comrades waned from sight. On the west dike were many soldiers, standing or laying down. All of them wanted to at least go to Hela, or better yet, right to the west. But nothing like that occurred; they would have to wait for a very, very long time.

That night in the Hela harbor. There were dark shadows all around, cast by ships that moved without lights. There were a lot of them. Our barge stopped and lay still. For a long time nothing happened. Then an empty barge came alongside us and the captain of the ship ordered that half of the soldiers had to transfer to the other one, about 200 men. I turned to the captain, an *Oberleutnant zur See*, and asked him the reason for this and why the empty ferry wasn't going to Schiewenhorst. His only reply was a murmur — there was no clear answer.

Shortly thereafter a navy signal's mate approached me and whispered: "*Herr Hauptmann*, please don't say anything to the people, otherwise there will be a panic. An armistice started a half an hour ago. According to the agreement, we must go as quickly as possible to the nearest port that is in the hands of the Allied forces responsible for that area. I can't tell you what will happen next!"

Leutnant Stüwe stood at the railing. When I told him what I had heard, he was deeply shaken, just as I was. There were many empty barges around which were ardently wanted by our comrades over there. When and how would they receive the news? What would happen to them? What would happen to us? Question after question! How long had we longed for the end of the war. But this end, which was also the end of our brigade, we had neither imagined, nor did we desire. It was unbelievably sad!

It only remains to be said that during the night a large fleet of ships of all kinds was set in motion. The overloaded battle ferries, in teams of three and under the leadership of the aforementioned Oberleutnant, also lit out. A few of the vessels — not suited for sailing on the high seas with their flat bottoms — were lost with all hands on board in the stormy weather and the high waves. Many of them were attacked by Russian fighter planes near Bornholm and were damaged or sunk. Others sought protection and a place to stay with the Swedes. Later we found out how *neutral* Sweden treated the German soldiers and how many of them were handed over to the Russians!

21. Surrender on 9 May 1945 and the Path into Soviet Captivity from Schiewenhorst to Deutsch Eylau…
(Report by *Obergefreiter* Heinz Fleischer, *Sturmgeschütz* driver, *3./Sturmgeschütz-Brigade 276*).

The first days of May 1945! The trees behind the dunes of the fresh water Nehrung sound sprouted lush green colors. The beach grass lifted its tips through the sand. Spring announced its arrival. Would it be a spring for us soldiers? For a few weeks we had served as coastal protection east of Danzig in the near vicinity of the still waters of the Weichsel. We built bunkers in sand hills and…awaited things that would come. We had no heavy weapons. Which enemy would be denied a landing at Nehrung?

Rumors were flying among the bunker crews: The war would soon be over. The Americans would fight with us against the Russians. We were going to be picked up by American warships at sea and transported to Denmark, where we would be reformed. Someone said that there was an order from way up that all of our radio equipment was to be destroyed. Something was in the air. Were we finally going home? Or, what would happen to us? Would we have to go into captivity?

8 May 1945. Like a wildfire the news was passed along: The war was over! During the course of the morning we left our sector and moved with everything we still had to a small patch of woods on the Dead Weichsel near Schiewenhorst. Members of all branches of the service assembled in masses, arriving from all nooks and crannies. Their numbers steadily increased.

We were to be brought out into the open sea in ferryboats, picked up by large ships and transferred to Denmark. That rumor and similar ones circulated through our ranks. And we believed it and hoped for it. Who wanted to go into captivity?

Our hopes were strengthened when three ferries actually arrived at the coast. The masses stormed the water's edge and wanted to get on the boats. But there were military police present who, with all their might, only allowed wounded soldiers and the few women present on the boats. But not all of the onslaught could be contained. With their entire strength, many jumped over the railing. I estimated about 1000 people forced themselves onto the boats. And this on boats which only had a legal capacity of 500.

The water was almost even with the deck. The boat departed in that condition. Our orderly room clerk, *Unteroffizier* Pistor, jumped after the first boat had already cast off. He made it. Whether all of the boats made it, we don't know. Someone said to us that the boats would come back and pick up the rest. We waited and waited. But no more boats came. Many were supposedly sunk by Russian attack boats.

It was already afternoon. There were no boats to be seen. In the meantime a Soviet plane came along the river, flying low. It was a biplane, covered in canvas. We had called these planes "sewing machines" or "charge of quarters." Whoever was on the Eastern Front was familiar with this type of aircraft as the terror of the road networks. The pilot lifted his hand, as if greeting us, and waved. Surely he wanted to say to us: The war was over and we would all soon be going home. But who knows? Thousands of German soldiers stood there at the mouth of the Weichsel River near Schiewenhorst and hoped that a boat would come so that they could perhaps get away.

My comrades and I were among them, hoping for a miracle. It was 9 May 1945. During the night we never slept a wink and thought to ourselves, "What will the new day bring?" It was about 1005 hours when suddenly I heard behind me, "Rucki-werch!" I felt a cold chill go up my spine. Behind me was a Russian soldier holding a machine pistol at the ready. I put my hands up. In my right hand I still held my *Sturmgewehr*. While putting my hands up the sleeve slid down on my leather flight jacket, exposing my wristwatch. The Russian didn't think another thought about my *Sturmgewehr*, which I was still holding in my hands. He saw my watch and said "Uri-Uri." Then he took my arm and pulled my watch off.

I then saw that he already had four watches on his arm. The *Sturmgewehr* was of no importance to him. After that a jeep approached. In the back seat were two generals, a German and a Soviet. The German informed us of the capitulation. We lost the war and had to oblige the wishes of the victor. Our weapons were to be immediately handed over. A Soviet sergeant oversaw the execution of this order in our sector.

So we unholstered our pistols and threw them with the other weapons onto a pile. At that point we were defenseless. That was the end, or was it the beginning of the end? What would happen? None of our officers were to be seen. Only *Oberleutnant* Schäfer was in our midst. So we fell in under his command — we, the remainder of the once-so-proud *Sturmgeschütz-Brigade 276*.

We marched towards Danzig. Everything was moving in fits and spurts. Increasingly, more march columns joined in.

A sidebar: In the immediate vicinity of our holding area was a French prisoner of war camp. In our unit we had two from the Alsace region. They spoke perfect French. Suddenly they were gone; they had disappeared into the camp. We don't know whether or not they made it home, but we wish and hope that they did.

The "long march" began for us and the many prisoners — there must have been around 50,000. First we went west, then south. We always had hope in our hearts that we were going home. But our hopes continued to evaporate. By order of the Soviets, we had to form march columns of 10 in the streets of Danzig. At the head of the column was a single Soviet sergeant mounted on a horse.

Disciplined and singing, we marched through the Free City of Danzig. [Translator's Note: A reference to the independent status Danzig once enjoyed — "*die freie Reichstadt Danzig*".] A Soviet officer had ordered us to sing. As a result, songs like "Erika," "Edelweiß" and "Schwarzbraun ist die Haselnuß" (Black-brown is the Hazelnut) among others echoed through the streets. We didn't feel like singing, but we had to. And so we marched, singing, with our unique German discipline intact, through the streets in which we had hunted and knocked-out Russian tanks only a few weeks ago.

From the houses came girls and young women. They latched on to us, arm in arm, and marched with us, tears in their eyes. I was asked to stay behind, they wanted to hide me. They told us of the bad things that had happened to them and what they had experienced. There wasn't one who hadn't been raped many times. They were happy we were there. But we were powerless, after all; we were prisoners.

At the edge of the city they stayed behind with heavy hearts. After that, we marched south and through the villages of Gischkai, Rosenberg, Mühlhaus and on to Dirschau. In these villages we saw how the Russians had brutally abused the population that remained there and treated them like animals — from babies to children and up through women and old people. Some of them had been murdered treacherously. Groups of Russians raped women and girls above the age of eight; in some cases they then slit them open with bayonets and killed them.

In villages we had passed through or had spent the night, we saw women who had been raped and then nailed to the wooden floor of their homes with a bayonet through their sexual organs. They were left to bleed until death relieved them from the suffering. Women who defended themselves against being raped showed us their bodies; they were covered with puncture wounds from knives, zealously implanted by Russians.

In a village we wanted to get some water from a well. Some people from the village told us that we shouldn't drink any water from it. There were five young girls in it who had been raped and then shot. Afterwards, the Russians had thrown them into the well.

It must be said at this point that Stalin gave the order to his armies that all Germans were "fair game" for three days starting on 9 May 1945. That meant the Russians could do whatever they wanted with the Germans, whether child, woman or old man. Even girls between the ages of eight and fourteen were brutally abused and many of them died.

There were violent encounters between German and Russian soldiers, during which most of them were completely drunk and tried to rob us. We defended ourselves successfully with sticks in most cases. Once in a while, when this happened, a German soldier would be shot.

We also freed German women and girls from Russians when we saw that they intended to rape them. We pulled them into our midst to protect them. The Russians were still very afraid of us because we were not afraid when dealing with these animals.

I would like to mention another occurrence that I experienced firsthand. I was wearing a leather flight jacket. One day, two completely drunk Russian soldiers approached me. They wanted to have my jacket. Since I didn't want to give it up, and since they were afraid of killing me in the presence of my comrades, they pulled me to the side. At that moment a staff car with four Russian officers came along. My comrades pointed me out to the officers and said that the other two soldiers wanted to shoot me.

The officers immediately stopped their car and approached the two soldiers that had me in their middle. They told them to let me go and disappear. One soldier drunkenly pointed his weapon at the officer. He was immediately shot and killed by one of the officers. The other was arrested. After that they spoke to me in good German and said that it was better for me to give them the jacket so that I wouldn't have any more problems along the way. They told me that they would give me food for it.

The other officer saw my almost new boots. He asked me to give them to him. I would also receive food for them. Then he pulled off his boots, gave them to me, and put mine on. It didn't take long before another officer brought so much food that all my comrades had enough to eat. The rest was loaded on our Panje wagon.

It was nothing but innocent people these Russian killed. It was the same in every village that we passed through. Our hate grew more and more intense. But we were unarmed; what could we do to address the situation?

A comrade of the battery had "procured" a Panje wagon and horse. It was completely loaded down with the small amount of possession we still had. One of us had a blanket, the other a laundry bag. Everything was covered with a blue tarp. Above the possessions and under the tarp was a mantle clock. Who brought it along, I don't know. It was there we all had our fun with that clock. The Russians were always on the hunt for timepieces, of course, by that I mean wristwatches. The majority of us had already had our watches stolen from us. Meanwhile, the Russian soldiers were wearing four to five on each arm.

Once a Russian approached our radio operator and asked where his timepiece was. Then the radioman responded, "Hey, here's one" in Russian. Then he lifted up the tarp of our wagon and showed him the mantle clock. The Russian cursed and ran away and we had something to laugh about.

We continued to the south on dusty streets. In the meantime we had become very hungry and thirsty and our strength was fading. Once in a while there was a little hard bread for each person. Our emergency rations had long since disappeared. We always wondered why we didn't see any Soviet guards. Occasionally we saw a rider to our front, the side or at the rear. At night we saw the reason for the relatively few guards. To the left and right of the road, at a distance of about 50 meters, was a complete guard system. Camp fires could be seen at regular intervals. The marching columns of prisoners were constantly being observed. An escape attempt was completely out of the question.

After about eight days we approached Deutsch Eylau. We passed the small village of Sommerau. Exactly one year ago we had celebrated our battery's organizational day there. Happy memories were awakened. It was a one of a kind occurrence. In the village *Gasthaus* we had had a lot of fun. Now we marched without hope in the direction of Lake Geserich. During the previous summer we had bathed there. Now signs could be seen that said, "Taking water and bathing are forbidden!" Someone had found dead bodies in the water. And so we marched through the city in which our brigade had been reformed the year before.

Everything was familiar to us: The streets, the parks, the pond, the café in the city. It went slightly uphill from there. How often had we rushed up the hill when curfew was not to be broken? To the left the Blücher School greeted us with its gray-green façade. It was there that our *3. Batterie* was billeted. We marched on by to the right, on by the artillery barracks, with its red bricks. We could see the *SA* vacation camp with its cottages. Now it was a large prison camp, fenced in with barbed wire. We were finally prisoners of the Red Army.

There was no going to Germany, no "domoi" (going home). Forty-five comrades were stuffed in a small room with wooden bunks, two high. We were divided into groups in the order we had arrived. Our comrades were separated from one another. We were registered, interrogated and lists were drawn up. Translators worked us over, "Were you in the party?" These procedures lasted a long time. We let everything take its course. We were shoved from one place to another and finally we landed at a place where they had shears, razors or even an electric cutter. They cut all our hair off.

Oh my! That was degrading for us. We looked like the Russians. This was justified for hygienic reasons. Then, after so many days on the road, we had a water soup with potato skins. For that we waited in lines for a long time.

From our billets we often heard the wailing of sirens. It reminded us of ships. Where was there water around here for large ships? It was Soviet locomotives. Soviet engineers had already constructed the wider tracks for their trains all the way to Deutsch Eylau. They loaded up everything that was valuable or useful and transported it to their large country.

Three days after our arrival in the prison camp, we marched to the train station. Then we were loaded up, 46 men to a freight car. The windows were covered with wire, there was a little straw on the floor and on the benches. On the other side there was a hole in the sliding door intended for going to the bathroom. In an old blanket there was stale bread. There was also a bucket of water.

The door was closed and sealed. Whoever had hoped for a miracle was now certain of one thing: We were in Soviet captivity, prisoners of the Red Army. How long? Will we survive? Would we ever see our homeland again and when? Would we ever see our loved ones again? The locomotive started up. We were headed east and into an uncertain future.

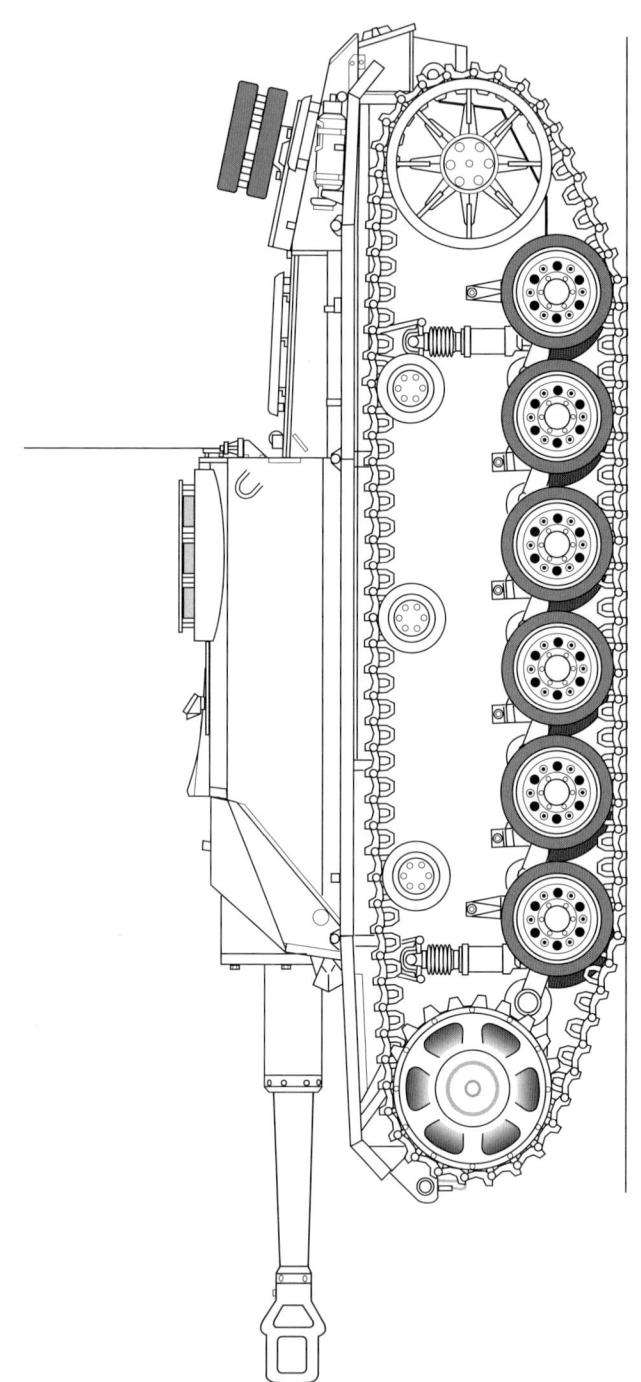

Sturmhaubitze 42
(courtesy of George Bradford)

Appendix 1: A Capsule History of Sturmgeschütz-Brigade 276

The History of *Sturmgeschütz-Brigade 276*
Feldpost Number 57769
Unit Insignia of *Sturmgeschütz-Brigade 276*

Sturmgeschütz-Brigade 276 was formed in the summer of 1943 at Altengrabow near Jüterbog. The cadre personnel came from the former *2. Batterie* of *Sturmgeschütz-Brigade 190*. In the late fall of 1943 *Sturmgeschütz-Brigade 276* was transferred by train to the Eastern Front.

The constant companion of the brigade during all of its fighting and until the bitter end was its unit insignia, a jumping black panther. The insignia in its original form could only be determined recently. Another unique insignia that was unofficially used by the brigade was a leaf-like symbol. It was intended to make the task of identification of the individual batteries easier.

Stab- und Stabsbatterie: A leaf symbol
1. Batterie: A leaf symbol with one stripe underneath it.
2. Batterie: A leaf symbol with two stripes underneath it.
3. Batterie: A leaf symbol with three stripes underneath it.

The officer corps in the summer of 1943 was as follows:

Commander:	*Hauptmann* Rünger
Orderly:	*Leutnant* Werner Semke
Stabsbatterie:	*Oberleutnant* Lötsch
	Oberleutnant Poldi Schäfer
Brigade surgeon:	*Unterarzt Dr. med.* Walter Cordes
Maintenance officer:	*Insp. Ing.* Otto Pöhlmann
Commander, *1. Batterie*:	*Hauptmann* Erich Schulte
Commander, *2. Batterie*:	*Oberleutnant* Ertel

Commander, *3. Batterie*: *Oberleutnant* Tobler

The following platoon leaders were present: *Leutnant* Nippes, *Leutnant* Kany, *Leutnant* Sehrt, *Leutnant* Erich Stüwe, *Leutnant* Gerd Albert, *Leutnant* Toni Erdweg, *Leutnant* Walter Schmitt, *Leutnant* Max Albrecht.

From May 1944 until 1 August 1944 *Sturmgeschütz-Brigade 276* was reformed in Deutsch Eylau (East Prussia).

The new officer corps was as follows:

Commander:	*Major* Norbert Braun
Adjutant:	*Oberleutnant* Werner Semke
Ordnance Officer:	*Leutnant* Walter Schmitt
Stabsbatterie:	*Oberleutnant* Lötsch
Commander, *1. Batterie*:	*Hauptmann* Axel Sewera
Commander, *2. Batterie*:	*Hauptmann* Bobo Schaubs
Commander, *3. Batterie*:	*Oberleutnant* Friedrich Stück
Brigade Surgeon:	*Unterarzt Dr. med.* Walter Cordes
Maintenance Officer:	*Insp. Ing.* Otto Pöhlmann
Paymaster:	Müller

The following platoon leaders were present: *Leutnant* Regeniter, *Leutnant* Sehrt, *Leutnant* Plaum, *Leutnant* Adalbert Müller, *Leutnant* Koch.

The following officers served as commanders of *Sturmgeschütz-Brigade 276*:

From 21 June 1943 until September 1943: *Hauptmann* Rünger (KIA)
From September 1943 until December 1943: *Hauptmann* Schulte
From December 1943 until 21 August 1944: *Major* Norbert Braun (KIA)
From August 1944 until January 1945: *Hauptmann* Axel Sewera
From February 1945 until the end of the war: *Hauptmann* Friedrich Stück

Sturmgeschütz-Brigade 276 fought on the central sector of the Eastern Front from October 1943 until April 1944 and then, from 1 August 1944 until 9 May 1945, in Lithuania, as well as East and West

Prussia. It was — as were all the other assault gun brigades on the front — always the vanguard and driving force of the counterattacks. The brigade destroyed enemy bunkers and helped the infantry in many operations in winning back lost positions. In order to give many members of the brigade an outward expression of recognition, many Iron Crosses, First and Second Class, were awarded for personal bravery. In addition, many other awards were presented.

The following comrades of *Sturmgeschütz-Brigade 276* were awarded the Knight's Cross to the Iron Cross, the German Cross in Gold and Silver as well as the Honor Roll Clasp of the German Army:

Knight's Cross to the Iron Cross

Oberleutnant Reinhold Ertel: KIA 22 January 1945
Leutnant Kurt Nippes: KIA 10 December 1943
Leutnant Alfred Regeniter: Platoon Leader, *3. Batterie*

German Cross in Gold

Oberwachtmeister Adolf Sausel: (496/32) 17 December 1943
Oberwachtmeister Alfred Koch: (625/42) 12 September 1944
Hauptmann Axel Sewera: (631/26) 22 September 1944
Hauptmann Friedrich Stück: (664/37) 30 November 1944
Oberwachtmeister Heinrich Glaumann: (664/36) 30 November 1944
Wachtmeister Emil Taschka: (675/57) 6 January 1945
Oberleutnant Anton Erdweg: (702/51) 22 March 1945
(The first number in the parenthetical entry indicates the award sequence for the German Cross out of all German Crosses awarded. The second number indicates the award sequence within the *Sturmartillerie* branch.)

German Cross in Silver

Heereswerkmeister Paul Linke: (1070) 20 April 1945

Honor Roll Clasp

Major Norbert Braun: (2969) 7 March 1944
Hauptmann Axel Sewera: (3795) 27 August 1944
Oberwachtmeister Emil Taschka: (5171) 20 April 1944
(The parenthetical entry indicates the sequence number of the award of the Honor Roll Clasp.)

Appendix 2:
Report of Internment by the Swedes and Transfer to Russian Captivity (Anonymous)

Foreword

This story is not a song of hate! Neither for the Swedish, nor for the Russians, nor for the Germans nor for any other race of people.

It is the story of the experiences of a man who wrote down all of this to show what we have come to as a result of our impetuous wandering on the path of advancement. And it will be left up to the reader to determine whether we have marched up the hill or down it. That means all of us: Swedes, Russians and Germans and also all of the other peoples that are mentioned herein.

But these are also the tales of a German who, in the search for truth and justice, would like to make it clear that not only members of his race, but also the members of other races, were responsible for wrongdoings, lies, deception and even inhumanity.

Search for the truth, be honest, judge fairly and forget the wrongdoings that we have mutually inflicted upon one another and build anew. This sincere wish should serve as the beginning of the story that you are about to read, sworn loud and clear for all to hear.

Great politicians like François Mitterand, who was a soldier and prisoner of the Germans during the war, said that the many German soldiers that he had gotten to know were simply German people. They had fought for bad goals, he said, but they marched forward at the risk of their lives. "They were people," he said, "who loved their country."

Everywhere I have traveled I have met people who thought and acted humanely — in Sweden, in Russia, in Germany, everywhere. Unfortunately, there were too few of them. They disappear in a whirlwind of indifference, which lets them be tyrannized by a few evil ones.

What the Swedish government did to the German soldiers who were interned there until December 1945 — horse-trading at the behest of Stalin — was against international law.

Heinz Fleischer
Sturmgeschütz-Brigade 276

Hunger, Barbed Wire and Walls Made of Plywood
Or
Swedish Horse-Trading

These are the experiences of one of 2,700 Germans who were handed over to Russia by the Swedish government in 1945, after it had interned them for half a year.

Prelude on the Baltic Sea
The Death of Danzig

"We'll definitely have to find a boat when we get there," said Hans. And with that, he said what we all were thinking.

It was the evening of 25 March 1945. We stood on the dunes of "Bohnsacker Island" on the Baltic Sea, a piece of land that surrounds the Dead Weichsel in a long, curved line, right before the mouth of the river. The channel, which spared many ships from having to take the long trip around, turned this patch of land into an island.

On the previous day we had left the poor city of Danzig and crept eastwards at a slow pace along congested roads that were filled with vehicles of all categories until getting here. My God, how the city had looked! There were demolished and burning houses, overturned trolley cars, hanging electrical wires, split trees and tanks standing guard. Here lay a dead man next to his demolished bicycle; there stood a burned out car with charred bodies. There were victims of intemperate and furious summary courts martial hanging in the trees. Enemy bombers and reconnaissance planes — barely even bothered by our anti-aircraft fire — "took a joy ride" all over the city, unloading their payloads at will. The enemy artillery was also not sparing with its massive greetings. In the middle of this inferno rushed frightened people, mostly women and children, dragging along the bare necessities. They sought to get to the harbor, so perhaps they could escape this hell by getting on a ship that would possibly reach Denmark or Schleswig-Holstein or…the bottom of the sea.

Empty, smashed out windows leered at us like the unfathomable staring of skulls. We were moving through Vineta!

No one walked — but rather rushed. No one spoke — but rather screamed. No one ate — but rather gulped down their food. No one laughed, no one cried — one was frozen. Trust, love, goodness — all had disappeared. One could only get the idea that life had flourished here once. The city lay in agony.

With a heavy heart and a wounded soul, we drove through it all without being able to help. There we saw the old city, our old homeland, sink, without being able to help.

It was over. We knew it. For five years our group had stayed together and we had always gotten along, because, I dare to claim, with us there was always a constant decent outlook. This shared level of being had also given us a firm ground upon which to stand, and had — despite a few exceptions — let us live together in good camaraderie.

But now it was over. We couldn't do anything to prevent it. Everything that was still being sacrificed could not be justified. The shadows of the approaching end displayed themselves on the features of our homeland.

Everything that we would undertake was driven by this realization. The only thing left that mattered was to make sure that we and as many women, children, old and sick people and wounded German soldiers could escape this chaos as was possible.

The Big Plan

So there we were on the beach on the Baltic with our trains on that day — 25 March 1945 — and held a "war council."

"The situation is serious, but not hopeless, gentlemen," said Hein, playing the general. Our irrepressible comrade from Hamburg continued, "because even if we are pressed together and into a corner, the open sea remains our emergency exit. Let's withdraw across the water for a change!" "You can talk a good line," others said, interjecting themselves into the conversation. "Do you have a tug boat that will take you along or do you plan on swimming to Flensburg?" "OK, gang, I highly doubt we will be able to hitch a ride," said our commander suddenly. "We have to see to it that we can rely on ourselves when it comes to our departure. Hans and Hein, I suggest that you arm yourselves with a few bottles of booze and take off."

And so it happened. It was our good fortune that we had lost neither our common sense nor a certain amount of lightheartedness, despite all of the disappointment and disillusionment. Perhaps it was the subconscious feeling that we had always traveled down the right path before; perhaps it was the will to live that held us together! We were all still young. Barely any of us were more than 30.

And even in those dark days it was demonstrated that it wasn't only discipline, but also an inner comradeship that bound us together. It bound us together even when all of the things we had committed ourselves to in honest conviction disappeared like foam on a beer. During those days we felt closer to one another on a human level than we ever had before. This occurred even though many others felt divorced from their surroundings because external order had been shattered.

After three days, the two came back from their expedition. Their success was amazing: They had "chartered" a small yacht, a police boat and an old tugboat (made in 1890). Schnapps had always held a strong attraction for old sea salts (in this case "Weichsel salts").

We posted two men on each boat as guards so that further shipments of spirits from somewhere else would not cloud the memory of the "captains" concerning the just completed "contract."

Then, with the help of hoses, pumps and canisters, the necessary diesel fuel was easily acquired from the full tanks of the abandoned buses and trucks that were left everywhere. The full canisters were then shoved onto our old rickety wooden boat and, with that, the problem of fuel was solved.

The Suspicious Roll of Cable

In the meantime, the situation in the delta of the Weichsel River became increasingly confusing. The rest of the *4. Armee* streamed back from Pillau and over the Frische Nehrung, which was still clear of the enemy. By doing that it helped to overcrowd even more the land that was already occupied and overcrowded by the rest of the *2. Armee*. The supply of rations became worse and worse. There was mainly bread, some margarine and horsemeat. Luckily, we had all kinds of supplies in our vehicles, so that we did not have any problems in that respect.

One day we received a strange order, which was passed on to us as more of a "recommendation," since everyone was shying from their responsibilities. The trains were to change location and move over the Weichsel Channel and into the vicinity of Stutthof. Several vehicles were to be left behind in this process. The vehicles left behind and all remaining equipment and supply-room items, however, were also supposed to be made unserviceable. My idea — to pull the leftover vehicles into the dunes, load them with gasoline and hand grenades and ignite them when there was an air attack — was not accepted. It was decided to smash the electrical equipment and the carburetors and fuel systems of the vehicles, slit the tires and hoses and shove the equipment and the gear into a hole after which someone would go around and chop everything a bit with an axe. Then the whole thing was to be covered with sand.

It was our misfortune that on the next day after the main body had already departed — we had been left behind with a small group — a few higher-ranking officers — I think there was an *Oberst* with a monocle among them — showed up at the beach. The *Oberst* stumbled over the end of a cable that was poking out of the sand. They approached this corpus delecti with the facial expressions of high judges, who divined — and with some justification, as we know — that they were on the trail of some monstrous crime. Like small, puny finance office officials who, during an audit, indeed finally do find the missing bean they have been searching for, they blurted out the token half-theatrical "Ha!" upon the appearance of the brand new roll of cable. "Fate, take your course!" I thought to myself.

"What kind of unit is this? Who is your commander? Who are you? What is your name? Who buried these things? Who gave the orders to do that? Who, what, where, when, why…" And so it rained down on the poor *Wachtmeister*, even though he had nothing to do with it. Everything had to be dug up again. After each new piece was discovered, the "high powers that be" took in a breath of air in disgust with an expression of extreme indignation on their faces. "This is…this is outrageous! Sabotage! What can I say! Subversion! High treason! This is, well..." It was too bad that the rules of grammar didn't account for an ultra superlative! To me it was just like the passenger of an airplane which is making an emergency landing making accusations against the pilot, because he threw all the baggage overboard.

The situation was sticky. We were still breathing, but…our names had been taken down! And that is worse than when you can't breathe. Because when you can't breathe, you know what is wrong. But when you have been written up, however, you don't know what the consequences will be.

As a result, we sent two comrades to the commander. They came back after a few hours with orders for everyone to come to the command post. Every half an hour we sent a group of ten men. We traveled cross-country and avoided contact with others. They were picking up stragglers everywhere and we didn't want to fall into their hands. People with no ability to judge the true situation still believed in a miracle and took senseless measures to grab hold of every last available man; even then, even though it was much too late. By being careful, we reached the battalion command post which was located in a farmstead that was overflowing with refugees and soldiers.

Our "Splinter" Tactics

One day, I was sent to the trains. On the way, I met up with one of the splinter units from the brigade: The maintenance contact team. Our commander proved to be a really sensible man in the end phase of this unholy war and, above all, he did not lack the necessary guts in standing up to some of the really stupid generals. He spread out the brigade into as many small groups as possible, so that there would never be too many people around to be picked up as stragglers to be sent elsewhere. So, besides our actual combat elements, which were forward with the remaining assault guns, we had the ammunition section, the supply section, the command post, the maintenance contact team and the trains. In addition, the members of the combat elements that didn't have any more guns were assembled into an anti-armor hunter/killer platoon. Members of the trains who weren't absolutely critical were assembled into an infantry platoon. As a result, everyone was always able to prove to the military police that they were essential members of a unit.

Due to this slick maneuvering, we were able to keep our group of men together in a single unit until the very end, despite all of its dispersion. And I still ask myself to this day: Who did more for the homeland, those who kept someone's sons alive or those who sacrificed them senselessly?

The maintenance contact team had a *Muli* (half-tracked truck) which was in need of repair and which was to be transported to the trains. That worked out well. I drove the rickety vehicle to Nickelswalde. There we crossed with the ferry. Then we went on through Steegen and Stutthof and into a patch of woods on the coast where the trains had settled in.

We spent a few quiet weeks there. We spent our time building nice bunkers with creature comforts. Also, we got a well working and had our youthful fun in the clean, fresh groundwater.

French and Russian prisoners of war were running around amongst the German troops. The Russians helped us build bunkers and received something to eat or a few smokes for their work. The French worked as hairdressers, shoemakers or mechanics. They traded coffee beans, chocolate and bars of soap, which came from their care packages, for bread and food. I had a Frenchman cut my hair and used this opportunity to engage in conversation. He had been on a farm in East Prussia and had it good there. The woman on the farm had been like a mother to him, he told me. "Hopefully you will be able to get your hair cut at home the next time!" he said as he departed.

In general, things were peaceful. Ivan no longer attacked. He threw out pieces of paper from airplanes, which said that we were his most inexpensive prisoners, since we guarded and took care of ourselves.

One day the bomb went off; the *Oberst* at the dunes was the one who had tripped over its fuse. Wilhelm, the *Spieß*, was ordered before a court martial. He was blamed for the whole episode concerning burying the equipment and the uniforms in the sand. With much effort, he was saved from the worst of it, this was fortunate because the officiating judicial authority was quick to judge at the time. It was decided that he was to be given a suspended sentence of one year. He then went to our infantry platoon and, with that, he had satisfied the goddess of justice.

The Trotting Race

I once again visited the combat elements still stationed on Bohnsacker Island. Upon arriving there, I got a chance to see our old rickety wooden boat. It was made entirely of wood; it appeared to be an antediluvian apparatus indeed. It was the size of a normal river tug (about 30 meters long). Built into the stern was a small diesel engine, which was able to propel this bulky monstrosity to a speed of between ten and twelve kilometers and hour. And with this thing we were to possibly…no way, it was impossible, I thought.

On the bow, the letters BERTA were proudly displayed. "Oh yes," Karl and the rest of the guard crew called to me, "that is BERTA, our battle cruiser!" Someone had already taken the small yacht from us in the meantime; high-ranking generals had confiscated it from us.

On the trip back to the trains, the following terrible incident took place: We took a horse-drawn carriage. Due to the lack of fuel we were forbidden from driving any type of vehicle. We were trotting along towards Steegen at a comfortable pace not unlike a Berlin taxi from yesteryear when a military policeman stopped us. We had indeed noticed him from far away, but we felt so completely innocent in our non-motorized one-horse carriage we did not suspect anything to be wrong. But the resourcefulness of the police has always been celebrated (especially by the police themselves). The resourcefulness of the military police cannot be expressed with words; it has to be experienced.

"Your march orders!" "Here you go." Oh yes, we had them. If only there hadn't been anything more to it than that, but the policeman had other, unuttered wishes. And then we heard them: "And where is your certificate that allows you to use this carriage?" At first, I didn't think that I had heard him correctly. We must have really stared at him in a dumbfounded way, since he repeated the question with extreme clarity. After a further embarrassing pause, Fritz, who was the driver, made it clear to the eye of the law that we belonged to a motorized unit and therefore we didn't have the slightest idea about the necessity of such a certificate or any prohibition against using horses. The good man then appeared to have even more far-sightedness than his high superiors did and let us drive on. He let us go, even though he really should have brought us before the powers that be. Because of the lack of feed, the nags were supposed to be protected. *As a result, you had this strange nonsense that made the trotting of a horse dependent upon special permission.* Only a horse was being fed so well at the time that it was capable of performing a capriole. Good old red tape. Even at that time it could gallop around! So, we shuffled along at a slow tempo, until the eye of the law could no longer see us, upon which we picked up the pace to a gallop to make up lost time.

The Last Days of Pompeii

Then came the 20th of April. Dr. Goebbels spoke on the radio about swaying cornfields and blooming gardens and about a more beautiful Germany. Was it sarcasm or the delusional beliefs of a pathological idealist?

On 29 April 1945, an order was issued that there would be even stricter limitations regarding driving motorized vehicles after 1 May. In order to use the last chance to change position, the trains moved into an area three kilometers in front of the Weichsel Channel on 30 April.

Then one night, something strange happened. We were awakened and received the order to prepare to move. We were to take weapons and gas masks and only the most necessary of equipment. March orders were being prepared in the orderly room, which had been set up in a built-up truck. Reason for departing: Employment as infantry. "What's that supposed to mean?" asked the *Spieß*. "No idea" was the answer. We waited an hour, then two, then three…Finally we were allowed to go back to bed. What had happened? The news of Hitler's death had given our officers reason to prepare for a quick departure. But the message that Dönitz had taken over the leadership of the government made such a quick departure unnecessary and even dangerous. So we continued to wait.

The Eerie Crossing to Hela

Finally, on 5 May it was over. Even the Army had approved our departure. Only the still serviceable guns and a few supply vehicles were to remain behind. So the headquarters battery and the trains of the three assault gun batteries were sent to Schiewenhorst, where our good "BERTA" also swam.

All stocks of food — and there weren't inconsiderable — were brought on board. The rest of the vehicles were rendered unserviceable. Armed with a backpack or a knapsack, we marched to the Weichsel Channel. Then we were on the coast and watched as *Sturmgeschütz* ammunition, which we wanted to use as ballast, was loaded. There was a loud "hello" as our Zahlmops, a man who intuitively knew how to make a fool of himself, arrived at the wharf. He was beaming with delight as he displayed the cartload of hardtack he had brought with him. They were some tasteless naval zwieback, just like the ones that we were issued with our emergency rations. He had dug them up somewhere and thought of the happiness that they would bring to everyone.

Next, it appeared that St. Peter did not have a very favorable opinion of us, because the heavens opened their gates as we waited to embark, ensuring that our clothes would get wet. The rain continued until 1800 hours, when St. Peter put an end to it. We then balanced our way over the swaying loading plank onto the deck of our "BERTA."

Finally, the line of geese found its end. The planks were pulled in and "BERTA" departed majestically from the wharf. Only two of us remained behind. The commander's German shepherd and our little "Spezi," an affectionate Terrier-Dachshund mix. The two ran back and forth along the coast, whining and bellowing to the old wooden crate which took away their masters. It really bothered some, but it was generally decided that no dogs would be taken along. And what should have been done with them? Should they have been shot? No one would have done that. So they stayed behind.

A complete flotilla cruised silently out into the Bay of Danzig on this evening 5 May. Just as we left the mouth of the Weichsel, the last rays of sunshine disappeared behind the horizon. In the sunset I saw an unusual vessel eerily whoosh on by. It was a "sea snake," as someone said to me. It looked like a long, narrow raft and was pulled by a tugboat. Hundreds of German *Landser* were pressed together on top of it and had to continually put up with cold showers from the sea. I was still completely absorbed in the sight of this ghostly vessel when someone called out: "Everyone below deck! The skipper can't see anything!"

So we climbed down the bulky wooden ladder into the loading room, in which a few had already made themselves comfortable on the bags of hardtack our paymaster had brought. With much cunning and treachery, we were able to sort out our limbs after a while so we could sort of sit down. We crouched, sat, slid around and lay on crates, rails, ladder rungs, knapsacks and anything else that was appealing that was there. A gas lantern dangled from the middle of the ceiling, so we could look around a bit. A quite extensive supply of food adorned the walls all around us. There were crates filled with canned food, sacks of fruit, flour, sugar, noodles, whole piles of bread and much more. Rows of pieces of smoked ham hung at odd angles from the ceiling beams. We were well supplied.

Meanwhile the boat began to rock gently. If the lantern hadn't given it away, then my stomach, which was for some reason not very fond of this kind of rocking, would have noticed it. Anyway, I felt a strange lifting and sinking in my stomach, but it was bearable.

I had become absorbed with myself and with the interior of the ship when suddenly the shooting of a light anti-aircraft gun was heard — an enemy anti-aircraft gun! All at once, we were aware of what kind of a situation we found ourselves. The Russians were already in Danzig and Gotenhafen (Gdingen). They occupied the entire west coast of the Bay of Danzig. Only the mouth of the Weichsel, a part of the Frische Land Spit and all of the Putzig Land Spit were still in our hands. Our trip to Hela led us across the Russian sea supply lanes. I must confess that only then did this dawn on me. Heretofore our thoughts had been completely occupied with preparations for the departure and the idea we were finally going to leave the contested mainland.

Luckily, there were only a few salvos. Then there was stillness. Finally, we heard in the distance a long, drawn out call: "Hold starboard!"

What had happened? Our good Weichsel captain, who indeed knew how to shove off and dock his boat, had no idea how to navigate the open sea. Thanks to the enormous speed of our "BERTA", we had overtaken all of the other boats of the flotilla. Thus we were dashing about on the open water all by ourselves. Our old freshwater sea captain had depended on sailing to Hela by dead reckoning. As a result, he had sailed more and more to the west and was near Gotenhafen — be it as a result of the darkness, the bad visibility or the wind. There he had landed in the sights of a Russian coastal battery, which greeted us with a few friendly rounds. Our "sea salt" then quickly turned the rudder and soon discovered to our delight a German cannon boat. This boat told him to hold starboard.

Soon our nerves were calm, but we couldn't sleep. So we relaxed and began a lively conversation under the swinging gas lantern, passing time, waiting for our Weichsel captain's next surprise move.

We had been underway for quite some time. We figured we should have already had the 35-kilometer stretch to Hela behind us, even when you calculated the "detour to Gotenhafen." Upon asking the helmsman of our boat who, at the same time, was also serving as the helmsman of our fate, what was happening, he said he didn't understand it either. He just wanted to hold starboard a little longer. After another half hour, our frigate decided to rebel against this trip. She reared, creaked and cracked. It became uncomfortable. We heard a spine-chilling howl in the distance. It gave you the creeps.

"Oh my goodness!" We heard the voice of our navigational strategist. "There's the whistling buoy!" We had reached the furthest point of the Putzig Land Spit as a result of his sharp course to the right and were about to sail out into the open sea. He heaved around quickly and sailed a bit towards the harbor, until we reached calmer water. There he cleverly dropped anchor and decided to wait until morning, since he could not find the entrance to the harbor in the dark. It was a bit risky even for him between the shallow areas and the rocks. As the sun rose we pulled up the anchor and sailed into Hela Harbor. It was 6 May.

The "Ant Hill" in the Hela Woods

Extremely relieved to once again have our feet on firm ground, we moved back and forth on the wharf. And everyone swore never to sail another mile on that old boat.

Then we marched into the woods, where we were to stay as long as needed, until *Oberleutnant* B. could find further transportation of a naval vessel. I then took all of my belongings, since I knew that you only continued to own what you carried on your person. Who could say whether we would be coming back to the harbor? And so I panted and puffed along with my heavy backpack, slowly hiking into the forest. Omnia mea mecum porto! The others were well ahead of me. I only caught up to them when they took a short break.

We pitched our tents in the vicinity of a rest area and awaited whatever came next. Once in a while we heard the heavy impact of an incoming round. Our friend Ivan was doing some firing exercises from the mainland. He also looked around occasionally from the air to see what was going on. There were German *Landser* swarming everywhere. The woods were as busy as an anthill. Yes, like ants — and just like ants which are known for running around when there is no purpose to it, so was everything running around aimlessly here.

On the morning of 8 May, Richard came to me and asked me to accompany him. He wanted to search for a *Leutnant* he knew who was supposed to be somewhere in the vicinity. I was happy to have the chance to do something different and said I would come along. After searching for a long time, we found him. When he saw us coming, he next made sure that no one was around. Then he laid his hands on our shoulders and began:

What I am about to entrust you with, you are not to tell anyone under any circumstances, except for your unit leader. The message just came through that tonight at 2400 hours is the capitulation. Go as quickly as possible to your unit and arrange for the necessities. Make sure that you somehow get through. Tonight at 1800 hours the last official flotilla will be departing. There are mostly rickety dinghies. Surely you all can join them with your "BERTA". So, run along quickly now. Time is of the essence. Who knows what will happen at the harbor when the news filters.

We stood there and were taken completely aback. Even though we knew this would happen sometime and even though it was in the air, it was as if we had been hit in the head as we finally heard the horrible news. We thanked him and went, no, we rushed — we ran. We passed by marching columns, from the rows of which the troops gave us all sorts of ribbing for rushing so fast. But that didn't bother us. If they only knew…

We arrived breathless at our unit. We informed the two officers present. Just as one of them was about to depart with his motorcycle to search for *Oberleutnant* B., B. arrived, breathless, and gave the order to depart in five minutes. He knew. We snatched our belongings. I left some things behind that would slow me down and left. At the field kitchen, anyone who wanted to fill his mess tin with butter could. Everything was laying around in a mess. This time our column was bigger than when we arrived, since on the day after we had departed, the remaining units of our brigade came over on pontoon ferries.

Every Man for Himself!
A Cruise into the Baltic on a Weichsel Riverboat

At the harbor, a crowd had formed and things were jammed up. Everyone was hurrying and grabbing. In spite of this, everything went pretty well at our loading place. At other loading places there were horrid scenes, as we later heard. Then the fateful separation of our unit: Everyone who came on "BERTA," left on "BERTA." Everyone else went on ferries. As willing as lambs, we climbed over the long plank onto our craft. What else was there to do?

All the big ships had already departed. And so it was in our need that we clung to our "BERTA" and to the goodness of God, of whom everyone asked for protection. Some ran at the last moment from the boat and found room on a ferry. Everyone is the master of his destiny. We knew that we — 180 men — could not leave the "BERTA" as a group and go somewhere else. So we surrendered to our fate and were happy to have this swimming "thing" under our feet and with it the chance to escape captivity. The dangers we would encounter on our journey paled into insignificance in comparison to the fear, deprivation and horror of what would occur in the woods of the Nehrung in the next few days. The intoxicating promise of seeing our homeland and our loved ones let all arising concerns disappear.

At about 1800 hours the flotilla departed. A larger ship tugged us, so we wouldn't fall behind. The majority of the comrades went below deck. I remained above and sat on the end of the bow, because I wanted to breathe fresh air as long as possible.

The sea was calm. We sailed around the whistling buoy at the tip of the spit. In front of us and behind us, the water was swarming with small and very small boats. It looked like a swarm of mosquitoes that had settled on a pond and let itself be pushed around by a light breeze. A few ships of varying quality did belong to our convoy, however. The only thing that brought a little life to our immobile swarm of mosquitoes was the maneuvering of the fast, small U-boat hunters that had taken over the duty of protecting our caravan. In addition, you could see a small motor yacht busily moving back and forth. It was the commander's boat.

In the stillness of the approaching evening I began to recognize increasingly the daring aspect of our operation. We were sitting on a wooden boat that was built in 1890 for freight operations on the Weichsel. It had a flat bottom and was, in every respect, completely ill suited for the open sea. We were fortunate someone was towing us along. We weren't alone in our predicament. There were similar fragile vessels swarming around and people were in them as well. This feeling of being in the same situation together eased my nerves a bit.

A gorgeous, clear sky full of stars surrounded us. I sat there for a long time and enjoyed the view, the beauty of which was so far away from civilization. There was none of the noise of the city, nor smoke from the smokestacks of factories to tarnish the peaceful, clear view of nature's extraterrestrial world. It was a symbol of a timeless order, ruled by God. There was light and shadows, but nowhere did darkness triumph. That was the reason why even the dimmest light stood out so much. And every light had its own path. It was powerful and completely contained in itself. And no light overtook the lights of the others, even if some light desired to intrude upon the others. Many had latched on to a family and sailed together, without bothering one another or others. Everywhere there was energy, movement, work, but nowhere was there disorder. Strange that this was even possible.

I spent the night thinking these and similar thoughts, which made me both happy and sad at the same time. They made me happy, because they gave me hope. But they made me sad because behind all of these thoughts was always the disappointing realization that those beliefs had been trampled upon. Perhaps I even slept a bit now and then. I don't know. I only know that we had set our course directly for the north, obviously to get away from the land. Later we turned off in a northwesterly direction.

Dawn broke. It was a beautiful, fresh spring morning. All around us were cobalt-blue skies. On the gentle swell of the Baltic Sea our brave boats continued to paddle along. Now and then we heard distant detonations. I thought to myself that it had to be the Russians, drunk in victory, firing off rounds in jubilee. Later I found out they were bombs intended for other convoys. Terrifying things must have taken place. Fighter planes and dive-bombers conducted low-level attacks. Many ships filled with fleeing soldiers and civilians were sunk. On other boats there were dead and wounded, not to mention the material damage. This happened on the day after we had capitulated. The armistice had already started. No one held back from pursuing and killing people who only had one wish: To go home.

But why should that have surprised me after everything one had already experienced: The horrifying actions against the Jews, the pilots hunting down helpless farmers or civilians who were, at the most, only carrying a walking stick. Those were things we experienced during the waning months of the war. And now this hunt on humans! All of it stemmed from the same root: The de-humanization of the human soul, as produced in our *advanced* earthly domain. Truthfully said, the advances in these domains have far outstripped those of technology. Not only in any given area, but in all of them!

During the afternoon things the sea traffic became a bit livelier. Despite that, everything continued peacefully. I thought I was on a seesaw, the way our "BERTA" lifted and sank. The fresh air ensured that I would stay at my post.

The commander's boat approached us. It came up along the side and *Oberleutnant* B, as well as an *Oberwachtmeister*, who had been on the ferry, climbed on board. They wanted to get some food.

The evening came and a delightful red twilight lit up the horizon. "That means good weather," prophesized a voice. "Nonsense! That means bad weather!" said several others. There was a lively exchange concerning what everyone thought. Everyone was a meteorologist, citing their own inviolable experiences. Unfortunately, the pessimists were right.

An uneasy wind came with the onset of night, which gradually made itself unpleasantly noticed. The sea was agitated. Our old wooden boat danced from the tip of one wave to another. "Everyone below deck!" someone called. Only our commander, *Oberleutnant* B., who could no longer return to the ferry, as well as a few courageous ones, remained above. I crawled down the ladder and, after searching for a long time, found a small place for myself where I could lay down somewhat. I had to lay down completely, since my stomach made itself known in any other bodily position.

Our dim light swayed. "BERTA" heaved and sank, bringing my stomach along with it. Perhaps it was good that my stomach's uneasiness increased with the uneasiness of the sea, because my indifference to everything else around me increased proportionally.

From above you could hear Helmut's voice, who was telling the poor Weichsel captain whether he should steer to the left or right. The captain was again at the rudder, after others had taken turns giving him a break during the day. To the rear in the rudder house, you couldn't see much due to the fog and the darkness. "Leeeffttt!" he rung out. Then again, "Riiiggghhhtt!!! The boat creaked and moaned at every joint.

Then you could hear the hubbub of voices. And it took a while until Helmut's monotone "llleeeefffftttt" and "rrrriiiigggghhhhtttt" rung out again. The towrope had ripped and, with much effort, a new one was tossed over. In the meantime, the intensity of the waves increased. The towrope ripped again. The motorboat informed us that it could no longer tow us along, but would try to find a replacement. Soon another river tugboat puffed along side and hooked up. (This was all told to me later.)

An eerie stillness crept over our cargo room. No one said a word. Everyone was involved with their own thoughts…or their own stomach. The moaning and creaking of the boat's hull was enough to drive you crazy. I slowly pulled myself up and groped my way to the ladder. My bladder was full. Luckily, I made it topside. As I looked through the hatch, I saw only rising masses of water and a dark horizon, then everything slipped into another distorted picture of yesterday's peaceful order. It was all I could do to crawl on all fours until reaching the railing. You had to cling to the deck and use your hand to look for a hook or a piece of rope to hold on to, otherwise you would slide off. To the right, I saw the little Weichsel steamer that danced around at a short distance from us. Someone was in the process of throwing over the rope after it had broken again.

After I felt my way down the stairs, I felt a bit better. In the dim light from our lantern I saw an entangled mass of bodies. Really, it didn't seem there were people there any more. It was simply the impression I had: Corpses! I remembered the galleys from the Ben-Hur film.

I had barely laid down again, when I heard loud voices from above. Something wasn't right. The intensity of the waves had been constantly increasing. But no one seemed to care. But in all actuality, horrible tragedies were taking place on the ocean at that very moment. Many of the small boats of our flotilla were not capable of withstanding the rage of the waves and sank. Even the small tugboat that had helped us thus far was lost. How many innocent people had to lose their lives in such a terrible and tragic fashion? Were they the plaything of some undefined tribunal that sent the peoples of the world — now and at all times — onto the stage of war from the security of its prompter's box? Did you ever consider, you, firebrand, that all of these people will testify against you some day?

"What would happen if there was no one left to tow us along?" I thought to myself. "Don't go to Bornholm! Don't go to Sweden!" was the last radio message Albert had received in Hela on the radio from the commander. There must have been a reason for it.

And I wasn't wrong, either. We would soon find that out. Otto, our lively and jovial friend, was sick of lying around. With much effort he built a mountain from the sacks of hardtack. He then got on top. He shoved a few planks to the side and took in the view. The raw morning air must have completely awakened his spirit. In any case, you heard him say, "Down there you'll breathe your last breath. I don't give a shit if I have to vomit. I'm staying here!" He held onto a crossbeam so he wouldn't fall from his pile of hardtack bags. At that point our "BERTA" rose high out of the water and splashed down on its flat bottom with such force that you would think everything would have to burst apart momentarily. Our "BERTA" was as helpless as a fat duck waddling around on the ground out there on the raging Baltic.

But this only served to give Otto even more energy. Unbelievable as it sounds, he played radio announcer and reported in a breathtaking sequence what was going on in the sea and on deck.

Gentlemen, we find ourselves in an terrible situation. Because, as I see it, the tugboat has ditched us. We are moving along all alone in the raging Baltic. Far in front of us on the distant curve of the horizon are the members of our convoy. A boat, no, a ferry, is quite far behind. Give me the binoculars! Yes, someone is waving! He's one of ours. Sail on safely noble warriors! Hopefully you'll have more luck than us! Dawn is breaking. Land can be seen to the right; it's unmistakably. Sweden, if I'm not wrong. But what is that? Land to the left as well? That must be Bornholm! Certainly! Of course! Bornholm! What now my friends? "What should I do," says Zeus, "the gods are drunk!"

Reading these lines, some would think Otto had cracked up. Perhaps others would label his chatter as frivolous. Still others would think that I made up his "broadcast" to spice up the events that were going on. But all of these assumptions would be wrong. It happened exactly as I reported it, even if I did not capture Otto word for word. And to those who would label his "radio report" as frivolous, I would like to say this: He did all of us a good service by doing that, because the general tension and resignation in the air were eased.

Meanwhile the bad weather raged on. It was not a hurricane, but it was increasingly becoming a bit too much for our fragile and rickety old lady, "BERTA." She pounded, groaned and reared up, splashing down again and again. That boat's propeller was more above water than under it.

"But my friends," continued Otto, "we are not as alone as I thought. To the right has appeared a warship of middle caliber. A Swede, apparently. Give me the binoculars! Yes, it is a Swedish destroyer. What should we do? Sail on or approach land?"

The opinions were split. Most everyone said we should land. But there were others who thought that despite everything, we should continue on. Who knew what was happen to us in Sweden? Some had had bad experiences with the people of the twentieth century.

But in the end the majority ruled. Red flares were fired to make the Swedes notice us. It took a long time for the Swedes to approach us. They approached in accordance with all of the formalities, they thought they owed us. They pointed all of their guns at our old lady "BERTA," as if she were deserving of that kind of respect. Who knew what kind of a trap was being set or what kind of monstrosity was about to be committed? They definitely had to have good binoculars! Then someone asked the really smart question from a very respectful distance: "What do you want and who are you?" Someone should have called out: "We are the big, bad wolf and we want to gobble up grandma!" But we didn't do that and asked where the nearest harbor was. Someone pointed and said "There!" And then the brave guardians of the coast disappeared from our sight.

Our good rudder man, who could barely stand on his own two legs, set a course for where the Swedes had pointed and tried to reach the salvation of the harbor. But that was scarcely possible under our own power. The weak motor could barely move us from our spot, especially since the propeller, as previously mentioned, was more out of the water than in it. The wild waves did the rest in preventing us from reaching our goal. What was left for us to do? We once again fired red flares and made a course for the destroyer lurking in the distance. After another long pause the destroyer approached us and asked us what we wanted now. It was like Serenissimus in the face of a drowning man asking: "Well, tell me then, why is the man yelling so?"

Finally they were satisfied and threw a rope over. Then there was a horrible jerk. "BERTA" gave us reason for concern when she lay on her side, reared up and splashed down again. She moaned, cracked and trembled. Water splashed in. A woman's voice screeched (it was the wife of the owner of the boat). Everyone grabbed the inner tubes they had brought along and forced themselves up the ladder and Otto's pile of zwieback to the top. I only remember taking off all my clothes. I thought: If I have to go in the water, then without my uniform on! That all happened in a matter of seconds. Fortunately nothing else happened, so a panic was avoided. And then the shrill voice of our comrade Emil yelled out: "SOS, SOS, he is taking us to Bornholm!" While all this was going on he fumbled about with a flashlight, thinking he had signaled SOS. Some mean-spirited types claimed later that there was no bulb in the lamp.

The destroyer had not given any consideration to what speed it towed us. It had described a narrow arc with us. The sudden yank occurred when the rope pulled taut. Not until we had fired off some more signal flares and directed his attention to the fact that he would have to slow his tempo somewhat if he placed any value in getting us to the harbor in one piece, did he let off the gas. After about an hour and a half, we reached Ystad, a small harbor on the south coast of Sweden, east of Trelleborg.

In the Harbor of Ystad

Having arrived at the Harbor, everyone and everything had to remain below deck. All weapons were handed above. Finally we were allowed to crawl topside and get some fresh air.

Our good "BERTA" was in the wharf at Ystad. But she was not the only one. Right next to us was a small luxury yacht that might have done well at Lake Wann in Berlin but certainly not on the Baltic. A bit further away I could see a submarine hunter. It had towed the yacht, which had run into trouble at see and, in the process, had also become immobile. The towrope had got caught in the propeller.

In addition to the stranded ones, there was a Swedish freighter of medium size in the harbor basin. The Swedish national colors were painted on the hull of the ship, and underneath was painted "Sverige" (Sweden) in large letters. Otherwise, only smaller fishing boats were under sail. I went onto land to finally have firm ground under my feet.

Even then it felt peculiar; hours later I still had the feeling I was being swept back and forth by the waves. A group of German soldiers walked around the pier. The submarine hunter had also brought a general along. In the background you could see the exit to the city and a barrier, behind which many curious civilians were standing. There was also a cannon, pointed towards the harbor! Watch out! But for the time being I went back on board with a lot of the others where we unloaded the assault gun ammunition we had brought along before the eyes of the staring Swedes. In the meantime we had realized that we were running around dirty and in need of a shave. Also, our pale faces must have contributed to our battered appearance. We therefore tried to make ourselves look a little more human.

We felt much better and even became hungry. So, we went into the ship's salon and ate something. Then we talked with the Swedish officers. They were very surprised that we looked so good and that our uniforms were reasonably clean. When we offered them some of our "schokakola" (chocolate with a high nutritional value and extra caffeine) and showed them our supplies on the "BERTA," they were stunned. They didn't consider it possible the exhausted and badly bled *Wehrmacht* could be still be so well supplied in the sixth year of the war. When we asked them what they would do if they were in our situation, they responded in unison, "Allow yourself to be interned. Sweden will treat you well." Our concern that we might be handed over to the Russians was indignantly dismissed. No, they gave us their word that Sweden would never do something like that. I didn't doubt it then and I don't doubt it now that these men truly believed what they had told us.

During our conversation, another wooden boat similar to our "BERTA" and filled with German *Landser*, arrived in the harbor. A larger tugboat pulled it. It was lively movement back and forth. We exchanged views about what should be done next. Finally our commander arrived and gave us the following alternatives: Every man could decide for himself whether he wanted to allow himself to be interned in Sweden or whether he wanted to continue on with him in the "BERTA." He said

I spoke with the skipper and the Swedish harbor commander. After repairing a few things on the boat, we could depart in the morning, if the sea calms down a bit. I want to sail westwards along the Swedish coast, outside of the three-mile zone, and try to reach Copenhagen. There we would be with the English and wouldn't have to wait a long time to get home. Whoever stays here will be interned and will not have to deal with the dangers of the continued trip on the "BERTA." I'm sure whoever stays will also be well taken care of. But, by staying here, it is hard to say when you will be allowed to go home. In any case, it will take a long time. Those are the two possibilities. The war is over. I no longer have command authority over you, nor do I want it. Everyone can decide what he wants to do.

A half-hour later he assembled everyone again. About 25 men of the 180 total decided they wanted to continue the voyage on the "BERTA" (I was among them). The rest preferred their Swedish "life insurance policy." No one could hold it against them after what we had been through together.

Free Passage for Deserters

Then from the Swedish side came the question as to whether there were deserters among us. We didn't know what that was supposed to mean and looked at each other with shaking heads. But, look! There's a few who suddenly discovered in their hearts the desire to be deserters. From our battery there was a "Beutedeutscher" [Translator's Note: A pejorative term for an ethnic German from outside the confines of the Reich.], a recently graduated secondary school teacher from the Sudetenland, who had an insincere and underhanded personality. Our friends, the deserters, were immediately separated from us; we never saw them again. Someone heard later that they were all sent home a short while later. At that time we were infuriated at such behavior and I can still hear Sepp, an Austrian, say: "Bah, such bastards! We have stayed together through thick and thin for five years; we need to stay that way until the very end."

Perhaps the deserters did the right thing. The success of their actions appears to have deemed them to be right. They had obviously recognized that you could go the farthest in this sad world through lies and treachery. Whether one remains happy inside as a result of such actions is unknown. But such thoughts mean nothing to many, because they never were happy with themselves; perhaps they never had any substance to them at all.

"Stockholm ordered it!"

The next day we were told that we would all be interned. Our departure was forbidden by Stockholm. A short time later, the ship which arrived the day before and was the sister ship to our "BERTA" departed from the harbor. It was once again filled with *Landser* and pulled by the same tugboat. We called out asking them where they were going, and they all called back in unison, "To Denmark!" Strange. They let those two boats go. We had to stay. Upon asking, the reply was a regretful shrug of the shoulders and the words: "Stockholm ordered it!"

We had to take it as an "act of God" and surrendered to our fate. And I have to say that I was almost content that it had come to this, since I didn't quite like the thought of continuing the journey by sea. At that point lists were drawn up: Last name, first name, date of birth, when and why…

After we spent another night aboard the "BERTA," we finally marched on 12 May with our bags and baggage to a tent camp behind barbed wire that was right next to the harbor. We took our army-issue radio and placed it on a wall. "Aha, our *Führer* is speaking!" someone said. (It was a speech given by Churchill.)

The next morning the delousing began. It went very slowly and we had to wait a long time. At about noon the commander came to us with the message that we indeed had permission to continue our journey. In 20 minutes he had to submit the names of the soldiers who wanted to continue along. But before the 20 minutes had transpired, the next decree had arrived from Stockholm, which reversed the latest one just given. It was the last and irreversible official decision that we would have to remain! Alea iacta erant!

It was strange, this back and forth concerning the orders from Stockholm. The Swedes did not seem to be complying to the norm of established international law, otherwise there would have been a clear yes or no. It appeared to me that there was something else at play that had to be figured into the equation. But I didn't think about it much further. We were in Sweden, after all, a neutral country, the land of the Red Cross, home of the "Angel of Siberia."

The delousing equipment was discontinued in the evening. We had to spend another night in the tents. It wasn't our turn until the next day. All of the delousing equipment was set up in a provisional manner in tents. A truck with the actual delousing chamber was part of it. After we had finished the procedure, we were led to a large warehouse, where the deloused ones had already settled in on layers of straw. There we were subjected to a doctor's examination; it was limited to a throat culture to determine if we had diphtheria.

After enduring this business there was a more pleasant activity: The first issuing of rations in Sweden. The Red Cross issued them. If I remember correctly, there was a sweet porridge and blood pudding with cranberries. The blood pudding (obviously named after the English "black pudding") was a lightly sweetened blood sausage, fried in fat; after what we had been accustomed to, this was a unique experience. Besides that, everyone received a bag with open-faced white bread sandwiches for the trip.

We were not allowed to take any of our supplies from the "BERTA." Customs was against it. That is no joke. On the other hand, our packs were not inspected any further.

THE TRAGEDY — PART I
Malmö, Göteborg, Skafteröd

In the evening around 1900 hours we climbed aboard the train that was switched exclusively for us in the area of the harbor. They were nice train cars with upholstered seats, like our express train cars. An hour later the train set off in motion. In an approximately 12-hour trip, the train brought us to Skafteröd, after traveling through Malmö and Göteborg. Skafteröd was a small station about sixty kilometers north of Göteborg, near Uddevalla.

The ride was unbelievably beautiful. We were enchanted as we rode through this clean and well maintained country, which had not seen war in about 130 years. No bomb craters, no burned-out tanks, no trenches — no wrecked cities or villages, no refugees suffering their plight. Oh dear Sweden, I don't think you know how lucky you all are!

We steamed along through well maintained fields and colorful villages. Soon it was dark. Then came Malmö, one of the three largest cities. The first thing that was dazzling — in the truest sense of the word — was the abundance of lights. Everything was brightly lit: Storefronts, streets, movie theaters and advertising signs! There was lively traffic everywhere. Well-dressed…and well-nourished people. You really didn't know if you were dreaming or awake. Something wasn't right. We had a lump in our throats. Was it happiness? Homesickness? Bitterness? Fear?

We sang. Our voices echoed happily in the main train station where we had paused at for a long time. Across from us was a passenger train. On the running board stood an older, stocky gentleman who gawked at us with a more than cold expression. He would fill in the pauses between our verses with a theatrical "It's a long way to Tipperary." As his train began to depart he tipped his hat and called out: "God save the king!"

Whether he was really a member of "God's own people," I don't know. In any case, I found his behavior quite foolish. If it was really a British subject, then he did not look like he had personally contributed very much to the victory of his country. But if he was a Swede, then his behavior was inexcusable.

On other occasions various civilians greeted us with a strange greeting, or whatever it was. They held up their hand, displaying two fingers that made a "V." Clueless as we were, we mostly nodded our heads in greeting back. Later someone explained to us that the "V" meant "victory!!!" Please excuse me, but when I heard that, I had to laugh out loud.

I didn't see Göteborg since I fell asleep during the trip. I woke early in the morning when it was bright out. That was 15 May. We drove through a slightly hilly springtime landscape that looked like it had been raked and watered by a gardener. The electric locomotive allowed us to look out the window without being punished. It could only be described by one word: Clean! Soon we were at our destination. Our bags were loaded onto trucks and we marched on foot through the dewy morning about three or four kilometers to our camp, "Backamo." It took a while for us to learn how to use the left-hand side of the street.

Arrival at "Backamo"

The prison camp appeared as a large piece of land surrounded by two barbed wire fences. There were large two-story wooden barracks that were painted red and also medium-sized barracks. The landscape fell off to the rear and led into a forest. Behind it to the right there was a shallow dip and there was a large lake surrounded by forest.

In the camp there were already a few comrades running around, the majority of whom were sailors from the Kriegsmarine. There were crew members from a "Snorkel" *U-Boot* that had an emergency off the Swedish coast, as they told us.

Naturally, we wanted to know how things were there. "There is roll call in the morning. Otherwise, nothing else happens. But we have only been here a few days ourselves."

We could not take the discussion any further since we were told to fall in for a greeting from the Swedish camp commander. A slender, tall, older man with friendly, even warm-hearted facial expressions appeared. His smooth white hair lent him the respect of age. He introduced himself as Major Uno Jacobsson. "Another contingent has arrived at 'Backamo.' You should find peace and relaxation here after the many things you went through in the terrible war!" Then he also told us that "Backamo" had been a training camp for the Swedish army since 1813, we should immediately write home and everything would be done to make life in the barracks bearable. Further, he expected reciprocity from us by our maintaining order and discipline and we would soon be going home. And so on, and so forth…

Forgive me for repeating the Major's words with an accent similar to which he spoke to us. They were repeated in this manner not to be meant as a mockery, but because they remain unforgettable to the comrades and myself. The words "peace and relaxation" continued to ring in our ears. I would like to emphasize: I never doubted the sincerity with which these words were spoken. Actually we did find peace and relaxation. It's just that the terrible ending should never have been allowed to happen.

After the usual formalities (medical examination, recording of personal data) everyone looked for a bed in the large barracks for the first night. We were to be split up into companies the next day.

During a walk around the camp we found (besides the previously mentioned barracks) the following buildings: one mess hall; one canteen with a larger room for events; one small barracks building (where a barber shop, dentist office, library and the editorial staff for the camp periodical were housed); a large aid station; and, finally, a large wooden structure in the woods to the rear where our officers were housed. Wait, not to be forgotten was the small sauna. The areas between the barracks were not maintained. We were not permitted to go to the lake.

We found ourselves behind barbed wire — that much was now clear. Thank God the camp was so large one did not feel so confined. There were enough places where one could not even see the fence or the guard posts. Despite that, there was a limit to our freedom of movement. There was a fence, and that was the limit. It was a strange feeling, an unusual situation.

Soon we were called to eat and for the first time we experienced a meal similar to the practical, organized manner we had experienced in our own military installations. In front of a long counter and to the left stood a table with a pile of metal trays and a container of silverware. We marched past and took a tray and the necessary utensils. Then, men standing behind the table handed us a plate with soup, sausage, sauce, potatoes, bread, etc. We looked for a place to sit down at a table in the mess hall and ate our food. After eating we placed the edible remains in a trough and placed our dirty silverware on a special table in the middle of the room, from which those who were assigned to be dishwashers in the kitchen picked them up.

The food was a little bit strange for our tastes. The three mealtimes usually consisted of the following: Breakfast — one bowl of sweet milk porridge (oats, semolina, rice), one piece of white bread, one piece of rye bread, one little star of butter, one cup of coffee with three cubes of sugar and lots of crisp bread. Lunch — one bowl of sweet porridge, grilled sausage, vegetables, potatoes, a cup of milk. Dinner — one bowl of sweet porridge, one bowl of fruit or vegetable soup, two pieces of bread, one little star of butter. On Thursday evenings we looked forward to delicious pancakes with cranberries; on Sunday afternoons the goulash and on Sunday evenings the rolls with butter and cheese.

The food was qualitatively very good. It was the same as what the Swedish army received, as far as I know. It was just that our *Landser* stomachs were used to larger quantities, especially of bread and potatoes. This is not an ungrateful complaint. I would just like to give the best representation as to how it really was. We just had to get used to it. Above all, a lot of people had a hard time with the "blood pudding." After a while, I couldn't even look at it any more. But you couldn't really complain. Our homeland could have never offered us such food back then. I gained about 12 pounds in the first six weeks.

The next day we were split up into companies. We requested we be allowed to remain with our comrades. We were housed in a large, austere room that had only two-tiered bunk beds and a few tables and benches. The washing area was very simple and impractically set up. We couldn't understand it, because the camp had not been built just for us, but also for the Swedish military. Later we were to find out why that was. The average Swede did not place much value on the military. The result was that the Swedish parliament only gave its war minister a small budget. The animosity of the Swedes towards everything military went so far that it was not unheard of for a civilian to spit at an officer on the street, even though the officer had not done anything personal to the civilian. An officer who had been attacked in such a manner could do very little about it. The regular soldiers were crudely and sparingly equipped. The relationship between superiors and subordinates appeared to us to be too casual. Our impression was summed up in the following: what we had too much of, they had too little of.

The Fatal Lists

And so the first days transpired without incident. That is, discounting the fact that that they asked us to fill out questionnaires concerning when and where each of us had set out to sea, the end of which had resulted in our arriving in Sweden. As dumb as we were, our

"BERTA" crew answered that we had departed from Hela on 8 May at about 1800 hours. Without making myself out to be the misunderstood prophet, I thought that something wasn't quite right. I can't say what gave me this impression, and I also do not claim that I presumed to know the exact purpose of this questionnaire. But some kind of feeling of mistrust forced me to say to our commander that I considered these facts to be very important and that we would have to really answer the questions carefully. Everyone was of the opinion that we could state the truth with a clear conscience, since we had indeed not departed after the beginning of the official end of hostilities but at a time when we were still under the command of the army. We were such harmless fools! Such legal considerations might have been appropriate in earlier times. But not in the progressive twentieth century...

We sat together in small groups and thought about loved ones at home. What was it like there? What could have happened to them in the final days when chaos broke out? The uncertainty was tiring. Were they racking their brains about our whereabouts? We wrote home. Was there a reason? Did our letters even arrive? Were the recipients even alive?

Pentecost arrived. A Swedish military pastor held a service in the open air. We stood under trees in the fresh grass and listened to his words. One could hear the sea below. Birds sang their songs. And we joined in the songs of praise: "Praise God!" You would have thought there really was peace on earth.

An Encounter

A few days later, the German leaders in the camp requested volunteers from those who were in the position to be able to teach something. They should make themselves available for the greater good of the camp. A sort of layperson's university was slowly formed, in which the majority of the teachers were also laypeople —- at least in a pedagogical respect. Courses of all kinds were formed: English (for beginners and advanced students), French (ditto), Russian, Polish, mathematics, German, history, geography, stenography, shorthand, business courses, courses for technical occupations, etc. During the breaks between hour-long classes which ran according to a prescribed schedule, you could see those eager to learn with notebooks and pencils hurrying from barracks to barracks. Often there were curious scenes: The general, the colonels and the majors sat there straining to hear every word of the low-ranking *Obergefreiter* who was passing along his business knowledge to them. Tempora mutantur et nos mutamur in illis!

Soon thereafter a band and a variety troupe were formed. They worked hard to provide a little change of pace. They constructed a stage in the canteen, painted backdrops and fashioned stage props of all kinds. They practiced, planned and offered entertainment that was quite good. Besides many good cabaret performances — considering that it was almost exclusively amateurs who performed them — there were also self-penned theatrical pieces and adaptations of plays.

For example, they performed Spoerl's "Feuerzangenbowle" after adapting it for the stage. Unforgettable for us all were Anton and Peter Pitt. The two comrades, whom they personified, never lost their new nicknames. A choir was also formed, which was led by comrade P., an endearing person, who was a teacher by profession.

Above all I have to mention a person who took care of us in such an unselfish way during the weeks and months of the internment, Father Nielsen; who was born in Germany and felt especially bonded to us. Sure, we were not suffering any bodily harm. We had more than enough good food and could live as we wished within the confines of the camp. (I will report about our duties later.) But what was it really like on the inside? There was the uncertainty concerning the fate of the next of kin, the dark thoughts about the collapse and chaos at home and, finally, the uncertainty of our own future! All of that gnawed at us and wore us down. One thought of law and order, justice, guilt and innocence…belief and disbelief…love and unkindness…

A few days after our arrival at "Backamo" Father Nielsen appeared for the first time. He was a medium-sized, stocky man with a serious and spiritual look about him. And from then on he came on a regular basis. Every Wednesday he held a lecture, often with slides, about a particular area of knowledge or a personality. He spoke about Sweden, its history, constitution, economy and culture. He taught us about the life of Goethe, he spoke of German painters and poetry. Every lecture was a pearl for us, a pearl that we desired like spiritual nourishment after going without it for so long. Every 14 days he would also come on Sunday and hold a church service for us that was often enhanced by the camp choir. On two occasions he obtained permission for us to have our church service in a nearby village church. That was a special occasion.

Moreover, one could turn to him for anything. He saw to it that we got handicraft equipment, teaching materials and he also dragged along a large amount of books that he had collected from his circle of friends. Our library, the construction of which he was largely responsible for, had not fewer than 1000 titles. Everything was available, from the classics to Karl May. One time Father Nielsen was successful in getting the band of the Swedish regiment which was in charge of our care to come into the camp. It made our church service even more beautiful with its chorales; afterwards the band gave a small concert.

So, it can be easily said that our Father was like a guardian angel who looked after us. He took care of us during the days when we felt so abandoned by the world, and that did us good. Oh, if only we could lead a Christian life like that one. Things would look a lot different on our planet!

The Culture Circle

In June, a Catholic priest visited us. He was unable to dedicate himself to us as intensively since he had to come from Stockholm. He came every third Sunday and sang mass in the camp.

Sometime later — probably in August — a small circle was formed which dedicated itself to ensuring more intellectual things had their say in the camp. Morning recitals were conducted with readings of poetry and prose, which were accompanied by chamber music performed by three pianos. The selection of the readings and music was already exciting enough as it was, but when the canteen hall was decorated with flowers and green cuttings, you felt like you were somewhere else for a while. The morning recitals — which always had a theme — were always well attended and there probably wasn't anyone who ever left dissatisfied. It was always a small celebration. I still have one of the programs in my possession:

Noch tröste mich mit süßer Augenweide der blaue Himmel und die grüne Flur; mir reicht die Göttliche den Taumelkelch der Freude. Die jugendliche, freundliche Natur. (Hölderlin)

Oh console me still blue heaven and green meadow as a sight for sore eyes; the divine one extends the giddy goblet of joy to me. Youthful, friendly nature.

Sequence of Events for the Morning Recital
Sunday, the 16th of September
10 O'clock
in the Canteen

Heinrich Albert (1642)	Choir: Desire forced me to…
Johann Wolfgang v. Goethe	from: Faust, Second Part
Ludwig van Beethoven	Violin Sonata in A major, op. 30/1 First movement: Allegro
Josef v. Eichendorff	Poet's Spring
Pater Lippert	from: Letters form the Engadin
Wolfgang Amadeus Mozart	Canon: Everything falls silent…
Hermann Fürst v. Bückler	Animals
Max Dauthendey	Nightingale and Rain
Theodor Storm	from the novella "St. Jürgen"
Josef v. Eichendorff	The Summer Thread
Ludwig van Beethoven	Violin Sonata A major, op. 30/1 Second movement: Adagio
Friedrich Hölderlin	One Half of the Life
Martin Greif	About Nature
Franz Schubert	Ave Maria

Conclusion around 11 O'clock

No applause please!

In addition to these morning recitals (three took place), extracts of Don Carlos were read aloud with different people playing different roles. On a beautiful Saturday afternoon Iphigenie was read aloud. Another evening was dedicated to German humor and featured the works of Goethe, Wieland, Mörike, Morgenstern and Winkler. Every Monday there were lectures from all fields of knowledge. I still remember some themes: "Heaven's stars," "The world of bacteria," "Questions of upbringing," and "Infectious sicknesses and their treatment."

During all of these presentations the presenters were completely aware of their status as dilettantes. The goal was not to be a good reciter; more important than a perfect artistic performance was allowing important works of German literature to be heard in the camp.

Several staffers put the camp newspaper together. It presented the most important news in a sharply curtailed form on two sheets of copy paper. The camp subscribed to Swedish, English, French and Russian newspapers. For every language there was someone responsible who translated the most important things and forwarded them to the editor-in-chief.

Besides this newspaper, there was an illustrated gazette for the camp. It poked fun at political events and things which happened in the camp.

But even with that I have not exhausted the magnitude of things that were offered to us. The Swedish camp administration provided us with a movie projector with sound, which was supposedly acquired through the German legation in Stockholm. Unfortunately, the films, for the most part, were not very worthwhile. Besides a film about Johann Strauß and a Marie Antoinette film as well as a German and an English film, which were bearable, for the most part, we saw nothing but American color movies which mostly revolved around a dim-witted dancer in gaudy war paint by the name of Carmen Miranda. Either the Swedish film distributor wanted to give us a lecture in culture or, what was more probable, he wanted to use the convenient opportunity to make a profit from his old stocks of movies.

Work and Soldier's Wages

In addition to all of these opportunities for entertainment, a lot of sports were played. Soccer, handball, volleyball, track and field, boxing, swimming…every sport was represented. Camp championships were held and there was even a large sport fest held with all of the associated trimmings. The play-offs were held over the course of many weeks. There was also a swimming competition after the German camp leadership convinced the Swedish camp administration to allow us access to the lake.

Down below by the lake, prisoners could take nice walks on the narrow pathways through the thick pine trees, a refuge for when prisoners wanted to be alone.

After the first two or three weeks, during which we only had to perform camp work, an order was issued which ordered 600 men daily — the number of internees was about 1200 men, including the 130 officers — to clear a nearby piece of land. But only 300 men were needed to work in the morning and 300 in the afternoon. This allowed a half a day to participate in instruction.

For those who didn't know how to occupy their time, this change of pace was really good. By the way, not really all that much was required from the work. It was more "make work" than anything else. At any rate, if you didn't hurt yourself, it was a pretty good thing. There was no special remuneration for the work, but we received (according to the Geneva Convention) the soldier's pay that we were entitled to, the amount of which was based on rank and at the lowest possible Swedish rate. We were paid every 10 work days: enlisted men received 10 Kronen, *Gefreiter* through *Unteroffizier* 12 Kronen, *Feldwebel* 15 Kronen, *Oberfeldwebel* to *Leutnant* 20 Kronen, *Oberleutnant* 25 Kronen and so on. With the money you were able to buy tobacco products (rationed), toilet articles, stationery and candy in the canteen. Later you were able to buy clothing and even suits and coats. All kinds of charitable gifts wandered their way into the camp, be it due to former or newly made acquaintanceships.

Swedish Odds and Ends

One day we read in the Swedish newspapers that Sweden had declared itself ready to take in several thousand former concentration camp prisoners from Germany and to take care of them for a few weeks. Apart from all of the horrid things that may have taken place in those concentration camps, it is perhaps indeed worth mentioning what was printed in the Swedish newspapers a few weeks later: The

Swedes had had bad experiences with their "guests." A large number of the former concentration camp inmates had been found guilty of theft, embezzlement and swindling. The Swedes saw themselves forced to considerably restrict their freedom of movement.

A German pilot, who made an emergency landing shortly before the capitulation, had gotten engaged to the daughter of an ethic German estate owner who had settled in Sweden. The farm was in the near vicinity of the place where the plane had landed. As the story goes, he would disappear from the camp for a few days at a time. His bride waited nearby for him in the car. In the darkness he would go over the fence during which the guard would close both eyes. His fiancé would then be waiting with a car in the vicinity. The guard turned a blind eye to this and another officer took his place during roll call. (The officers were individually counted in their rooms in the evenings). Vivat tolerantia!

Not all of the Swedish guards — and we got to know quite a few of them during the constant changing of guards — were so generous. One time the guard who watched over us while we were swimming shot at one of our comrades, who, in his opinion, had crossed beyond the border marker which was the outside limit of our freedom of movement. It should be mentioned, the comrade was still swimming about two meters away from the buoy. There was a local hearing during which the incident was reconstructed in excruciating detail in the presence of all of the higher Swedish and German camp dignitaries. Without any further consequences, of course! It may be interesting to note that the enthusiastic rifleman was a Jewish student.

Another incident occurred on a Sunday when a comrade received a visit from some Swedish civilians. The officer of the guard at that time was a little bit unfriendly (!) to Germans. In any case, he didn't put up with conversations between those who were interned and his acquaintances, although other such meetings were approved. You could converse in Swedish administrative buildings or even go on a short walk outside of the camp, during which a guard followed at a respectful distance.

But this time, as said, there was a Cerberus at the gate who did not tolerate such behavior. He forbid the comrade from approaching the fence. When the comrade then went to another place on the fence with the intention of making contact with the outside world, the *friendly* officer who observed this shot a hole through his thigh.

After that there was a commotion at the camp gate. The captain who was the acting commander for the traveling camp commander felt compelled to read a statement in front of the assembled internees which had been prepared for him by our officers. In it, the Swedish camp administration distanced itself from the behavior of the officer of the guard and promised to punish the perpetrator.

Otherwise we had no cause to complain about the Swedish camp leaders. They behaved correctly and loyally towards us and granted many of our requests. Also, the camp leadership allowed some things for the improvement of our quarters as well as the beautification of the entire camp.

A group of men under the leadership of an *Oberleutnant* who had been in construction was sent to the Norwegian border with a truck to pick up barrack construction materials. A bunch of small 10-man cabins were constructed from these materials for the last groups of men who arrived at the camp. Until then, they had camped out in tents. Also, medium-sized barracks were constructed; a second and third kitchen (the third one with a dining facility) and a barrack for instruction.

Other comrades were responsible for the gardening in the camp. And so, after a period of time, our "Backamo" digs turned into a well maintained, almost home-like, barrack village, with clean walkways and beautiful greenery and flowerbeds.

The friendly major, whom I reported about earlier, was unfortunately relieved shortly after our arrival at "Backamo." He had probably earned a negative reputation with his superiors due to his all too fatherly treatment of us. The good old man, who quickly earned the name "Uncle Uno" among us, had attended our first variety show and had handed the "male prima donna" a bouquet of flowers after the performance. Was this friendly gesture the bone of contention between him and the Swedish administration? I don't know. In any case, Uncle

Uno had to depart soon afterwards. It is a sad world in which humanity and goodness are offensive to some.

But I'm sure there were reasons at play for that as well! — A colonel by the name of Niels Brunsson was his successor. He was a tall and strong man of middle age, whose strictly business-like behavior was not perceived to be straightforward and candid, but rather as ice-cold and impenetrable. If he were to read these lines, I'm sure he would consider those characteristics as a plus. I, however, considered them to be on the negative side of the scale.

He liked to trot through the camp on his horse with a riding crop in his hands. I never saw him laugh. His red hair and his utter unapproachability, behind which there appeared to somehow be some kind of undefined arrogance hiding, earned him the nickname of the "Red Czar." I would like to emphasize that these are only impressions of him. His behavior in public in the camp was always dispassionate and…proper (a great word!).

I also do not want to forget the funeral for an older comrade that passed away in the camp's hospital. The funeral was conducted by a pastor, the Swedish camp administration and the entire camp community and was more like a state funeral.

Information Anyone?
Herr Hellmann fills us in

Just a few weeks after our arrival in Sweden — I believe it was in June — the rumor surfaced that we would be handed over to the Russians. As one could imagine, the rumor spread like wildfire and took the camp by storm. The Swedish camp administration tried to calm our fears by denying it, but after those days in June we were unable to rid ourselves of the stifling feeling of uncertainty.

A new source of rumors was the fact that the ethnic Germans were separated from us and housed in a smaller camp ("Grunnebo"), about 25 kilometers away from us.

In September, Stockholm sent a certain *Herr* Hellmann — nomen est omen — who was to bring light to the dark thoughts of our future. [Translator's Note: Hellmann means *light* or *bright man* in German, hence someone who could enlighten you.] He was, as the announcement preceding his arrival claimed, in a position to answer all our questions — not only about the situation back home but also with regard to our own fate. But we found out that *Herr* Hellmann was more like the opposite of what his name would indicate. In a string of convoluted words — he spoke a completely accent-free and fluent German — he made it clear to us that nothing final about our return home was known. Note well: He didn't say words to the effect that nothing had been decided yet. No, instead: Nothing was known at the present. Of course, we didn't need the very respectable Herr Hellmann to tell us that. But at the end of his talk with us he added something to his convoluted elocution which, despite the cloak of his soothing friendliness, did not lack a soft hint of cynicism: We were being supervised by all four of the victorious powers, including the Soviet Union.

How we could be under the control of all four of the victorious powers, let alone only one of them, was a mystery to me. Was Sweden not a sovereign state? Everything that Herr Hellmann said was so obtuse, so intentionally unclear. When *Herr* Hellmann departed from us we knew exactly as much as before, or perhaps, indeed, a little bit more, namely: There was something foul in the state of Sweden. Our suspicions, which up to then had only been a "Sleeping Beauty" in our subconscious mind, became a difficult-to-extinguish glowing red heap of burning coals which began to glow at the edges of our conscious mind.

It was horrible, this groping about without any clear idea of what was going on! And what was happening at home? No one had any contact, even by this point. And even with all the things we had done to try and get in contact! Besides our simple letters we had sent out Red Cross missing-persons inquiries (which cost one Krone each). A Vatican search form was filled out. I had written to a lady I knew in England. She regretted to tell me that there was no mail service with Germany. I wrote to a Jewish family I knew in the Netherlands. A person unknown to me answered that he was sorry to inform me that family X had died on such and such a date in a German camp. No mail service with Germany was available.

There was chaos everywhere! Finally we were allowed to fill out a few English military postcards that were handed out to German prisoners of war. But they also remained unanswered. Later we found out that these cards brought our loved one the first signs we were still alive. Unfortunately, it was at a time when a drama was taking place in Sweden.

Storm Clouds

The camp life at "Backamo" had just reached a high point. Following an appeal made by the Swedish-German Society, a group of gifted do-it-yourselfers under the skillful and devoted guidance of *Hauptmann* P. (who had a master's degree in engineering), was allowed to make toys for German children, which were to be sent to Germany for Christmas by the society.

With a good amount of enthusiasm and hustle and bustle, beautiful toys were made from simple materials and just as simple tools. Doll stoves were made from old tin cans; complete sets of furniture were made from plywood (kitchens, living rooms and bedrooms). There were also tumbling figures, trains, ships, airplanes and puppets and many other nice things. Besides this series of small things there were also unique, artistically carved items.

When all this was completed, the entire group of toys was put together to be shown. It was quite an experience to go to the instruction barracks, where the toys were set out for viewing. You would have thought that you were at a Christmas arts and crafts show, just like at home. The rooms were separated into diverse alcoves with direct and indirect lighting. The entire camp made a pilgrimage through the hall and, for a time, they were enchanted. Our pastor, the Swedish camp administration and the German-Swedish Society appeared in the camp to see the display. And they all enjoyed it.

Men who had so many hard times behind them — and in front of them — had created all of this. They were homesick and had carried their homesickness with them wherever they went. Now, their homesickness was given an external form after it had made itself known so strongly in the quiet contemplation of internment. It was homesickness for peace.

Mean-spirited people will say: Why did you all then wage war, if you were so peaceful? Dear reader, who wages war? Only some people! Here and there! You and I, we are only specks of dust in the tails of raging comets. Moreover, the peace we yearned for was not to be granted. Those in Stockholm were making sure of it. And so a fateful, stormcloud filled sky was brewing over our display of toys, just like in 1914 during the international exposition.

Totally unexpectedly, gloomy rumors stubbornly surfaced on Friday afternoon. They whistled around the camp like poisonous arrows. There was whispering everywhere. No one wanted to believe it, but no longer did anyone doubt it. The work time had already been extended to the whole day for some weeks now. They indeed wanted to get something out of us. And for weeks all of the newspapers arriving in the camp were censored. Often there were articles missing that someone had cut out. The much friendlier Lieutenant Colonel G. had stepped in for the "Red Czar" for a while. But then he reappeared in all his magnificence.

That had already had a strange affect on us, but our inner defenses against the things that might happen were so strong that we simply shut out any negative thoughts. No one wanted to think about it. We fought against the negative thoughts and the dire consequences that would result from them. We also fought these thoughts because we believed that we were in a country rich in culture and under the auspices of Christian-thinking and, more importantly, Christian-acting people. People who still maintained a healthy sensitivity and a proper attitude with respect to law and order, justice and fairness — people for whom humanity, goodness and love were still to be greeted as virtues. How bitterly — how infinitely bitterly — we would be disappointed!

The Government of His Majesty Announces…

24 November 1945. Saturday morning. The camp prisoners, as always, dressed into their work clothes and lined up for roll call. We all knew that something was in the air. Rumors from the previous day had impregnated the atmosphere. It took a while and then the Swedish camp commander, Colonel Brunsson, appeared with his adjutants, and read aloud a decree from the Swedish government, that generally went

as follows:

> *The government of His Majesty informs the interned German soldiers in Sweden that in a few days they will be handed over to the Allied Forces against whom they last fought in the field before they came to Sweden. The exact time of departure will be announced later.*

I don't remember if there was more to it than that. But it doesn't matter. Following that the camp commander discussed the procedures as to how the Stockholm order would be executed. The names of those who would go to the "West" were to be posted on the outside of the barrack that housed the barbershop. Our belongings, which we did not want to take into captivity, were to be packed well and labeled. The Swedish-German Society had declared its willingness to store them and ship them to Germany at the first possible opportunity. Address labels as well as package mailing cards could be picked up immediately. (Oh yes, they made sure that they would take care of our packages!) Finally, he warned us to be calm and maintain order! Upon our arrival they had wished us peace and relaxation! For us! For our departure they wanted calmness and order! For themselves!

Thoughts of an Outcast

And, in this way, the long feared lightning bolt crashed through the atmosphere that had already been brimming with disaster. It set off a horrifying thunderstorm that would now rage.

For the time being, everyone stood there, frozen in place. Was it a ghost that had just scoffed at us? And by scoffing at us, was he scoffing at his creator? Ah, what, a ghost! Reality was all too real. A person had spoken, a person in flesh and blood — just like us. He had read us our sentence — perhaps our death sentence! But how was that possible? I thought judgments were handed down to those who had broken the law. Did we do that? We, who had obeyed the powers that be just like those standing before us, who now thought they were allowed to condemn us? Perhaps I was traveling down the wrong path; perhaps it was not a sentence at all. Because where was the plaintiff and what were we accused of?

But did there exist another form of judgment when one held the fate of another in his hands? Surely in the dark ages there existed unscrupulous individuals who sold off people as merchandise at will. This is how some deals were made back then. Yes, deals! What an ugly word it was, but it was indeed a word that accurately reflected the emptiness of the souls of many people of that time. This ugly word stood in large letters before me. That explained everything. Indeed, it was a deal that was taking place, the possibilities of which were great. It was a one-time offer, never to be repeated. There were great possibilities for profit! Indeed, God knows, it was a fine coup. Twenty-seven hundred souls — perhaps in reality just twenty seven hundred robots — stood on the trading block, being offered for a little bit of goodwill.

If someone could have offered us a word of goodwill at that moment (because it would barely be a minute during which our future was haggled for), it could have gone like this: "Please stay, you are so nice!" But in reality it was: "It was fun while it lasted, but such easily acquired trading items may not be available to us ever again." For 130 years the Swedes had been able to stay out of everything. (I can't hold it against you, Sweden. I'll grant you that!) But then, the situation grew tense. All sorts of dreadful things had happened during the horrible war. Many people were often forced to hold not only one eye closed, but both, so that they did not see what was rolling on the Swedish railways in the direction of the Finnish front. These same people now thought they could hear the upset growling of the evil bear, which had already extended its claws in a threatening manner. So, you had to throw it a little treat in order to make its growling sound somewhat better.

That's how things stacked up for me. And I still suspect that it was indeed this possibility that had made the Swedes be so hospitable to us on 14 May 45 at Ystad. After thinking it over for a while — consider, for instance, the long delay in giving us permission to depart from the harbor at Ystad — they had finally figured it out. And so it was that they requested with compelling politeness that our floating shipwreck — supplied by the Firm of Mars and Neptune — remain in their official trade organization for a longer stay. Indeed, they had caught wind of the possibility of future favorable business transactions.

It was in June (or was it July?) that the contract was supposedly made in Stockholm. Undoubtedly it was an opportunity that was apparent to the Swedes in the days after our arrival at Ystad.

It could be that there were other external influences that played a role. It could be that I have presented these things to the reader too crassly. My only excuse is that I was one of those directly affected. But even today I harbor bitter thoughts about what they did to us, and it is truly difficult not to cross over the line of objectivity. But, for the sake of fairness, I will try to report on what happened without emotion.

I cannot help but raise accusations due to the injustice that was done to us. But can one argue that it was really an injustice? I do not demand revenge. Where will we wind up if the cries for revenge are not squelched once and for all! I demand justice. The phrase "audiatur et altera pars!" was always true. Please take the time to have a look around for once. Injustice and malice are established everywhere where humans are found…

As stated, I dare not claim that the hypothetical thoughts I have stated here score a bulls eye. But I choose to — I am forced to — present them as the most obvious reason for the course of action of the Swedes. My suspicions that all this represented was political horse trading were strengthened by the offer that well-meaning Swedish industrialists made for us. Supposedly they offered shipments valued at 10,000 Kronen per person as ransom money. The offer was turned down.

It didn't matter how it was, it didn't matter what it was, it didn't change the situation. Indeed a strong pressure may have been exerted, but alas, nothing, absolutely nothing, could change the fact that 2,700 people were to be sent into misery. And nothing could change the fact that these 2,700 people were now being kicked out by the people of *a civilized, humane* society. They were kicking out people who had been subjected for years to the most difficult physical and mental stress, who had only escaped the cruel fate of life in Russian captivity after an adventurous trip across the Baltic, who had been interned in a neutral country after an emergency at sea and to whom lullabies had been sung for six months. They were being kicked out from the same civilized world to which they thought they had returned.

Why did they even take us in? So that they could fatten us up like Hansel and Gretel and then put us to the knife? Why did they send *Herr* Hellmann into the camp with his repertoire of pharisaical verses to reassure us? The wolf put on the good grandmother's bonnet so Little Red Riding Hood would be lulled into a false sense of security for as long as possible. How embarrassing it would have been if she had smelled what was up and had caused a commotion in that well-maintained house! It was just these thoughts, the justification of which can barely be disputed, which allow me to place the behavior of Sweden — the government of Sweden — in such a low light. It used its good reputation, which we all gullibly believed in, to carry out the planned evil deed more easily than would have been possible under other circumstances.

Some might say: How was Sweden supposed to stand up to the external pressure? If that was true, how could Switzerland survive? Switzerland never betrayed anyone. It's fortunate that there are still a few small states here and there which serve as an oasis of decent convictions…

One must view the affair from two sides: It had a legal element and a purely human element. Viewed from a legal point of view, we are talking about the breaking of international law. But completely apart from that, the human side of the Swedish course of action was so completely shabby that I am at a lack of words to describe it. To a certain degree I can put myself in the shoes of the gentlemen in Stockholm: It was necessary that peace be preserved for the future. That is a completely understandable point of view. But I believe that one should, despite everything, consider what price he is paying! To the gentlemen in charge in Stockholm this entire episode may not have been more than a simple gesture; a gesture, though, which recalls the thumbs-down displayed by Nero. One only took into consideration the maintaining of peace and was willing to haggle for it at any price. The opportunity presented itself to throw some weight onto the scales of peace without burdening the treasury department. A burdened conscience was gladly exchanged for it. The evil end, which justified the means, found its gruesome translation into reality.

All this happened in Sweden, in the much-praised Christian country of Sweden, the country that spelled out the word "humanity" on its flag, the land of Elsa Brandström, the land of the Red Cross! When I say that, I don't mean to attack Christianity in any way; I only intend on making it clear where Christianity lives and where it is only talked about. You can find both everywhere, and in Sweden too! With terrible clarity one has to realize where we have ended up today. Blatant egocentrics are everywhere. Coldness is trump. Long live the freedom to elbow others out of the way! Down with feelings!

International law has now incorporated so-called "crimes against humanity" into the list of indictable offenses. Progress in the battle against the misuse of progress — it is definitely welcome. But if one wants to punish all of these types of offenses, the most important thing is missing: a procedural rule requiring the creation of a completely independent tribunal which would then bring every crime against humanity to trial and judgment in an honest fashion. Please, if one would just open their eyes a little or think a little bit about the war years; that is all it would take to fill the files of such a tribunal.

We want to forgive and forget in the hopes of a better future; hopefully, one not built on hate and the desire for revenge. Moreover we would have to demand the same thing from everyone. Only honesty, decency — a really Christian attitude — can provide the fundament for living together peacefully. Everyone should look inside himself and do some housecleaning. In that way he will make himself more useful to his fellow man than any government finger pointing.

The laughable argument "an eye for an eye, a tooth for a tooth" only makes sense to those who bring it up. How can one accuse another of a crime that he himself commits?

I don't want to be unfair to the Swedes or ignore the fact that large portions of the Swedish population, and above all the Swedish Church, were against the actions of the Swedish government. In all of the Swedish churches, prayer services were held on our behalf. Many newspapers distanced themselves from Stockholm's actions. But it is indeed one of the many strange phenomena of our time that all over the world small committees of politicians are allowed to play politics without the approval or knowledge of the people they represent. How else can one explain the fact that one war is waged after another, even though barely any of the people of any nations — the "mere mortals" among us — have ever desired such a thing?

Every one of us in the Swedish internment camp had thoughts like this and similar ones during those hours. Then came the thoughts about home. My God, everything had become a dim outline of its former self in a split second. Just a while back one imagined going home and now?! What were those at home doing at the moment? Did they even know we were alive? How good it would be if they did not know what was transpiring here! But were our loved ones at home even alive? Did they have a roof over their heads? And what did it look like for those who came from the East in what was now Poland? One had to fear the worst for their loved ones. Ah, the dreadful uncertainty! When had such things ever happened before? We call it the 20th Century. The era of great human progress! God only knows what kind of progress it really was! Tears of sadness were more appropriate than tears of joy! This entire desolation! This inconsolable hopelessness! This bitter disappointment! One could really lose his faith in goodness; at least in goodness on earth.

Yes, that was the only thing that kept us going: The feeling that everything was in the final stages of a sensible master plan we could not comprehend. The belief in goodness around us was shattered. The belief in that above us gave us new strength. In that belief we almost recovered the balance within our souls.

A Hunger Strike and the Call For Help

But belief in God is not resignation or fatalism. Thus, the desire to defend ourselves rose.

In a public meeting of the internees, which took place just a few hours after the notification of that dark decree, it was decided to conduct a camp-wide hunger strike. Only a few — I believe it was about 10 men out of about 1,200 — did not go along. The Swedish camp administration was informed of the decision.

Furthermore, *Major* H., who had assumed command of the internees, announced the preparation of several memoranda and requests for reconsideration. The first of these writings was a petition to the Swedish king, which was read out loud a few hours later. In it, all legal and humanitarian points of view were represented in detail and vividly. An officer of the Swedish camp administration flew to Stockholm on his own with the petition so he could personally hand it over to the king. The officers of the Swedish camp administration paid for the flight out of their own pockets.

Further writings were directed to Count Bernadotte (chairman of the Swedish Red Cross), the Swedish Minister President, the Evangelical and the Catholic bishops of Sweden. In addition, telegrams were sent to the Pope and the Archbishop of Canterbury.

On the next day, Sunday, our two pastors appeared. They remained with us until the very end and held prayer services. They gave us something to hold on to during those terrible days. Every evening there was a gathering during which the latest from the Swedish press arrived — once again uncensored. It was read out to us. With this we were able to form a picture of what the public thought about this affair, because the newspapers and also the Swedish radio news programs devoted a lot of their reporting to us. There were very many voices to be heard that took our side, especially in Christian circles. But other groups also let it be known that they were primarily in favor of the politics of neutrality and considered everything else to be secondary in nature. At any rate, the affair resulted in a lively debate in the country and showed that the voices of conscience were making themselves heard everywhere. Despite that, they did not stop the government from its trade in humans. And that is once again proof they didn't have the courage to put it all on the line for their convictions. One can see how far we are from a truly proper, assertive and unmistakably unwavering attitude — even in Sweden!

Our commander called all those who had been on the "BERTA" together and talked to us. He told us that Swedish officers recommended we direct petitions to the government stating that our claim we had come from the Eastern Front was incorrect. We had only said that at that time in order to prevent being handed over to the victorious powers and escape captivity. At that time we considered being handed over to the Soviet Union to be completely out of the question and therefore stated that we had come from the Eastern Front. Even if submitting this story seemed to be a completely hopeless attempt to change their minds, we were willing to try anything we could.

I myself made a last attempt to possibly escape the fate of being handed over to the Russians. I had myself sent to "Grunnebo," a neighboring camp, where one of our doctors was used as a surgeon. I wanted to be operated on — it didn't matter what for! What one wouldn't do when in despair! I knew that others had done similar things but, when I arrived at "Grunnebo," it was already too late. Stockholm had sent a telegraph, forbidding every operation dealing with non-life threatening health issues. (Yes, they thought of everything!)

So I returned to "Backamo" with mixed feelings, but at least I knew inside that I had done everything in my power. Besides, there were thousands who shared my fate. That gave me consolation. But I will never forget the sight I saw when I arrived at "Grunnebo": I saw a group of depressed comrades who stood around the laid out corpse of one of their comrades. He — an older gentleman, father of several children — had hanged himself in the latrine!

Illusions Go – Policemen Come

After arriving back at "Backamo," I heard of a large gathering that took place in the camp on the night before. It was announced that the date of our being handed over had been delayed. "Supposedly" a commission from the Red Cross had inspected the just-arrived Russian steamer "Kuban" and determined that the ship first had to be set up to carry people before it would allow us to depart. And therefore it was necessary to delay the date. The camp had viewed this message as a sign of success of the memoranda we had sent out and in its frenzy of enthusiasm even went as far as to give out excited cheers for King Gustav. Father N. was thanked for his great work on our behalf with a large Iron Cross that was hung around his neck. Poor "Backamo" Camp! How quickly would the excited cheers disappear! During the following days a paralyzing despair crept into the camp. Nothing happened. And that was worse than if something had happened. An escape was out of the question after the Swedish national police took over guard duties. The Swedish armed forces declined to get their hands dirty with this political slave trading. So from then on policemen as tall as trees in black uniforms with silver tress stood guard. Moreover, the camp was guarded in depth over a very large area. During my trip to and from "Grunnebo" I saw large field camps with all sorts of weapons and ammunition. At least we were respected!

The hunger, which was very difficult to bear during the first two to three days, became easier as time went on. Our stomachs felt numb and, in any case, we hardly felt the gnawing in them any more. Only an increasing weakness and sense of resignation made themselves felt. Many still had biscuits and such things, which they probably ate secretly. But the majority of us took their little stockpiles and laid them at the camp's gate as a demonstrative measure.

Quod licet Iovi non licet bovi

During the days when Damocles' sword cast its eerie shadow over us, I thought about the extremely embarrassing court session that took place a month before in the camp. A couple of young toughs from the navy took an *Obersteuermann*, whom they could not stand for various reasons and who had ratted on them to the Swedes about their lax approach to their work, lured him into a trap, jumped him and then beat him black and blue. The *Obersteuermann*, a braggart who received little sympathy from the rest of the camp, called loudly for help and walked a long time thereafter with a limp. I think he thought it was fun to limp around like that. Be that as it may: The Swedish powers that be appeared and summoned the offenders before a tribunal that met in the camp. They interrogated the witnesses, made accusations, heard the defense, took breaks for lunch, interrogated anew and finally retired for consultations. That evening, after an approximately eight-hour trial, they sentenced all 20 of the boys to two months behind bars, with the exception of the one man who, in my opinion, was the leader of the gang, but who also knew how to defend himself the most skillfully. His sentence was only one month.

I did not tell this story with the intention of misrepresenting the deed of the young boys as acceptable. In fact, I find the way in which they acted to be mean and petty (jump him and overpower him). But I found a certain parallel with our shared fate. Hadn't the Swedes also, in a way, lured us into a trap, so that they could more easily hand us over to the Russians!? The misdeed perpetrated by the rash young soldiers who had been coarsened by the war was severely punished by a Swedish judge — a judge who, moreover, liked to point out that no one in Sweden sympathized with such reprehensible behavior. In the same breath, however, one did not hesitate to do the same thing — or even worse — to 2700 people through a sovereign act of the state.

The Morning of Terror at "Backamo"

Many were at the camp aid station, since they had collapsed from exhaustion.

Plans had been forged. When it was time — and gradually we were all sure that this time would indeed come — we were to link arms and form a solid mass. Other proposed the idea we were to arm ourselves with razorblades, sit down and inform any approaching policemen that at the slightest sign of action we would slash our wrists all at the same time.

Large banners had been hung up on the barracks buildings facing the road. But on Swedish orders they were removed. Two courageous ones made a halfway successful attempt to escape. One of them, who spoke perfect Swedish, jumped onto a Swedish ambulance while the other one lay on a stretcher and pretended to be unconscious. They were able to get through the restricted zone unnoticed thanks to their Swedish uniforms (we all had been issued a uniform, a coat, two changes of underwear and two pairs of shoes) and the one soldier's Swedish language abilities. Later someone caught the two on a train when the one who could not speak Swedish could not find his ticket and then started to curse in German.

Until then the Swedish officers had assured us every night that the next day nothing would happen. But one evening these assurances did not occur.

The following night I encountered something strange. I woke up and had to go to the latrine. But at the exit of the barracks four (perhaps six) bayonets stared me in the face. After lengthy negotiations, Cerberus and his friends finally let the group that had assembled in the meantime by.

The time had come! What would the next day bring? We could no longer think about sleep. We lay there and brooded. Our entire lives darted quickly through our memories like fast-motion camerawork. What would happen? The end? Eternal slavery? Would we be wasted away in a drawn-out ordeal? Or was there still hope?

Our company *Spieß* came in and informed us laconically we should get ready. The Swedes would definitely appear soon. We had to know what we were going to do. Then he disappeared. That was during the first hours of Friday, 30 November, 1945. I got up and went to the other barracks where our company was, to see what was going on there. The majority was laying around apathetically on their beds and staring at the ceiling. Some of them appeared to be sleeping. One guy was trotting around, looking for something. I asked him what he was doing. "I'm looking for a hatchet or something!" I spoke to others and inquired what they were thinking of doing, but no one gave a rational answer. I noticed that nothing was really going on there, so I went back.

It was pretty cold since no one had the desire to light the furnace any more. Our suitcases stood there, well packed and addressed. Also, the backpacks that we were supposed to take with us were arranged in a corner. We were in agreement that we wanted to stay in bed to wait for what was coming. They could drag us out of bed if they wanted to. In any case, we would not go willingly. We didn't consider active resistance; it would have been senseless.

So we lay in our beds and shivered due to the cold and agitation. I became sick and vomited.

Then, suddenly, the most horrible thing I ever experienced in my life began. You would think after the horrible war that had just ended I would have experienced worse. On top of that, it occurred in a neutral country which had been spared all of its devastation.

I heard cracking, booming, screaming, whimpering, groaning…

people running up and down the stairs. Someone yelled for a medic. Outside people were running excitedly back and forth. The cracking, booming, screaming and whimpering went on. Finally, after about 10 dreadful minutes the worst was over. Only the whimpering and moaning did not die down. Indescribable, inhumane, terrible!

A high point in the annals of Swedish history! Now Sweden would sadly be famous for being a home to the largest act of self-mutilation that was ever provoked in a civilized country!

In the other barracks, soldiers had used the blunt side of an axe or heavy rocks rolling off a table to smash their shins. Some did it to themselves; others did it to one another.

I found out later what other horrible things had happened. Many had slit their wrists and had to be quickly bound. Some had lost so much blood that they were found completely unconscious. Some took poison and were all balled up, suffering from severe cramps. An old *Hauptmann* — it sounds unbelievable, but it really happened — hammered a nail into his foot and pulled it out again five times. The old man had obviously gone mad. Another person stuck a dagger in his breast, but didn't strike his heart. An *Oberleutnant* who had lost his wife and child as well as all of his possessions in the war hanged himself in the attic of the officer housing. That's what happened in the Kingdom of Sweden in the year of 1945 AD.

Saved?

A little cat jumped around in our barracks and finally found a warm place on a bed. It began to purr in delight. It was a happy creature, a creature that had not been given any human reason by our Creator. It had no idea as to what kind of a blessed effect human reason had. It also did not know anything of the satanic sophistry human reason possessed which dealt all trumps into the hands of the forces of destruction and degradation.

It didn't take a long time. A Swedish commission of doctors came in. I closed my eyes and made myself appear to be even more unconscious than I already was. They went from bed to bed and asked everyone about their state of health and their personal data. Suddenly I heard groaning and a rush of people. Robert had slit his wrists and they carried him out quickly. Then they came to me and inquired about my health. They felt my pulse, whispered something, shook me and wanted to know my name. I said nothing. Finally they left.

We saw that someone had written the word "kvar" on our beds. That meant "stays." We had won! For the time being, anyway. And then? Who knew what would happen next. Like cattle that earned a week's grace, we laid around in our miserable straw beds and conjured up further measures. For the time being, however, we felt like we had been saved.

The Black Omnibuses

So we lay there endlessly, or so it seemed. Outside there was a coming and a going. We could care less. I felt like someone who had been shipwrecked and who lay powerless and naked on a raft, abandoned to the will of the waves.

After a considerable amount of time, the door opened. A few policemen or medics packed us onto stretchers and wrapped us in blankets. The stretchers were then laid on a cart that was attached to the back of a bicycle. I was driven around on this strange form of transportation for a while. Along the way I heard the word "collapse." Finally someone brought me into a barrack and laid me on a straw bed. I opened my eyes a little bit. We were in the instruction barracks, in which shortly before our pretty display of toys for the children had been displayed. Perhaps one of the medics who was working here had seen them; perhaps he was making comparisons, like I was, between the display that his government had set up in this building and the one that had been here before.

They gave us water with sugar so that we could regain some of our strength. Then somebody suddenly screamed. It was one of our German doctors. He had taken poison.

Then there was quiet. The day went by. The night went by. The first day of December began. Large black omnibuses came. We were placed in them on stretchers. I had a second good blanket with me. They took it away from me. I protested, but they said that I was not permitted to take more than one blanket. It was not even a Swedish blanket, but a German field hospital one. I had made the extra effort to carry it around with me. The lack of rights continued to become ever more refined!

In the omnibus there was room for nine stretchers. They were placed three high next to the sides of the bus. No fewer than 6 policemen were sitting on a long leather seat. Besides them there was a medic. He was a friendly young man who spoke passable German. He talked to us during the entire ride and was obviously trying to say positive things to us. God, he couldn't have had anything to do with what they thought up for us in Stockholm. I would have gladly said that to him, but I was in no condition to talk. So I let the others do the talking.

They took us through Göteborg and Boras to Ulricehamm, a small south Swedish market town that was about halfway between Skagerrak and the Baltic. The trip was long. I think it was about 250 kilometers.

After arriving in Ulricehamm, we were unloaded. It was really dark. Civilians carried us in the stretchers into a school building that had been converted into a provisional hospital. Next they placed the stretchers into a lobby. Three agile nurses had completely undressed me and put me into a fresh nightgown before I even knew what had happened. My old rags were stuffed into a paper bag upon which my name was written. I was then taken to a freshly made bed. Twelve fellow sufferers were already in the schoolroom. Then I remember that a large plate filled with great looking sandwiches was brought in. No one touched them. Just imagine what it was like to turn away such delicacies, especially after you had eaten virtually nothing for an entire week! But I didn't have a long time to think about such things, because I soon fell asleep — exhausted by the long drive in the large black omnibus with its nine stretchers and six policemen.

Inter arma caritas!

This beautiful slogan, which the international Red Cross carried on its flag, was embraced for the most part in this provisional hospital. Despite that, there were also people here who were entrusted with our care who acted very strangely towards us.

On the next day, our two pastors appeared and visited us — for the last time. They went from bed to bed and offered words of encouragement. And we noticed that they knew more than they were saying. Then we were alone.

It didn't take long and they announced that the beds would be changed around. I asked a nurse to make sure that I would be placed alongside my comrades. They honored this request and, after being carried around from room to room and floor to floor, we found ourselves in a group of three in a larger schoolroom among twelve others.

With the exception of a career nurse, Sister Ingrid from Stockholm, numerous women and girls who had offered their help as volunteers cared us for. The majority was indeed friendly and concerned about our welfare and making our lives a little better. Some of them acted reserved. All of them worked very hard though.

I thought that three of the doctors displayed very strange behavior. Two other doctors were helpful and friendly. These three though — one of whom was a Jew — acted not only extremely reserved but very cold. There was something arrogant about their behavior. Surely they had every right to think whatever they wanted to of us, but what infuriated me was their behavior as doctors. Every day they visited us during our short stay, and they made us recite our entire medical history a total of three times — from the time we were born to the present — all dictated on paper. They also interrogated us about every complaint, and every day they were shown the data concerning our pulse and temperature. They spoke of all possible measures that could be taken and…what came of it? Nothing!

The only thing that we could have was castor oil and anti-neuralgia and sleeping pills. I didn't see much else in our rooms. In our room there was a comrade who complained of intense pains in his head. A few years before he had been operated on in the back of his head and he had a silver plate back there. The chief doctor had everything explained to him in great detail; he spoke of taking x-rays and another operation…and what came out of it? Nothing! I don't know what to think of such behavior. If they didn't care about us, then they should have left us in peace. But no, they attended to us until the last minute with their hypocrisy, at least officially. They wanted to lull our senses in order to have an easier time with us. That is what makes me feel especially bitter when I think back on those days.

On the other hand, the female caretakers, with Sister Ingrid in charge, looked after us in a touching manner. It bothered me every time I turned down their nicely presented food with the exception of tea and hot milk. But I didn't do it to offend the nurses.

After it was announced on 3 December that the "Kuban" had departed from the Trelleborg port, a general sigh of relief went through the hospital. Many, the majority of us actually, were naïve enough to believe that we were out of danger. They stopped their hunger strike and had a new lease on life. Short notes were written and the nurses wandered from room to room with them. There was chatting and people were in a good mood. Across from me was *Leutnant* P., a middle-aged man, small, thickset, with glasses. He had learned a few words of Swedish in his vocabulary and made sure he used them every time a nurse or a doctor came by. He got on our nerves with his silly chatter and never missed an opportunity to disturb us by telling everyone the complete tale of his woe. Besides that, he constantly went to the bathroom and visited the other rooms. One day we heard him fall to the floor in a convulsion. He was an epileptic. But that didn't change the fact that he had to share our fate.

A middle-aged woman, who spoke really good German —she was the wife of one of the two friendly doctors — visited us on various occasions and brought books. She had somehow known how to get into the building that was otherwise shut off from the outside world. (They didn't even let the two pastors in anymore.) One noticed that she pitied us and also wanted to do something good for us. She had often been in Germany, as she told us. On St. Nicholas Day she gave each of us a bag with a bar of chocolate, an apple and a pack of cigarettes. Then suddenly she no longer appeared. Either a few good souls made sure that her visits would be forbidden or she had found out something definitive about our fate and didn't have the heart to lie to us about it.

There was a strange atmosphere in this hospital. The Swedes were at pains to show us that people in their country were still conscious of their humanitarian duties. The government of Sweden was trying hard to convince us of the opposite. It was trying to get the ball rolling again on its agreed-upon exchange, in order bring an end to this unpleasant, but politically important business. As a result, the very tall policemen in their silver-trimmed black uniforms were there in addition to the nurses and the doctors. As the representatives of His Majesty's Government, they made sure that we did not leave the building in our dressing gowns. (Solely to prevent the public outcry, of course!) One beautiful evening we heard singing in the distance. It slowly came closer until the nurses appeared in our rooms playing their guitars. They were singing Swedish Advent songs. The angels!

"Other News" from "Backamo"

The days were filled with stories from other comrades about what had happened on 30 November. I found out a lot of other things in the provisional hospital, some of which I have mentioned previously. But a few more of these things are worth mentioning: Some of the comrades hid themselves in the camp, a few in the attic of the barracks, others under the wooden floor planks. They looked for them everywhere and, for the most part, found them. But a few were not found right away. Due to that a camp officer appeared at our hospital to determine exactly who was there.

A small group of comrades had clandestinely dug a small tunnel under the stage. It was difficult to do and took weeks, but the work led to the digging out of a small cave. It was there that the "conspirators" had fled and hid themselves on the last day. They closed the stage boards up behind them so you couldn't tell they had been removed. They brought hardtack, chocolate and water with them; they would have been able to hold out for a while. They wanted to wait until the coast was clear and then make off. Of course more people caught wind of what was going on than the original group would have preferred. So, the group was forced to take in a number of "sub-tenants" against their will. There was, indeed, no argument, but at any rate, the situation was indeed not very cozy. Finally one of the "me too's" did something stupid despite being warned. He decided to make an assault on the outer world. They didn't catch him in the act of leaving, of course, but he left behind his scent which the police dogs tracked. (Oh yes, they spared no costs or effort in the hunt for the criminals.) And that led to disaster for our cave dwellers. They found them quickly thereafter and so the dream ended. At any rate, they had held out eight days, if I remember correctly.

Unbelievable things took place in the other camps as well, above all at "Ränneslätt," as I later found out. In this context I would like to mention them. At "Ränneslätt" comrades joined together, arm in arm, in the camp grounds as a form of passive resistance. This had no effect on the Swedish National Police, who used their rubber clubs to beat everyone apart and ship them off.

This all happened, as previously mentioned, in the Kingdom of Sweden in the year 1945 AD. Whoever doubts the credibility of this report can inquire in Sweden. If they are courageous enough to tell the truth, then they will confirm it.

The Last Breath of Humanity

Soon the last night in the hospital arrived. We noticed that the nurses were becoming increasingly uneasy. They came with a large tea wagon and brought a cup of good coffee and baked goods for everyone. They had paid for it themselves. It was their farewell gift, they said. Medics relieved them.

What that meant was easy enough to figure out. During the afternoon the doctors were there and decided to do some regrouping. From our room one was carried out and put in the room of those who were to remain. Everyone else was to be transported off the next day. I had begun to eat again a few days ago, since I felt that the hunger strike had become meaningless. Perhaps I would have stayed with the others if I had continued with the hunger strike. But what would have really happened? It would have just delayed my ultimate fate. It would not have been a definitive solution, or better yet: salvation!

The nurses had meant well with their baked goods, but I couldn't touch a thing. I had a lump in my throat. Everything was against me. Everything made me sick!

Practically all of us spent a sleepless night. The dread of not knowing and the thousands of possibilities of what would happen to us stirred new thoughts in our heads. I felt like I had a high fever. Blood rushed to my ears and put pressure on my temples. I sweated and tossed and turned from one side of the bed to the other. In the morning I finally fell asleep, only to be brusquely awakened again.

The light went on. We heard energetic voices. A huge policeman in a black uniform with silver ornamentation and silver buttons stood in the door and read something to us. At the same time a large number of policemen ran to the beds, obviously to thwart any possible attempts of self-mutilation. But what could we have attempted after they had taken everything from us? We only heard the message from the state, which only served to agitate us a bit more: "You are being transported to another camp by the name of "Gälltofta" in southern Sweden…" Then each one of us was thrown a paper bag with his clothes. The only thing in the bags was the clothes we would wear on our backs. My last good blanket had wandered into the assets of a bankrupt community comprised of those who had lost all their rights.

After we got dressed we marched down the stairs. Below, in the hallway, the nurses had lined up to shake everyone's hand. Many had tears in their eyes. It was the last breath of humanity we were granted.

In the Pen

Then once again we were loaded into those monstrous omnibuses which brought us to "Gällofta" after a long trip. "Gällofta" was a small camp — a part of the "Rinkaby" internment camp — not far from Christianstad.

It was already dark when we arrived. The omnibuses drove right into the camp so that no one could escape. An icy wind was blowing. We were happy when we arrived at the barracks. But it wasn't cozy inside. The large room was separated into cubicles with two double-stacked bunks that were situated left and right of a hallway in the middle, like a sleeping car in an express train. After we turned up the stove as high as it would go, it slowly became warm.

There we sat like bombed-out victims gathered in a bunker which had saved their lives. But we were just property owned by the country of Sweden, which was about to pass the right of ownership to another power.

I went out to look at the place from the outside. And there you could see that they had made a right proper little pen for us. The small camp was made even smaller by enclosing it with thick barbed wire fences. Three barracks, which stood in a U next to each other, were all that remained for us. The officers were housed in one of them and we were allowed to inhabit the rest. The barbed wire fences were well lit. There was an enormous bank of lights brought in which were set up every five meters. There was also no lack of police officers to make sure that the "white ivory" did not get caught in the barbed wire.

One would think one found himself on the set of a filming of a colonial war somewhere in an arctic region, during which the "representatives of civilization" had driven the local troops or insurgents into a camp. The policemen, who were wrapped in their white fur coats, didn't seem real! The glaring spotlights strengthened this impression. Only the ice-cold wind from the sea, which mercilessly blew over the open area, reminded us of the horrible reality. I went back into the barracks and lay down.

The next morning we were called to breakfast. We went out and found out the dining hall was outside of our fence. We were connected to it through a passageway ringed with barbed wire. It was similar to the ones you saw in the circus for bringing the carnivores onto the stage. An iron door was opened and we were allowed to go into the dining hall while being guarded by the policemen. Once within, a policeman handed out the necessary utensils to everyone. Then we marched past a shabby counter, behind which two grumpy civilians plopped food onto a plate with noticeable coldness. The eye of the law was constantly looking at us — with a corresponding effect on our appetites. While leaving we had to return the utensils to the representatives of state power. This game — truly worthy of a civilized nation — repeated itself three times daily.

The Last Straw

Since everyone else did it, we did it too: Once again we wrote a petition to the Swedish government and also one to the British, American and French ambassadors in Stockholm who, according to international law, had to protect our interests (as representatives of the powers that were charged with administrating the districts in which we had lived). It was seemingly senseless; nevertheless, we were able to pass some time and draw the final straw, which we believed we could cling to.

Actually one day a few telegrams arrived from Stockholm that brought salvation to a few. But these were the successes of the petitions that had already been written at "Backamo". They always had only to do with the occupants of smaller boats. While submitting the total count of the number of men to the Allies, some breathing room had been allowed so that a few men could fall through the cracks. There was no need to surrender to illusions with regard to those who had been on the "BERTA" — all 180 of us. Was the conscience of those in Stockholm getting the better of them? Or was this also just a premeditated gesture of noble compassion, so that their very dirty record would look a little better? It is sad that one has to draw such nasty conclusions, but our experiences taught us this.

Other than that, we basically received no response to our letters. Only the bishops had answered: They wanted to do everything in their powers for us, but their veto alone could not tip the scales in our favor. Besides, it was known that King Gustav had personally requested Stalin that the extradition be delayed for a year, as Sweden wanted to house us for another year. The categorical "no" from Russia had been the answer to the well-meaning intervention of the old man.

That which mocks the actions of the Swedes the most is the ironic things that resulted from the long time it took for our petitions to circulate: A smaller boat crew, which had not departed with the "KUBAN" on its first trip out due to self-mutilation or collapse, was now being redirected to the West while its contemporaries were already in the hands of the Russians.

Better evidence for the completely confused state and uncertainty of the Swedish government, as well as for its lack of moral fiber, cannot be produced. It was said the mainspring for the entire operation was the then-serving Swedish Foreign Minister, Günther.

And so transpired another day during which we gave the lucky ones who were to go home our addresses and the instructions that they were to inform our loved ones of the necessary details, while protecting them from the horrible ones. An inmate of our barracks undertook a last desperate attempt to deceive fate by swallowing a handful of shoe nails. Since that didn't produce any symptoms, he then ate something else (I believe it was a cigarette that had been soaked in oil), which produced some sort of results. When he became pale and his pulse increased, he went to a Swedish doctor who immediately sent him to the hospital. But he soon returned, since they determined with a smile that the swallowed nails would pass through him like everything else.

This is it!

On the next day a civilian appeared with a pile of clothes and he distributed based on what we needed. I had a pullover and a scarf given to me.

Later, another civilian appeared. (All our care by then was the responsibility of the ministry of the interior, since we were no longer military internees. We were then obviously regarded as criminal elements, which were shortly to be handed over to a foreign power.) This civilian paid us our soldier's pay for the last two pay periods. At our request, he appeared a few hours later with a carton full of chocolate, oranges and tobacco. But what did a carton of items mean when there were 150 men who wanted to spend something for their 25 Kronen!? I was lucky and actually got a bar of chocolate. I saved the remaining Kronen in the hopes of being able to obtain something later.

Then came 14 December. It was completely dark when suddenly some of us who were standing at the windows called out: "There! This is it!" Everyone ran to the windows and to the doors. The camp gate was thrown open and a swarm of 40 to 50 policemen marched in hurriedly. The majority of them went to the officer barracks, while only one of the giants came to each of ours. He gave each of us a simple hectographed scrap of paper, upon which stood the laconic phrase: You will not be transported today.

Aha! Not today! Very friendly. Very attentive. Very clever once again. Just no trouble, my friends! Just no complications! For God's sake, calm these people down so that they will not bring any disturbance to our land. It would indeed be horrible. No, calm them down! Oh, you kind-hearted ones! Be calm! We are really sensitive people and can't bear any noise.

We had already sensed that something would happen on this day because, first of all, they once again issued us our dangerous possessions (I received my pocketknife and my mirror back!) Weren't they afraid that I would swallow them? Secondly, it was noticeable that a lot of medics had arrived at the camp.

When the policemen pressed into the camp, something ghastly happened. We suddenly heard a scream and then moaning. We rushed to where the noise came from and found a comrade who had collapsed in front of the barracks' door. He seemed to be completely out of it, did not recognize anyone and moaned incessantly. We carried him to his bunk and fetched the Swedish doctor. He gave him a shot, after which the patient became talkative and laughed continually. But nothing he said made any sense. And so it went, the entire night. We asked the doctor, who was, by the way, one of the two friendly doctors from Ulricehamm, to send the comrade to a hospital. But his efforts in this regard were without success. Stockholm had given instructions: No one stays here! So they gave the poor guy a further injection, which put him to sleep, and shipped him off in an unconscious state onto the ship. Inter arma caritas!

The officers had already departed. For us there were only another 24 hours of grace. Then the game from the day before was repeated. This time there were no little pieces of papers handed out. That day we would all be transported, even the Austrians, although they had high hopes until the very end. They had all discovered they were really Austrians and not Germans and formed an exclusive society, which didn't associate with just anyone for a long time. There were exceptions of course. We couldn't hold it against them. We would have done the same thing if we could have. But all hopes were ruined, even theirs.

One at a time, upon the calling of our names, we had to climb into the horrid black omnibuses that were to transport us across the Swedish roads for the third and last time. Upon entering the bus we were forced to trade the good things that were in our possession for

POW supplies. It was our going away gift. This was the "crown of thorns"; I can say that without exaggerating a bit. I received a "spoon" made of iron that was almost completely rusted; also a Swedish mess tin which had a capacity of two liters and showed characteristics of being quite aged. My blanket was of the same quality as an old horse blanket; it was frayed and had small holes in it. In exchange, they kept my two good hospital blankets. It seemed as if they wanted to emphasize our destitution and defenselessness. Eat or die! A proper land, it was, the Kingdom of Sweden!

Property Transfer

Scene of the Deal: Slave Market at Trelleborg

And so we drove through the night in long ghostly columns, to face our fate. Between us sat policemen. Some of them spoke some German. One noticed that they didn't like performing this duty. They gave us a few words of sympathy and took down our addresses. On the way, in the village of Lund, the column stopped for a few minutes. One of us gave one of the policemen some money. He jumped out and came back with sausages that were being sold at a stand. That was the last food we ate on Swedish soil.

Finally the column stopped. We were in the port of Trelleborg, a small city that we recognized, having learned about it in geography in school: "Ferry Train Saßnitz — Trelleborg!" We moved on in fits and starts, until the Spanish rider closed behind our omnibus. There was a last handshake from the policemen, and we then departed from our bus one by one.

I stepped into the night and was pointed toward a corrugated iron shed, the entrance of which was directly in front of me. Inside to the right was a podium. Behind it was a Swedish officer and a civilian, obviously a Russian consul official. They completed the contract that had been made some time before. Under the supervision of the representatives of both parties, the "handing over of the goods," like the handing over of possessions, of "livestock," was completed.

"Last name, first name, date of birth," were required. They stamped an index card that found its way into the hand of the new owner. He then laid it on a pile. I was then directed to the right.

I walked slowly, as if dreaming, exited the shed from the other side and stood in front of the quay. I will never forget what I saw in front of me: A large ship, garishly lit, was in front of me. There was a long, steep gangplank that led up to it. Along the entryway were the oft-mentioned policemen in their solemn black uniform with the silver buttons — in our honor, of course! But it was more likely that in reality they were there to make sure that we did not jump off to the side. They stood there in an icy fashion, without any expression on their faces. That whole thing was surreal. It looked like a theater scene, built for the last act of the first part of the tragedy. Above, on the ship, stood what we expected: A Russian guard in the usual shaggy fur coat with a machine pistol hanging from his shoulder. Unfathomable. Immovable. A sphinx!

I was in a kind of trance-like condition. The hunger strike, the back and forth, the infinite disappointment, bitterness, abandonment, uncertainty — the entire psychological upheaval — and then the garishly lit up silhouette of the phantom ship!

Slowly and absorbed I climbed up the steep path. I thought of "Es Sireth" — The Bridge of Death — which we knew from Karl May's Arabian stories.

Then, I heard for the first time, as if from another world, "Dawai!" — "Hurry Up!"